I Come to the Garden

The Spiritual Quest of
Dorothy and Russell Flexer

A study in
Metaphysics, Mediumship
and Community

by

Gerald A. O'Hara B.Sc CSNU

Published by
Saturday Night Press Publications
England.
www.snppbooks.com
snppbooks@gmail.com

ISBN 978-1-908421-24-1

Printed by Lightning Source
www.lightningsource.com

www.snppbooks.com

Dedication

To Spirit

The Teachings

To You

And to the many people of Sarasota, Florida
whose lives were and are being shaped
by
Russell and Dorothy Flexer.

Acknowledgements

"Solitude is fine, but you need someone to tell you that solitude is fine."
Honore de Balzac

A writer needs solitude to write and music for inspiration but outside of privacy, the author needs advice and assistance of others! That was never truer than of this book. To research a theme that is concerned with the USA, presents to an Englishman in Yorkshire, a dire need of assistance. For a researcher to undertake his own research is as normal as Tuesday, yet, the author found that the research for this work cannot all be done on-line. The goodwill of friends in the USA was needed to undertake much of the work of research and much of the signposting.

The author traveled to the US and undertook research in the files at Sarasota. Otherwise, without the full assistance and considerable archive of Eileen Courtney this book would have been the poorer. I cannot sufficiently thank Eileen and the Courtney family.

Likewise, the Reverend Tom Newman has been diligent in his support and in the supply of research materials, information and advice as to research leads.

The excellence of Robert Carr's designs for the cover, speaks for itself. Robert's flair, skill and artist's eye have enriched the manuscript with a cover that enhances the final production.

I thank Elizabeth Rhodes for the unflagging assistance and collaboration on the manuscript. Elizabeth's internet 'ear' and gentle advice has been of great support. As has the work of the publisher Ann Harrison, who takes a manuscript collage and skillfully creates a book.

Others, have helped with the research and leads. In the USA, Piet Nickels of Camp Chesterfield and Professor Todd Jay Leonard for his thoughts on 'Natural Law' and his advice on the Camp Chesterfield Photographic Collection. Further, I thank Todd for his help with the Spiritualist Episcopal Church Convention of 1956.

In Sarasota, may I thank Reverend Marie Rowe for use of the family archives, both photographic and written histories. Their family archives added photographs that captured the community events of the SOM over the years.

The Board of the SCOL have been loyal in their support of this project. I would like to thank the Senior Pastor Jim Toole, President Kath Curtin and especially Lyn Mulder-Rosenberg, without whose generous support this book would not have come into being. The publications committee have been generous in their support; may I thank Jennifer Blecher and John Shores, and in the Center of Light office, I wish to thank Sarah and Reverend Jim Toole.

Cyndy Mayer contributed a graphological analysis of the hand writing for which I am obliged.

In addition, I thank Reverend Marilyn J. Awtry, NST who correctly pointed the author down the by-ways of US Spiritualist history and my thanks go to Reverend Bessie Hope and Rodger Parker of the SEC Michigan.

A number of US Institutions were helpful, in particular, Angela White of the Indiana Philanthropic Studies Archivist, Ann Gordon of the Metaphysical College, Anna Lys Proctor, Archivist at the University of Indiana and the Reverend Lelia Cutler of the Memorial Spiritualist Church of Virginia.

The author is never at a loss with Wikipedia's help and free assistance at hand. I am also indebted to the late J. Stillson Judah, for although his work on Dorothy and SEC is flawed, his ground-breaking work on New Thought and the influence of Metaphysics in the USA remains influential.

Thanks must go to the Indiana Association of Spiritualists (IAOS) and the Hett Art Gallery and Museum at Historic Camp Chesterfield, Chesterfield, Indiana, U.S.A for permission to use photographs and illustrations from their archives. Each illustration carries the following (CCC) indicating it is 'From the archives of Camp Chesterfield.' The author would like to express a heartfelt thanks to Marc Demarest and his colleagues of the IAPSOP, for the brilliant work they are doing in preserving Spiritualist and occult history.

The Courtney and Flexer family archives were an invaluable collection of photographic materials for Dorothy and Russell's early days.

I also thank the Sarasota Herald Tribune for the kind use of their images and indirect quotations.

In the UK, I thank my old friend Paul Gaunt, archivist at the Arthur Findlay College and editor of Psychic Pioneer, for his help.

Margaret Hodge contributed an insightful astrological chart for which I am grateful. I also thank, Sean Taylor for his research. And Luke and Kelly Conde for his typing and Kelly's research. Last on the list but always first in my thoughts, Eric Cargill for …..!

About the Author

Gerald O'Hara, nee Tubridy was born of uncertain parentage in Middlesbrough in 1951. Two years later, in 1953, Jack and Helen O'Hara adopted him. Gerald, now renamed O'Hara spent most of his happy childhood in the North Riding of Yorkshire at Marske-by-the-sea.

Perhaps television pre-disposed the him to an early interest in world affairs. Events such as the 1953 Coronation of Elizabeth II, the 1959 General Election, the election of J.F. Kennedy and the Cuba Crisis of 1962, form some of the author's earliest recollections. Jack O'Hara passed away in March 1963, and Gerald has one adopted sister. In 2002, Gerald traced his full-blood brother Ernest Tubridy, the brothers have been close ever since, and both share a deep interest in Spiritualism. Being adopted perhaps gave Gerald an interest in origins and beginnings and may have led to a lifelong love of history. The ideas of religion and the study of history are the writer's favorite subjects. He left school at 15 and following a job offer, he left home at sixteen, in favor of the fun to be had in 1960s Edinburgh.

At the age of twenty-one, after working for a year in Industrial Northern France, the writer left Edinburgh and moved to London. Gerald was overseas for much of the 1970s and traveled in India twice and throughout most of Europe. He obtained 'O' levels and 'A' levels, then a degree in Sociology from the London School of Economics in 1979. After that, he traveled in North America for a year. In 2006, Gerald and his partner Eric celebrated their 25th anniversary with a Civil Partnership and in 2015, on their 34th anniversary they were formally married.

In 2006 Gerald B.Sc. CSNU, launched his first book, *Dead Men's Embers*. This was followed, a year later, by his second book *Mrs Miller's Gift*, published to mark the 75th anniversary of the Edinburgh College of Parapsychology. In 2009 a further book to accompany the CD of valuable recordings found on 78rpm discs at the Edinburgh College was published. *I come to the Garden: The Spiritual Quest of Dorothy and Russell Flexer* (2017) is Gerald's fourth book.

Contents

Cover Design: Robert Carr of Santa Fe, New Mexico.
Robert studied art at the The School of the Art Institute of Chicago, The Kansas City Art Institute, and the College of Santa Fe. He holds a Master's degree in Art Education from The University of New Mexico and has experience with a wide range of media and processes.
For contact Robert: robertcarrart@gmail.com or www.robertcarrart.com

In The Garden

I come to the garden alone,
While the dew is still on the roses;
And the voice I hear falling on my ear,
The Son of God discloses.

Refrain

And He walks with me, and He talks with me,
And He tells me I am His own,
And the joy we share as we tarry there,
None other has ever known.

He speaks, and the sound of His voice,
Is so sweet the birds hush their singing;
And the melody that He gave to me
Within my heart is ringing.

Refrain

I'd stay in the garden with Him
Though the night around me be falling;
But He bids me go; through the voice of woe.
His voice to me is calling.

Austin Mills (1868-1946)

Austin Miles, in 1912, composed Reverend Dorothy's favourite hymn. An amateur photographer, while waiting for a film to develop, had a profound spiritual experience in which he saw a vision of Mary Magdalen visiting the empty tomb of Jesus. He saw her leave the tomb and meet the Master in the garden where he spoke her name. When Miles came to himself the words to a new song were filling his mind and soul. He wrote out the lyrics and that same night composed the music.

Quotations from the hymn are used at the beginning of each chapter.

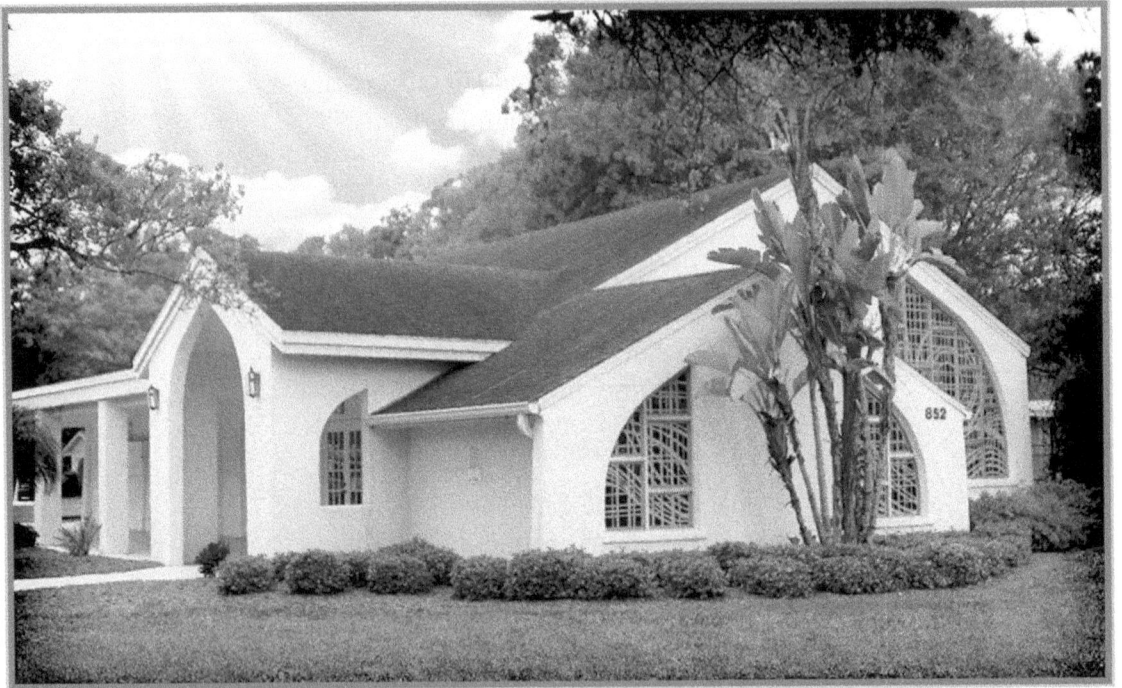

Sarasota Center of Light.

Introduction

"It's no use going back to yesterday,
because I was a different person then."

— *Lewis Carroll, "Alice in Wonderland"*

No one knew Dorothy and Russell better than they knew themselves and the couple cannot tell us who they were; their voices are stilled. Nevertheless, we are going back to their yesterday to understand the people that they were and determine what their legacy is. Yesterday was different; we are not the same. The truths of yesterday may be enhanced by the perspectives of today. It is up to the present to determine the meaning of Russell and Dorothy's life. Though their lives were lived and ended recently, nevertheless, the meaning of their lives remains to be understood. We will appreciate the Flexers on their own terms and assess what influences, actions and what motives come together in the final narrative to say, this is who they were.

There are still many who knew Dorothy and Russell, and they contribute their appreciation. Those who have come along after their story is over must rely on the serendipity of the records that are left behind. The records that are discovered may be contradictory, they will be incomplete and may conflict with the lengthening memory of others. Such is the material with which we shape the portrait. In the keeping of archives the present seldom takes thought of tomorrow and chance dictates the shape of our heritage.

What is written is an interpretation, albeit an interpretation based upon the records, memories and the author's empathy with the Flexers. If this is a good biography, the writer will have an intuitive insight into the couple's life. This is a portrait in ink; what is written is crafted in truth and acceptance of mediumship, for to do less would devalue the biographical process. Much of the routine of living, the setbacks, the hard work and disagreements are forgotten and went unrecorded. As such an ideal portrait belongs to these narrated events and not to those who lived the life. Nevertheless, you may have once seen a now vanished hand, yet still describe the fingers. In so far as we can empathize with the subjects, so may the portrait be truer. In so far as the writer can be objective so might the impression be more accurate. It is for the author to be Dorothy and Russell's envoy and to give new breath to their life. We are going back to yesterday and yesterday was different; people were different.

Dorothy and Russell devoted their life to Truth, and the truth is the goal of these accounts. One-sided views can never be exhausted because they are sectarian. The essence of the Truth for which Russell and Dorothy dedicated their lives was the 'Science of direct experience of God.' This work is intended to be factual and to be above factions in order to be acceptable to all. The hope is that this book will be part of a healing process. In so far as these narratives can be shaped without becoming embroiled in partisan views, so will the book create something that will stand as a living legacy and inspiration. In so far as these aims are realized, is for you to decide.

The author never knew the Flexers, maybe you did? Like most, this writer has come along after the couple left this world and joined Spirit. This story is written for those who knew the Flexers and for those who never met them. This book is intended for the reader who is immersed in Russell and Dorothy's ideas and for those who are new to their concepts. Their lives were lived amongst others in a New World different from the Old that the author was raised in. The USA is a foreign country, their way of doing things is different, the values and the people are different from the European. There is, therefore, a need to take into account all degrees of familiarity with the topics under discussion.

And yet, in not having the pleasure of meeting them the author has the advantage of being an outsider. The writer sees more context to their lives than the local view affords. New eyes see a greater perspective; themes can be explored and the picture not fixed. The interpretation of the Flexers' lives in these narratives does not follow a strict chronological order. Key elements of Metaphysical thought and events can be explored in different locations of time such as the role of 'Master Teachers' in Chapter Two, and the death of Russell and the mysticism of his thought in Chapter Three. Eric Butterworth, the Unity writer, quotes an oriental saying "to define a thing is to limit it," – a more linear approach would have been prosaic. The author's aim is to let the couple find their own voice through these pages as we explore aspects and themes of their life.

Some readers may have never visited the Shrine of the Master (SOM) or the USA but know of these topics from other backgrounds. Such interests in themselves make for other areas of perspective, for example, physical mediumship. Other readers may take an interest in metaphysics and spirituality and be attracted to this book to compare what they believe with the interpretation that Dorothy and Russell developed. The Flexers up to 1958 are part of the history of Spiritualism, as such their story is part of a larger story of that movement. Students of 19th and 20th century American New Thought and Metaphysical religions would be attracted to reading how these influences were synthesized in Christian Metaphysics.

Dorothy and Russell were not given to reminiscing, and theirs was a 'stand alone' church, yet no ship floats upon an empty dock. The Christian Metaphysicians religion of Truth was shaped by many influences. To begin the study, Chapter One is concerned with origins, births, the familiar townscapes and countryside of youth. How and what the families thought was influential in shaping of Dorothy and Russell's early lives. The closeness of family relationships, the economy of living and the subtle forming of emotional intelligence are looked at. These background influences shape the flowering of adulthood. 'The Truth' was to be a major theme of Dorothy's and Russell's lives and in Chapter One we look at what the couple understood by 'Truth' and how they arrived at their conclusions regarding the nature of truth. Also, we look at what took them on the road to meet the medium Ethel Post Parrish, probably the most influential person in both Russell and Dorothy's early life. It was at Ethel's Camp Silver Belle that the Flexers discovered a heritage that they could emulate, wonderful teachers and some great contemporaries.

The brief of the second chapter is to explore the move away from their home state of Pennsylvania and forward into their lives in the Spiritualist movement, in which movement Reverend Dorothy Grafff Flexer was acknowledged as a great mental and physical medium. That is one through whose mediumship the departed can physically manifest in this world. The author looks at the links that the SOM had with other Spiritualist groups, especially the Spiritualist Episcopal Church (SEC). The SEC, AGM of 1956 is looked at closely, and Dorothy's role in the events at that conference are examined. The internet is full of inaccurate disinformation, and the record is set straight. See also the appendices for more on this topic. Moreover, Dorothy and Russell began to develop their own path to truth and their own 'Science' of metaphysics. The early Shrine of the Master Churches that were founded (Norfolk and especially Tampa) are looked at in this chapter.

The emphasis on the teachings of the Metaphysical nature of reality is explored. The role of the Dorothy and Russell's personal Master Teachers and spirit helpers are included. The accounts of the weekly séance and procedures of communication as chronicled by Alda Madison Wade are examined.

In Chapter Three, the other influences that shaped the SOM are noted. Dorothy and Russell knew everybody who was anybody in the Spiritualist Movement, the subtle influence of such contact is assessed. There may have been an indirect influence of Winifred Moyes, the English Medium who founded the Greater World Christian Spiritualist Association in 1931, such similarity of thinking is noted. New Thought and its influence on Metaphysical religions in the USA is explored and explained to readers who are not familiar with its ideas. The nature of metaphysical religion is examined and in particular its influence on the Church of Metaphysical Christianity's (CMC) ideas regarding 'Spiritual Law'. The important public service of Vibrational Healing in the

SOM is discussed and compared with the Christian Science approach to healing. The nature of Dr Russell's mysticism is considered and is regarded as the heart of Metaphysical Christianity, and Russell's final illness and passing are narrated.

It was the life that Dorothy and Russell shared with others in the community they founded that was of importance to the couple. Chapter Four looks at the founding of the Sarasota Sanctuary and the building of the community. The Flexers chose to dedicate themselves to their own churches, rather than serve other churches. The congregation and its welfare, the teachings of spirit and Dorothy's mediumship was their chosen path. Chapter Four looks at the foundation of the CMC in 1958 and the break from the SEC. In this chapter, we look at the communal aspects of SOM such as the choir, the classes and the Sunday schools, weddings and the phenomena of Dorothy's mediumship. This book is then not simply a biography but rather it is a portrait of a community and in this part of the book we look at the communal life that was lived.

In Chapter Five, we examine the idea, that, as the author was told: "it was never about the money." The motivation for the pastoral role was a vocation to serve the needs of others and not monetary. Money was not of interest to the Flexers, as a lasting community cannot be built on the greed of the leaders. It was part of Spiritual Law that "we attract to ourselves that which we are." Dorothy and Russell attracted co-operation and support because they lived the values they taught. This book looks at the many communal activities that were part of the daily life of the SOM. Dorothy and Russell held a pastoral role within their world, presiding over the birth, deaths and marriages at the SOM. The Reverend Dorothy Flexer was a counselor and social worker, and as the Master Jesus had said in the parable of the Good Samaritan "...insofar as you do these things to the least of these, you do them to me." (Matt.25:31-46). Care and succor of their commune were a natural part of who Russell and Dorothy were. In this chapter, we look at the events that brought about the closing of the Tampa Church, including the creation of the Featherstone housing project that formed a residential community around the sanctuary in Browning Street.

Reverend Dorothy's passing is recorded in Chapter Six and here we examine the challenges of taking the legacy forward and making the heritage relevant to a new generation. There were choices to be made and new foundations followed from those decisions. New personnel were chosen, and new people came forward and joined. In this final chapter, the flexibility of Dorothy and Russell's vision is examined in terms of how the spiritual enrichment and the psychic life of the member was and remains the key to developing both the individual, the community and the Center itself.

It was Reverend Dorothy and Russell's dearest wish always to keep the intention of the mediumship upon the teachings of spirit. It is right to honor that perspective. This book has boxes of text inserted throughout its pages that have quotations from the teachings as received mainly by the Flexers and a few others. The narrative may deal with details; nevertheless, the page may still point to higher instruction.

Subtly, there are several themes that run throughout the book, some themes are questions, and others are themes to think about as you read the text. Such themes are explored rather than answered directly. Answers emerge as the work progresses.

Firstly, the book is a photographic record of the people and the society that formed around the Shrine of the Master. These portraits of a community reveal who they wanted us to see and the activities that they were engaged in. Pictures reveal only so much but nevertheless are an invaluable record of activity. Some services such as christenings and weddings leave little in the way of written records. Images can often convey a mood and suggest a sense of what was occurring in the hearts and minds of the participants. This author agrees with Lewis Carroll's, Alice in Wonderland who said: "And what is the use of a book, without pictures or conversation?" The photographs in this book are chosen to complement the understanding of the narrative.

Another theme of this work is the character and personality of the Flexers. Dorothy is well remembered for having a decisive manner. There was 'only one way to peel potatoes!' And there are those who remember Reverend Dorothy not always suffering fools gladly. Dorothy Flexer was quoted as saying "don't let the door hit you on the …on your way out!" However, you can believe that the Reverend Dorothy never swore or used bad language. For nearly fifty years, Dorothy proved an able executive; there was direction and authority but also a capacity to engage support. Neither Russell or Dorothy were egotistic, and there was no sense of narcissism in their characters, such flaws of character are divisive and counteract the building of community. The theme of how the character and personalities of the Flexers contributed to the building of their elective or voluntary community is explored throughout the book. As Florence Strauss put it in 2015, with admiration and directness, "Reverend Dorothy was nice, she was something else."

The Flexers were not saints, but they were loved. Dorothy and Russell Flexer knew suffering, work, and hardship, indeed when Dorothy lost her husband, Russell in July 1977, Dorothy grieved and carried on with the mission of building the Shrine of the Master until Reverend Dorothy Graff Flexer died on 26th August 1996. As some have said, Dorothy was possessed of an inner illumination, it was the dedication, generosity, adherence to high standards and love of the spirit world that shone through. Such happiness as the Flexers showed was born of linking their lives to something greater and outside themselves. And those who have come along afterward, speak as those who knew them do; that they were happy for having this couple in their life. Indeed, the Flexers were loved. Is it the role of a biography to understand and explain why they were loved?

It is certain that Dorothy and Russell valued belief over experience as a basis for faith. That is, faith and belief were primary and essential to true Religion. It is arguable that the phenomenal aspects of Dorothy's mediumship, the demonstration of the Spirit world as a material force in this world, was the basis of conviction for those who joined the Shrine of the Master. It is a matter of personal account whether it was experience or faith that was tantamount in an individual's life. Quite possibly, the converts never considered the matter. It is, however, of concern to this book and differing perspectives emerge on the themes of experience and faith and form part of these narratives.

The subject of transcendence of death and communication with the departed, teachers and spirit helpers are themes that run throughout the book. Death, it was shown, was no longer an enemy to be feared but a friend that teaches us to live fully now. The theme of how to live according to the 'Spiritual Law' and thereby earn our future state in Heaven was to Dorothy and Russell a lifelong preoccupation and of concern to this book. Our inevitable end was not an ultimate invasion of privacy but a stimulus to learn how to live. The ultimate goal of us all was to the Flexers a realm of merited happiness far greater than we can comprehend in this world. This ultimate metaphysical reality challenged the Shrine of the Master member to live correctly here and now. Heaven did not undermine this present now, heaven gave value and meaning to all that had gone before it. To the people of this book the universe was no longer cold and indifferent, instead the individual found the world was a place of unconditional love and they found that they were never truly alone.

It has been said that 'fools are fools that think alike' and in this work you will find that there is much discussion of rare forms of mediumship such as full-form materialisation, levitation; the apporting or appearance of physical objects into the séance room; of direct voice and trumpet mediumship, where voices from another world speak to this dimension. The reader will read of saints, guides, masters and archangels and what they had to say to mankind. Dorothy and Russell were primarily concerned to bring the teachings of the spirit world to man. Mediumship as a vehicle for the known departed was of secondary importance to the teachings.

This social scientist and biographer accepts the witness statements of mediumistic phenomena as, being what the witness believed to have occurred. What they were taught is what they came to value and what shaped their lives. In philosophy, this is known as Phenomenology or the appearances and impact of things in our experience, and the meanings things have in our life. Reverend Dorothy from 1946 to 1996 demonstrated an extraordinary gift of mediumship that was literally witnessed by hundreds of people. To the people of this book the experience of such extraordinary mediumship changed their lives. A truth is no less a truth because only a few eyes see it. No doubt that the people who were witnesses found the answers to life's questions in Dorothy and Russell's work.

The members' lives were shaped by their participation and adherence to the teachings, phenomena, and community they experienced. To say, as many would that they were fools, that such things do not and cannot occur is to devalue the process of biography. No doubt, some writers would take the paranormal scientific researcher approach. Such would look for the 'tricks of the trade', collusion of the sitters and the paraphernalia of tomfoolery. Witness statements would be found to be invalid as they could not be substantiated by independent verification and so would be dismissed as worthless. Values, standards, and sincerity would be set aside, and intention would be reduced to – money. The life that was lived at the Shrine of the Master churches would be found to be 'Topsy Turvey' and a contradiction of common sense.

In the Appendices the reader will find material that supports and enhances the understanding and appreciation of the previous six chapters of the life and quest of Dorothy and Russell Flexer. Here are a few details of what will be found in them.

1. Many people devoted a great part of their lives to the Church of Metaphysical Christianity but did not receive, or have only a brief mention in the book. In this appendix, an effort is made to list those who served and their offices and where possible dates.

2. 'Mrs Flexor' and the Chinese Whispers, is a setting of the record straight. The information on the internet is almost completely or at least 80% incorrect. In this appendix, we trace the origins of the errors and give the facts with references.

3. Dorothy and Russell: an appreciation by Tom Newman.

4. An excerpt from Alda Madison Wade's *At the Shrine of the Master* that gives an impression of what it was like to be at a Class of Reverend Dorothy at Tampa SOM in 1952.

5. Four Sermons by Dorothy and Russell are given in the hope that the reader will enjoy and be enlightened by reading, in the original voice, the thoughts that shaped the SOM.

6. Dorothy's Astrological Birth Chart by Margaret Hodge.

7. Vibrational Healing Protocol: – given by Dr. Charles Davis.

8. American definitions of Spirit Guides from a Handout.

9. *How to be a Good Metaphysician*: a printout of the original pamphlet.

10. The Principles of Metaphysical Spirituality at the Sarasota Center of Light.

11. Books and Journals consulted by the Author in his detailed research for this book.

12. Reverend Tom Newman's booklist offers the reader a wide choice for extending his or her knowledge on the subject of Metaphysics, Psychic Awareness and the Afterlife.

The task of this author has been to empathize and understand Dorothy and Russell Flexer, and explain what motivated this community at the SOM and what their lives meant to them. Such empathy is, I believe, sound social science; that is to understand the subjects on their own terms. Let the skeptics 'sweat the small stuff', I shall sleep soundly.

Abbreviations used in the Text and Background Information

CCC: Camp Chesterfield Collection.

CMC: Church of Metaphysical Christianity.

CSB: Camp Silver Belle.

GWCL: Greater World Christian Spiritualist League. (later Association) British.

IGAS: According to the Association of Religious Data Archives, this organization had 90 churches linked to it in 1940 and 209 by 1956. It appears to have been a general umbrella association to provide a forum where Spiritualist organizations could meet to discuss matters of common interest.

ISA: Independent Spiritualist Association. Founded in 1924 by the Reverend Amanda Flower. It currently has 12 churches in association.

NAS: National Association of Churches. Reorganized as the NASC: National Association of Spiritualist Churches. (Some 87 churches in association as of 2015.)

NT: New Thought.

SCOL: Sarasota Center of Light.

SEC: Spiritualist Episcopal Church 1941. Today, the SEC is mostly in Michigan and has some 20/25 churches affiliated to it.

SNU: Spiritualist National Union, UK. 315 Churches in affiliation.

SOM: Shrine of the Master.

SHTC: Sarasota Herald Tribune Collection.

SST: School of Spiritual Truth. Founded by Ethel Post (Parrish) and had up to eight churches in association and issues ordination certificates to Ministers. Ethel's own church was incorporated by the NAS (NASC) in 1946.

USA: 1956. Universal Spiritualist Association. Nothing currently known, possibly defunct.

N.B. The SNU and the GWCL in the mid-1930s had over 1,100 churches in association in the UK, plus many independent churches, colleges, and associations of all kinds. The figure in 2016 is closer to 400, including all types of organizations.

Do all the good you can
To all the people you can
In all the places you can
At all the times you can
In all the ways you can
For as long as ever you can.

John Wesley

Russell and Dorothy Flexer

Chapter One

"While the dew is still on the roses..."

"Vision," Jonathan Swift wrote, "is the art of seeing things invisible," – that is to other people. When vision combines with character and resolve, then vision becomes a purpose in life. Such an individual has a sense of being part of something greater than the self.

The Reverend Dorothy Graff Flexer had vision, character and resolve but there was more, Dorothy had a great gift, that gift was service to others, and the tool of that service was her remarkable mediumship. None are born with gifts and talents fully formed. There may be a capacity for greatness, but if the subject has a want of character, then nothing may come of the talent. Dorothy and her husband Russell had to apply themselves to the work of developing their vision over many years. Their work is ongoing, never complete. Labor to maintain, to sustain and grow the dream is still needed; long after their earthly life was completed.

But to start; Dorothy Graff's family were Lutheran from German stock. The first known Graff in Pennsylvania was Henry Graff, arriving in 1736 from Germany and he died in Pennsylvania in 1763. The family became Presbyterian, and Dorothy's father, Otto Graff (b. 1884) was a Hosiery Mill Forman. Otto died in April 1933, leaving his wife and mother of Dorothy, Bertie to live on in Sarasota until her death in April 1972.

Dorothy's name translates from the Greek as 'Gift of God' and was amongst the ten most popular girls' names in the USA in the early 20th century. They were a large family. There was a well-loved sister, Ruth, who died in 1940 aged only thirty-five. She also worked as a medium. Helen was the next eldest (1909-1983), and there were also three brothers Paul, James and Richard. None of the brothers were interested in the psychic life. A few days after what has gone down in history as the 'Great White Storm' had devastated the Great Lakes area, on Monday 17th November 1913 Dorothy Graff was born in Reading, Pennsylvania. Dorothy's maternal family was also of German origin and were called Schweimler.

Reading is situated in the southern corner of the state. In the 19th century the town became important as a railroad hub for the shipment of coal. The Frick Coke Mills and Carnegie Steel Works at Homestead, which saw the bitter strike of 1892, were served by these railroads. The town was mapped out in 1743 and established by 1748, with the first Germans arriving soon after from southern and western Germany. The area has a mild, warm climate with humid summers and average high temperatures of 85F. Frosts can occur in October, and the winter can be freezing and snowy, but the winters are seldom severe. The population at the time of the 1920 census is given at 107,000.

1940s Postcard of Reading PA.

Reading sounds a pleasant town to grow up in, with two symphony orchestras (music was very important to Dorothy and Russell), parks and a public Museum and Art Gallery. In the 1930s the town boasted several movie theaters which Dorothy and her family would almost certainly have visited. But with the death of Otto in 1933, money may have limited visits to the silver screen. All but one of the cinemas have been demolished. The only surviving movie house that the Graff family may have visited is the Rajah, which was converted into the Sovereign Performing Arts Center in 2000.

Russell James Flexer was born in Quakerlake, Rush Township, Pennsylvania on 25th October 1914. This town, located in Schuylkill County, is a small place with a population today of 719. Most of the population is thought to commute to other larger towns for work. Doctor Russell was to die of a brain tumor on 22nd July 1977 in Sarasota. His father, Arthur J. Flexer (b. 1892) was a railroad conductor and had died on 22nd September 1953 in Philadelphia. His wife, Russell's mother, was Mary E. Flexer (1895-1977), and both parents were from Pennsylvania. In 1930, the census for that year lists two children, Russell and Virginia (1918-2007). Russell's sister appears to have lived and died in Hazelton PA, the town in which she was born. Hazelton was also the town in which, in 1920, the Graff family was renting a house. The town was noted for its coal mining and railroad connections.

Russell and Dorothy both shared a great love of music and, of course, a love of the spiritual life. Russell's family were Evangelical United Brethren Church members. This body has now merged with United Methodist Church. It is known that the Flexers were also interested in Spiritualism and that the interest pre-dates Russell and Dorothy's first meeting.

Russell studied violin as a young man and traveled by train to nearby Hazelton to take lessons. He enjoyed playing in the local dance bands and at other gatherings. Dorothy is well remembered for her fine singing voice and both sang. Russell would play the violin at home and in church services. Given Russell's love of spirit and harmony, the more *avant garde* 'plink-plonk' music would

Arthur Flexer,
Russell's father.

have sounded to him like a headache on a train. It was said that Dorothy could have been an opera singer. Music was a key element in their life together.

Dorothy said, "I was still a teenager when I learned 'The Truth', but mostly my interests in life were all in church or religion in one form or another. I think that makes a difference. The only other interest, other than religion, was music and that is also very important for development. It certainly adds rhythm and harmony, and lifts the soul and makes it a lot easier for relaxation and meditation."

Music is a shared language. It has a restorative power and music unlocks the world of better times. The wide stage of emotions, of deep collective harmonies, dark beauty, and joyous exuberance, can transport the individual who loves music into a variety of sound worlds. These sound poems give a sense of space, time and place. Dorothy and Russell's love of music has a deeper meaning, for music brings a sense of communion and mindfulness. There is an emotive force in music that transports and uplifts the soul. That emotive power to the sensitive can be a language of God that expresses itself beyond ideas and thoughts. Lovers of music understand that language as mood, invocation of atmosphere and textures of sound. Russell and Dorothy were united by their love of music. That harmony of sound echoed their devotion to the work of the Great Spirit.

There is a sense of vocation in Dorothy's life that became apparent at a young age. The whole of Dorothy's life revolved around the twin themes of spirit and music. Both are interior experiences that require sensibility. The Pennsylvanian hills must have echoed with music, that of the Puritan communities, the numerous churches, the radio, and music made at home. Russell and Dorothy would have understood the meaning of the verse of the old Shaker Hymn *Simply Gifts*, that a vocation shared with a partner is a joy for life.

> "And when we find ourselves in the place just right,
> 'Twill be in the valley of love and delight."

The other key aspect of their life together, and that which was to be their principle joy and motive in life was their quest for and realization of the Divine. Martin Luther King expressed the sense of connection to the community and to the divine that Russell and Dorothy also felt: "We are caught in an inescapable network of mutuality, tied in a single garment of destiny. Whatever affects one directly affects all indirectly."

The work of mediumship and teaching that the couple undertook gave them both a keen sense of connection to the spirit world and to the communities they founded. It was the life that Russell and Dorothy shared with others and not simply the life that they lived, that was of importance to the couple. The Masters and teachers whose voices were heard through Dorothy's mediumship and Russell's sermons were accepted by those communities as being ultimately connected to the source of all life, God.

To the medium, the mind is a channel connecting many discarnate sources. Dorothy's mind was touched by many worlds of being and through her agency many worlds of thought were expressed in this earthly sphere. There is a joy in Dorothy and Russell's work, in that their lives were touched by many other lives. They lived the truth that we are never truly alone. In understanding the role of music and the role of the Divine in their lives; we approach an understanding of them as individuals and as a couple.

Imagination, a good mind, and the capacity to empathize with other people are all part of the emotional flow that music lovers and good mediums share. Not to be overwhelmed by the emotions of others implies psychological resilience. Every good medium must have an internal mental order that understands and empathizes with the living and the discarnate but which retains emotional balance and mental independence. Everyone who knew Dorothy would agree that she was open, friendly and firm of character.

We know that Dorothy and Russell were well versed in Bible studies and such studies, were (as we shall see) taught at the Centers that were founded in Florida. The Presbyterian background of Dorothy's family must have been influential in Dorothy's education. We know that the family was free thinking, and open to other influences. Russell and Dorothy would reject many orthodox beliefs. Nevertheless, the primacy of Jesus Christ as a Master Teacher was firmly rooted in these early years and became a focus for the couple's whole life. These topics we will look at more closely in Chapter Four.

Notably, the Presbyterians taught that priesthood was everyone's job and that all should share the good news of the Gospels. Also, and important as an influence, the Presbyterian Church is governed by laity, clergy, women and men alike. For the purposes of the individual, the Bible and in particular the New Testament was the authority and source of Divine revelation. However, St Paul had said, "Let women keep silent in churches; for they are not permitted to speak, but are to subject themselves to the Law." (1 Corinthians 14:34). On this authority, the ministry of women had been suppressed in the early churches, as had healing and prophecy. In the 1930s this dictum of St Paul was still widely in force, except, in a limited way amongst Quakers and Presbyterian Church.

The Spiritualists in the mid-19th century were unique in that they empowered women's mediumship, church leadership, and ministry in all its phases. Emma Hardinge Britten (1823-1899), the British Pioneer Spiritualist came to America as an actress in the 1850s and became involved with a group

I will accept the responsibility of making my life productive, spiritually and materially, assured of the many blessings provided by the immutable laws of the Great Spirit.

of Spiritualist women in New York. In her highly readable autobiography, she had this to say about the attitude of the movement to women's mediumship, etc.

"But the whole of the women present chorused out that St Paul was a crusty old bachelor, who objected to women speaking out in public. Upon this, the entire party looked sympathizingly on me, and St Paul was dropped."

The leadership role that women acquired was dependent on their possessing adequate psychic abilities. Dorothy had great mediumship abilities, a vocation to serve and the ambition to be a Chief and not an Indian. It is worth recalling that the U.S. Susan B. Anthony's Amendment to give women the vote was passed in 1920 when Dorothy was 7 years old. Indeed, Dorothy could quote St Paul and loved the verse in 1 Corinthians 13:6 "Rejoices not in iniquity but rejoices in the truth." I am sure that Dorothy would have agreed whole heartily with the truth of the survival of death that St Paul expresses in 1 Corinthians 15:16, 3-6

"For if the Dead are not raised then Christ has not been raised … Christ died… was buried… and he was raised on the third day … and he appeared to Cephas: then to the twelve. Then he appeared to more than five hundred brothers and sisters at one time." *(shortened extracts).*

The Graffs were a close-knit, affectionate and supportive family. Such backgrounds breed emotionally secure and self-confident people. It is a sound background for someone such as Dorothy who had a natural ability and was attracted to the psychic side of life.

Otto Graff, was secretary to a Lodge, that Lodge we may assume was of the Freemasons. His future son-in-law Russell was also a Freemason, joining at Portsmouth VA in the early 1940s. It is worth noting that the principles of the Freemasons are similar to that of Metaphysical and Spiritualist groups, being based in egalitarian ideas of the Brotherhood of Man, living a moral life, freedom of religious worship and equality for all. Otto had responsibility for opening and closing the Masons' Hall when it was being used by others. It was while attending the Lodge hall that Otto came to listen to the messages given by visiting mediums. Otto was a religious and open minded man who told his children that "there was a lot more to religion than what the churches taught or admitted." Through following the responses of the audiences, Otto developed an interest in psychic matters and in the nature of the soul.

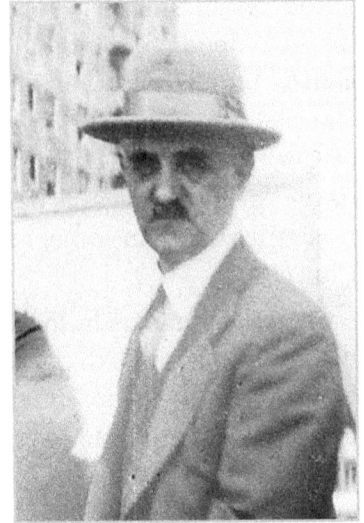

Otto Graff, Dorothy's father.

Dorothy and her sister Ruth with the other family members had experience of Spiritual healing which, along with prayer, was a resource that was often used at home. Instead of a doctor, a healer would be found. That kind of help works at a physical vibrational level, at an intuitive level and also develops the spiritual awareness of connections to greater forces. It was while training as a nurse that Ruth and other students developed an interest in mediumship. One woman they thought had unusual abilities, and the girls were much impressed by the woman's accuracy. Upon returning home, Ruth told the family what she had witnessed. Dorothy comments that the mediums at that time were frequently regarded as 'fortune tellers'.

As a 61-year-old Dorothy was to look back at 1930 and say, "With our interest in the messages that this woman gave, we began to search for other people who might have an understanding of what was then called Spiritualism. We then met a woman who was a healer and a medium. My mother received a great deal of benefit from her gift of healing, and when the woman held message services, we would go. We would receive guidance and messages which were very evidential."

In the spring of 1933, Otto Graff died suddenly on the night before his fiftieth birthday. Otto had predicted his own death saying that he would not live to be fifty. On the night before he died Dorothy's father was reading the newspaper and on the back of the paper Dorothy could see his obituary printed; that night he died of a heart attack.

The wild and stormy summer of 1933 was a season of loss for the Graff family; grieving was like a winter without Christmas. Dorothy was close to both parents and dearly loved her father. Our age believes in hugs and tears, but such emotional display would have been treated with suspicion in the 1930s. Tears outside of grieving would have been greeted with embarrassment. It was considered more dignified to keep crying within the privacy of the heart. Too much sensibility was regarded as a weakness; better prefer common sense.

In 1932, a summer school for training and education of mediums and public demonstrations was opened at Ephrata, Pennsylvania.

Camp Silver Belle Memorial Newsletter
showing the First Board with John Reese.

Ethel Post (later Post Parrish), a major influence on Dorothy and Russell.

Ethel Post (1888-1958), usually referred to as Ethel Post Parrish a was a physical medium and founder of Camp Silver Belle at Ephrata. (CSB,1932-1988.) The Reverend Dr. Myron Post (b.1875) it is thought, was Ethel's second husband. The couple divorced in 1939 and Ethel Post married a James M. Parrish (1906-1964.) For several years in the 1920s, Myron Post was President of the Board at Camp Chesterfield and Ethel Post served as a medium, starting her career there as a medium in 1925.

Ethel & Rev. Dr. Myron Post in 1929.[1]

Through Ethel Post's physical mediumship, Dorothy would have witnessed full-form materialization of departed spirits. Witnesses would have verified the identity of the departed. The communication between people of earth and the angels was experienced by Dorothy and family when her father Otto manifested physically and 'distinctly'. Dorothy wrote: "outstanding evidence was given so that I and the family knew it was he." This was the impossibility of which we all dream, a reunion with people we have loved and lost. There were messages from her father which for Dorothy and family were beyond any doubt.

Dorothy herself was a physical medium. As we will see Reverend Dorothy, would do what was necessary, then do the possible and finally achieved the impossible in becoming a Trumpet medium for other worlds. Through this mediumship, evolved masters found physical expression in this world. The Flexers founded a new center of excellence, which twenty years after her passing, still functions.

Dorothy and Russell were schooled in Bible studies and the experience of meeting materialized spirits, would have been a confirmation of what St Paul had written in 1 Corinthians 15:20 "But Christ has been raised from the dead, the firstfruits of those who have died. For since death came through a human being, the resurrection of the dead has come through a human being. For as all die in Adam, so all will be made alive [in Christ]."

1. Apologies for the quality of the photograph. It was the only one that could be found of the couple. (G.O'H)

'The Truth' was to be a major theme of Dorothy's life. The meeting with spirits confirmed the truth of scriptures with which the couple were familiar. We have seen that as a teenager Dorothy had 'learned the Truth', and what was meant by that is crucial to understanding the future that Dorothy and Russell created. The evidence from the mediums of which Dorothy spoke elsewhere indicates that 'the Truth' matched reality and was in agreement with the facts as Dorothy understood the world. Personal survival of death and communication were a fundamental part of that Truth. The meeting with the materialized spirit of her father, with other family members present, was that unique thing in life: an experience that changes everything. This was a conversion experienced by Dorothy that is expressed in John 8:32 "And ye shall know the truth, and the truth shall set you free."

Further, Dorothy realized that mediumship and therefore communication could be a vehicle for further revelations of 'the Truth'. In the manner of Old Testament prophets, spiritually evolved masters could teach and provide a direct link to the Divine. Revelation was not ancient but an on-going tradition. That is the revelations of yesterday may be enhanced by the perspectives of today. Each age has the same quota of intelligence as we have, yet each period of Man sees the evolution of the self, we are not the same as the ancients. Our field of vision increases as does our scope of inquiry. Further revelation enhances the breadth of the Truth. In terms of religion, further revelation is unorthodox as it requires the reassessment of what we understand to be the truth. No church's approval is required. Such revelation was a threat of anarchy to established faiths. Revelation to such religions was safely in the past. In this sense, Russell and Dorothy were rebels against orthodoxy.

I am thankful for every moment of communicating with my angels, for they help me to carry my personal burden of life with dignity and with hope.

Nevertheless, Dorothy and Russell's metaphysics was firmly rooted in biblical tradition. As Dorothy was to say Spiritualism or Metaphysics as an approach to religion was not new, but it was arrived at by Dorothy and Russell themselves through experiencing other mediums' work. Dorothy was following in the steps of the Master Jesus' teachings given in 'The Sermon on the Mount' when he said:

"Enter into thy closet and when thou has closed the door, pray to the Father which is in secret, and the Father who sees in secret will reward thee openly."

It was the going inward and the development of personal consciousness that was the key to the 'Quest' for Dorothy's relationship with the Divine. The material world proceeds from our thought, from the inner world of spirit to the outer world of the material. Metaphysics is a system of understanding individual consciousness in relation to universal principles. It meant 'Right Living', learning to live in harmonious and positive relations with the material world. James Allen put it this way:

"Man is made or unmade by himself. By the right choice, he ascends, as a being of power, intelligence and love, and Lord of his own thoughts he holds the key to every situation."

Through understanding Metaphysics, man learned that he was the master gardener of his soul, the director of his life. We will consider 'Natural Law' further in Chapter Three. Metaphysics, the spiritual inquiry into the nature of reality and man's place in the Universe and relationship to the creator, was to be Dorothy's principle focus and mediumship was to be a tool of that inquiry. This would lead the Flexers away from the Spiritualist movement to a metaphysical emphasis in their spiritual lives and in the lives of the centers they founded. It implied the rejection of Spiritualist phenomena as sensationalism and of sensation seekers. Though the phenomenon of trumpet mediumship was to be an integral part of Dorothy's mediumship nevertheless, that gift was to be an instrument of Higher teachings, St Paul in 1 Corinthians had written:

"If I have the gift of prophecy and can fathom all mysteries and all knowledge, and if I have a faith that can move mountains, but do not have love, I am nothing."

Dorothy and Russell looked to the teachings of the Master as a guide on how to lead their lives. And it was for the life they shared with others, that Russell and Dorothy were loved.

The certainty of the truth and commitment to that as an ideal, tells us that much of what Dorothy, Russell and their families had encountered in Orthodox churches was the opposite of the truth. There was a firm response in their minds to what they realized to be untrue. It is also possible that 'The Truth' and the desire to express the highest standards of mediumship was a refutation of fraudulent mediumship? As well as an affirmation of intent to communicate only the highest, the best and truest in spirit teachings. Russell and Dorothy would devote their life to 'The Truth'. The subject of fraud is one that we look at again in Chapter Two.

Adherence to a cause, a belief, a purpose in life is psychologists say a key factor in the happiness and well-being of an individual. Belonging to something bigger than oneself satisfies that inner urge to find meaning in life. 'The Truth' to Dorothy and Russell had several aspects. The continuous existence of the human soul after death, physical phenomena, the reality of communication between worlds, and the connectivity of all living things. The help and assistance of angels and those whom we have loved and a chain of being that linked creation with the divine. Truth and faith had been grounded in experience.

The loss of her father in 1933, saw the realization, at an emotional level, of 'The Truth' of mediumship confirming scripture, and Dorothy's arrival at Camp Silver Belle (CSB.) These three factors combined to create in the young woman a resolution of purpose and a sense of vocation. Dorothy must have thought, where there is an ambition and faith a way will open! That ambition in the early years must have seemed elusive, and the path unknown.

Prayer is the communion with the God Spirit and the accepting of the help that is given and that you have the blessings of good jobs and abundance and truth and good friends, to live in peace.
Those are the blessings, my friends.

Dorothy took a job at the hosiery mill, possibly the same mill that her father had worked in. It is said that Dorothy was the chief 'bread winner' of the household. Work during the 1930s was difficult to find and with two younger brothers (Ruth and one brother had left home) and mother to look after, Dorothy's work at the Hosiery Mill was vital to help support the family. After finishing high school Russell had attended a trade school in Milwaukee, Wisconsin where he learned to be a welder. At some point, Russell moved to Reading PA to find work and lived with his aunt and uncle. While there he worked for a magazine distribution company delivering magazines to retail outlets.

The Graff family had planned to visit CSB with Otto, but he died before they could do so. Nevertheless, in June 1933 with Ruth, their mother and friends they did visit the camp which lay twenty miles from Reading. The family was very impressed with the way of life and the new religion of Spiritualism.

The yearbook of Spiritualism for 1927, noted that Spiritualism in Pennsylvania dated from 1850 when an association was formed to study Andrew Jackson Davis's book *Nature's Divine Revelations*. *Hartman's International Directory of Psychic Science for 1931* lists the First Spiritualist Church situated at Seidel's Chapel, 117 N Fifth Street and later moved to 1047 Penn Street, Reading PA, where it was housed till at least 1961. The Church was advertised in the 1949 CSB program. This church closed for the summer and reopened in the fall, presumably because the congregation attended CSB. In 1947, Ethel Post Parrish and Peggy Barnes held a service with a choir at the Berkshire Hotel to dedicate the church for the winter months. Ethel Post Parrish and Peggy Barnes would then join the exodus and leave for the balmy climate of Florida. Another church, the Second Spiritual Alliance Church for Life was situated at Ninth and Franklin Street, Reading. It is likely that the Graff family visited these churches. Hartman's Directory for 1931, lists at least eight Spiritualist churches in the state of Pennsylvania, whereas Philadelphia listed as many as twenty-six different organizations.

Nationally, Hartman recorded nineteen Spiritualist organizations, not including Metaphysical or Theosophical bodies. The Reading churches no longer exist.

Between 1930 and 1933 the Graff family had explored and experienced the Spiritualist message as far as they were able at a local level. It had prepared them and educated them for the further work of developing themselves as mediums and channels for other worlds. They found in Camp Silver Belle, "a way of life that was not new to us." Dorothy had found in CSB and its founder Ethel Post (Parrish) a facility that would train her and her sister Ruth's abilities.

The new Camp Silver Belle was founded as a sister to Camp Chesterfield in Indiana which was set up in 1886 and is still functioning. As of 2014, there are still twelve Spiritualist Camps functioning in the USA, including Lily Dale NY (properly known as the Lily Dale Assembly) founded in 1879. These Camps are almost wholly unknown outside of the USA. Most are summer seminaries, though at least four have full-time residents.

The Camp Silver Belle Association was named after Ethel's Indian guide. Silver Belle, spoken of by Peggy Barnes Jefts as "a beautiful Indian girl". Ethel Post Parrish's mediumship saw many aspects of materialization, including direct voice where spirit voices speak in the room at a distance from the medium, full form materialization, and apports, where objects are brought from outside and materialize in the room.

'Silver Belle', Ethel Post's North American Indian spirit guide.

In 1935, with the help of local supporters, CSB was able to take over the Mountain Springs Hotel at Ephrata. The new property was incorporated in 1935 as the Mountain Springs Hotel. The hotel, built in 1882 and demolished in 2004, was set in 100 acres of grounds and boasted over 100 rooms with two external lodges with a further sixty-four bedrooms. The large auditorium could seat 500 people, and at the time of the 25th Silver Anniversary in 1957, it was said the local hotels in the area were kept busy with visitors to the Camp.

Mountain Springs Hotel, Center of Camp Silver Belle.

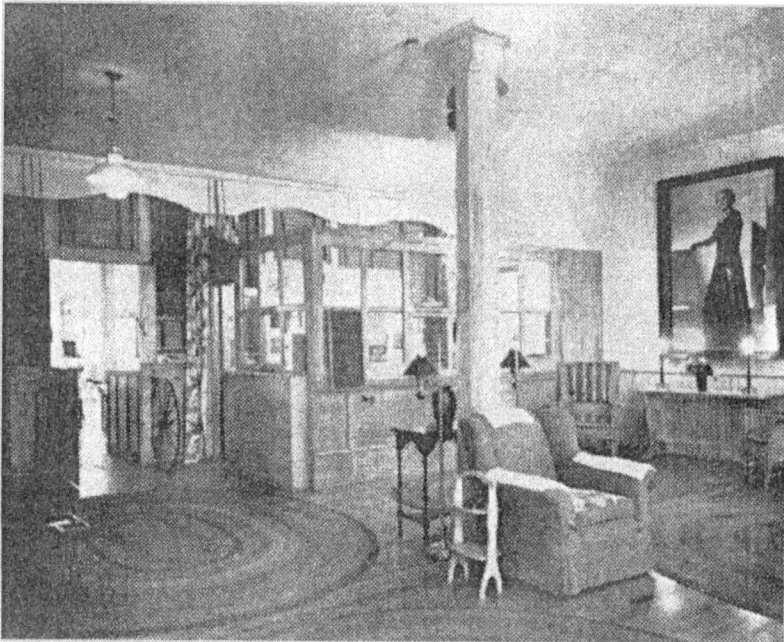

Lobby to the Mountain Springs Hotel showing the full-length portrait of Ethel Post.

The establishment at Ephrata became one of the largest in the USA, and Dorothy would have visited the Camp a year after it opened and had an association with the Camp that lasted twenty-eight years.

It is known that Dorothy got to know Ethel Post Parrish, though Dorothy seldom mentioned the lady in later life; there is no doubt that Dorothy's training really started in earnest at Camp Silver Belle. Ethel Post Parrish was described by Lena (Peggy) Barnes Jefts as "a pleasing personality, always well groomed, attractive and to know her is to love her." Ethel's photographs also show a woman of character with a firm look to her smile. Ethel also founded the Church of the Beloved chartered in 1946 by the National Spiritualist Association (NSA, after 1953 NASC) at St Petersburg, Florida.

Ethel was one of the teachers and Dorothy listed 'other outstanding teachers' as Lena (Peggy) Barnes Jefts, John Reese and Dr. Myron Post. Dorothy thought that they were 'fine mediums' and inspirationally responsible for much that Dorothy and Russell would develop and create. John Reese worked at CSB and conducted the 'Sunday Evening Song Service,' and was said to have a fine voice. Lena (usually known as Peggy) was the cabinet attendant for Ethel Post Parrish at CSB. Peggy wrote several booklets for the National Spiritualist Association of Churches (NSAC, formerly NSA, post 1953) which are still available.

The sisters were soon in regular attendance at the services and classes. A service would have been held each Sunday, possibly at 1 pm with worship in the camp chapel during which spirit messages would be given. These messages would involve billet readings. Upon entry to the chapel, the visitor would be given a blank piece of paper on which to write a question. With initials on the reverse, the mediums would give messages from the spirit side of life. There would have been classes on the development of physical mediumship conducted in the séance rooms. Attendance would have been by invitation, and the student would have to be thought of as suitable. Dorothy was to say, "we were told that we had gifts that could be developed."

Dorothy and her sister Ruth were spoken of as natural mediums, and Dorothy credited her progress to the fact of her starting out on the path of development at a young age and being devoted to the work. Camp Silver Belle closed at Labor Day (the first Monday in September), and the resident mediums went to their homes, many of them in Florida. But there was one medium who stayed through the winters, and he was invited to give classes once a week at the Graff family home in Reading. This may have been, Ernest Holden who lived at Ephrata. We have no record of which family members sat, but it clearly helped the sisters to sit in a private development circle. We don't know what form these classes took and whether they involved the development of trance states of consciousness. We do know that it took forward the work of mediumistic states and understanding of Spiritualism and Metaphysics. As we know, Dorothy had a grounding in Bible studies, and more than likely there would have been access to books on related subjects. Dorothy also took religious studies at the Albright College in Reading. Originally an Evangelical College and Seminary, this beautiful College had been founded in 1856, and has links to the United Methodist Church.

In addition to the classes at CSB, the sisters were also attending a local Spiritualist Church in Reading PA. The girls were occasionally asked to give messages and sermons. Dorothy and Ruth both enjoyed the work. Though the girls found that other (more experienced?) speakers were invited 'week after week' to take the platform. After two or three years, it was suggested by 'many other people' that the Graff girls start their own church. Meanwhile, Dorothy and Ruth took their ordination examinations with Ethel Post's husband, Reverend Dr. Myron

Lord, make me an instrument of your peace, where there is hatred, let me sow love; where there is injury, pardon; where there is doubt, faith; where there is despair, hope; where there is darkness, light; where there is sadness, joy.

(Prayer of St Francis of Assisi)

H. Post. In December 1928, Ethel and Myron Post opened the Spiritual Temple of Truth in Miami. And in 1929, Peggy Barnes tell us that the couple 'seeing a need' opened a School of Spiritual Truth. Further, Peggy Barnes says that that School being incorporated under Florida Law, had 'the right to ordain Ministers and issue certificates of Mediumship; that standards set are of the very highest, both mentally and morally.' There were eight churches within the school.

Dorothy was to say that Ruth and herself were ordained in 1939. Peggy Barnes Jefts, in *Telekinesis, Ectoplasm and Materialization*, probably printed in 1939, tells us that Dorothy and Ruth Graff were graduates of the "School of Spiritual Truth". This must have been a correspondence course as the distance to Miami is close to 1,200 miles. There was a course of religious studies at Albright College, and there was seasonal training at CSB. Additional training, as we shall see was gained in Norfolk VA.

'Truth' became the watchword and the standard by which Dorothy and Russell lived their lives. This writer believes that the emphasis on truth was learned from Ethel Post's influence and teaching, and became the standard against which ethical conduct, mediumship, values, morality and preaching was set.

Dorothy's first church in Reading PA. was founded in 1937 and was called the Friendly Church of Truth. Dorothy Graff was twenty-three years old. Lena (Peggy) Barnes Jefts states that "the eighth church, Reading Penna, in charge of Rev. Ruth Schatz and the Rev. Dorothy Graff." (Dorothy's sister was married with four children.) The association with the Post's School of Truth was, it is thought, a loose one and that Ruth and Dorothy's church remained independent. Nevertheless, Ethel Post's (Parrish) teachings, seminary, and approaches to Spiritualism – one that emphasized Truth as a principle value, was influential on the sisters. The name above the door was chosen to speak for their aims for the church. Somewhere, between the living and the dead, Dorothy and Ruth were to be a new bridge connecting two worlds of being human.

We don't know what types of mediumship were being practiced, though Dorothy herself spoke of 'great interest in our development' which suggests that there may have been unusual phenomena at this time. It has been said that in the USA, Spiritualism was 'all physical' at this time. How true that is, is hard to judge.

The sisters and Russell always possessed a sense of mission in life, and there were to be many unknown roads ahead that led from that first church. The first occurred one Sunday, Dorothy wrote: "The weather was very bad, and Ruth and I were late to church." There were not many in attendance. Dorothy decided to dispense with the sermon and move to the messages. But "after getting a sentence out, I went into a trance, and Dr. Davis gave the sermon." Dorothy, could not account for how this had occurred? Never again would Dorothy give a service without a sermon.

Dorothy was to tell her friend Reverend Tom Newman that Camp Silver Belle services would be given outdoors in the summers. These would be attended by the sisters with their mother. At one such event, a woman medium went slowly into a trance, until the woman's forehead banged on the table! Dorothy found this to be undignified and vowed never to follow the example.

Trance has many phases, though true deep unconscious trance is rare. There is no doubt that Reverend Dorothy had the ability to suspend awareness of external surroundings. Dorothy was unconscious in the Trance State and could set aside normal mental processes at will. This allowed the discarnate to communicate verbally and to physically manifest their own voices via a metal trumpet. The discarnate could materialize their presence; spirits could materialize and move objects and communicate through Dorothy yet independently.

Dr. Charles Davis is not to be confused with the 'Seer of Poughkeepsie', Andrew Jackson Davis whose pioneering work as a trance channel from the mid-1840s empowered many of both sex to follow his example. Dr. C. Davis was to be Reverend Dorothy's Doctor Teacher and spirit guide for Metaphysics. The early appearance of Dr. Davis speaking through Dorothy in trance state in 1937/38 shows a level of sensitivity and receptivity which allowed Dorothy to pass into a trance and say afterward "it just happened." As Dr. Davis was to say, "We always welcome those who come freely in search of the Truth."

Dorothy remarked that they tried to keep it a 'Friendly Church of Truth' ... "and we did our best to do just that." The fate of this little church remains unknown, but when the Flexers left the area in 1941, they were able to pass on the ministry to a gentleman medium from New York. It had been planned that Ruth would become the Minister and administrator of the church, but that was not to be.

It is said that Russell reminded Dorothy of the father that she lost when she was only nineteen. This may have been in temperament and character or in interests shared in common with Otto Graff. There is always someone in need of a good heart, and the future Mrs. Graff Flexer was to say, "A nice young man attended our church..."

On 15th June 1940, Dorothy and Russell were married. Russell at this time would have been around twenty-five. With a pleasant face and of average height, a little taller than Dorothy, he gives an impression of being firmly built. Their true colors shone through, and they matched each other. Russell and Dorothy were married for thirty-seven years until Russell's death in 1977.

As Sister Nicci said in *The Sword of Truth:* "Love is a passion for life shared

Dorothy in the 1940s.

The young Russell Flexer.

with another person. You fall in love with a person who you think is wonderful. It's your deepest appreciation of the value of that individual, and that individual is a reflection of what you value most in life. Love for sound reason can be one of life's greatest rewards."

It is typical of Reverend Dorothy that the description of their courtship is brief and to the point. Mrs. Graff Flexer had a name for not talking about the past. It is apparent that this was a woman who lived in the present and had a mindfulness that was not given to reminiscing.

Unexpectedly, as we have said, Dorothy's much-loved sister Ruth became ill and died suddenly in 1940 aged thirty-five. In an era before antibiotics, the condition of 'Strep-throat' (streptococcus virus) could and did prove fatal. Generally, this is the same virus that causes colds, influenza, and pneumonia. Dorothy and Russell had planned to move to Virginia, but these plans were delayed by Ruth's death. We can only guess the impact that the loss of Ruth had on Dorothy and the family. However, in Dorothy's work as a medium, it was said that Ruth worked closely with her sister throughout the rest of Dorothy's life. There is evidence of Ruth's continuing support for her sister, as we shall see in Chapter Two. Fyodor Dostoyevsky expressed the pain of grief as: "The darker the night, the brighter the stars, the deeper the grief, the closer is God!"

In 1941 the couple moved on and, settling in Virginia, they poured themselves into their life's work. The city of Norfolk Virginia, had a population of 144,000 in 1941, which was to grow to 213,000 by 1950. The rapid growth was fueled by the ready employment offered by the Navy and the industries that the Navy supported. The US naval docks were and still are the largest in the world. With the outbreak of World War Two in Europe in 1939 and the US/GB/China 'Lend-Lease Act' of March 1941, work was to be had at the docks. Russell's skill as a welder was in demand, and as a war service, it gave him exemption from military conscription for it was vital in repairing battle-damaged ships.

Russell and Dorothy found their way to the Memorial Spiritualist Church, Norfolk, which is one of the few churches which was built as a spiritualist church. The Church was founded in 1938 and chartered by NSA in 1939. The Memorial Church is located on the corner of Llewellyn Avenue and 37th Street in Norfolk, Virginia and is the

Memorial Spiritualist Church, in Norfolk VA.,
where Dorothy worked in the 1940s.

'mother' church of many other metaphysical churches in the area. Russell and Dorothy knew the Minister, Kitty Baxter, when the church was known as the First National Spiritualist Church. Kitty had been unwell and asked Dorothy for her help in running the church. In 1945, the name was changed to that of the Memorial Spiritualist Church, by which name (via a few changes) it is known today. Dorothy's experience at that church was formative, and she referred to the experience of working there, without pay as 'tremendous'. As is often the case the archives of the church have vanished long ago, thrown out by a church secretary.

Hannen Swaffer, the British journalist in his book *My Greatest Story*, writes that there was another church in Norfolk run by a remarkable healer, Fred Jordan. His supporters to whom Jordan had given healing, had provided the funds to found a church. This was the Light of Truth Church of Divine Healing. Jordan was a retired Navy Commander ordained by Arthur Ford in 1937. Ford had founded the International General Assembly of Spiritualists (IGAS) in 1936, Jordan succeeded Ford as President in 1938 and fulfilled the role until 1974. Russell and Dorothy would have known Jordan and Arthur Ford from working together at Camp Silver Belle.

It is possible that Dorothy and Russell worked at Jordan's church, given that the couple were living in the same town and working in the same religion. Dorothy tells us that people from the neighboring city of Portsmouth VA asked her to start a church in that area. The city which is on the opposite side of the bay from Norfolk had no church and the locals found the journey to Norfolk to be troublesome. Portsmouth had a population of nearly 51,000 in 1940. This is the location of the docks and repair center at which Russell worked.

Here emerged a key difference in Russell and Dorothy's approach to Spiritualism. Dorothy was to say that this church in Portsmouth was the first to be known as "The Shrine of the Master" (SOM) and that the name was received 'Inspirationally' by Russell. It appears that the Portsmouth SOM was independent, although a member of the IGAS. The title reflects their shared Christian background, their roots in the Bible and in particular the 'The Sermon on the Mount'. The Shrine was to be devoted to Christ as a Master teacher, and as an example of how to live one's life. This approach emphasized spirituality as a way of living. It sought to create conditions for the inner spiritual growth of the individual. There was to be no idolatry at the Shrine of the Master, Christ did not die for our sins. And the light from the lamp of other Masters was allowed to shine and teach through Reverend Dorothy's trumpet mediumship.

Dorothy was to recall that in around 1935, a medium was to predict to her that her home would be made in Florida. Dorothy knew that 'it was spirit led', but the couple were not finished with Virginia and Pennsylvania yet. In 1944, the two of them, Dorothy and Russell became three when their daughter Eileen (now Eileen Courtney) was born. In the following years 1947, 1948 and 1949 the Flexers were again invited to work at CSB to work. Their daughter Eileen was with them, and research shows that Russell volunteered in the camp cafeteria. As always, music was to the fore and both assisted with the music at services. Dorothy is listed as a 'Spiritual Counselor and Lecturer'. The couple knew and worked with famous names such as Arthur Ford, Hugh Gordon Burroughs (President of the CSB Association), Peggy Barnes Jefts, John Reese, Virginia Falls, the British Spiritualists Paul Miller (editor of Psychic Observer) and Horace Leaf, and, of course, Ethel Post Parrish.

On Saturday, 27th August 1949, Dorothy is listed along with Hugh Gordon Burroughs as giving an 'auditorium séance'. Dorothy is also listed amongst the Spiritual Counselors for 'Clairvoyance and Direct Voice'. The final demonstration for the summer

CAMP SILVER BELLE PSYCHICS AND LECTURERS---1948

Camp Silver Belle workers, Summer 1948.

season on 5th September 1949, was listed as a "Demonstration of Direct Voice Mediumship (in the auditorium) by all the mediums." Some twelve mediums are listed as having this ability. We cannot be sure of what occurred but if direct voice is understood to be objective, manifested and heard by all present in the room; the event must have been something to witness.

There were to be differences between Ethel Post Parrish and Dorothy. Dorothy had written to Ethel in 1949 and asked Ethel's advice regarding the possibility of a new church at Sarasota. Ethel said that others had tried in the area, but the people had not proved receptive. However, by the time she received the reply from Ethel, Dorothy had visited the city and had decided to go ahead, feeling that she was following spirit's advice. This caused a rift between the Flexers and Ethel Post Parrish. Russell and Dorothy attended that summer season at CSB in 1949 and did not visit again until after Ethel's death in 1958.

Page 24   Camp Silver Belle—1949

PROGRAMME (Continued)

—Direct-Voice Seance (in Auditorium)
Ethel Post-Parrish, Bertha Eck road, Elizabeth Fabian, Raymond Burns, Emma Munch, Dorothy Flexer, John E. Reese, H. Gordon Burroughs, Ernest Holden, Mary Fulton, Frank Decker.
10.00—Closing Service
    Lowering of Flag
    H. Gordon Burroughs

Relevant entry from the programme for 1949.

The couple served at CSB, in 1959 and 1960. In 1960, Russell and Dorothy were again listed as Spiritual Counselors, lecturers and teachers and as part of the musical team. Here Dorothy is also listed as 'Materialization' and Russell is listed as 'Clairvoyance', and Eileen this time volunteered in the cafeteria. It is thought that 1961 was the last time Russell and Dorothy visited Ephrata PA. The Shrines of the Master were left in the care and service of Roy Kaywood of Bradenton and Miss Myrtle B. Faithful.

*Advertisment for Reverend Dorothy,
Camp Silver Belle, 1949.*

Though Ethel and Dorothy were destined to travel different paths, nevertheless Reverend Dorothy always paid generous tribute to the teacher and mentor, Ethel Post Parrish. Hugh Gordon Burroughs (of DC) is known to have succeeded Ethel Post Parrish as CSB Board President in 1959. Peggy Barnes Jefts was Treasurer and Reverend Virginia Falls (Indiana) was Vice President. Peggy was noted by Dorothy as one of her teachers in the 1930s. The Board members must then have held Reverend Dorothy and Dr. Russell in high regard, to invite the Flexers to return and work at Camp Silver Belle. The payment, terms and conditions made to Dorothy and Russell, for their services are not known.

The program for 1960 lists a near contemporary of Dorothy and Russell's, the Reverend Virginia Falls of Indiana. Virginia (1925-1977?) was to work at CSB and Camp Chesterfield giving materialization séances until 1977. In 1960 membership of CSB was said to be nearly 500 life members. Camp Silver Belle was to close some thirty years later in 1988.

In 1960, the family appear to have been at the Camp between Friday, 1st July through to Tuesday, 2nd August. The couple took a morning philosophy class at 10.00, a short afternoon lecture for 15 minutes at 2.45pm and at 3 pm Dorothy was available for 'Spiritual Counsel'. This was presumably a private sitting with Dorothy. The program for 1960, without a hint of irony, lists for Monday 5th September at 8.30pm, "Bazaar Séance: Cabinet demonstration of Physical Mediumship by Camp Mediums." There are seventeen mediums listed with 'Direct Voice' and or 'Materialization' abilities. Though mediums came and went throughout the season, it is likely that a good number would have demonstrated on the 5th September. The Bazaar Fund was a revenue raising venture for the Camp's benefit. Why the word Bazaar was chosen is unclear. Dorothy, it has been said, was a materialization medium i.e. able to materialize spirit individuals. On Monday, 25th July the following is listed in the program – "Bazaar Séance, Russell and Dorothy Flexer" listing Reverend Dorothy as "Direct Voice, Clairvoyance and Materialization." It seems that CSB endorses the opinion that Dorothy was a materialization medium.

We can assume that Russell acted as circle leader conducting the evening's proceedings. As Dorothy was to say, Russell was her 'battery'. Meaning that Russell conducted proceedings and gave his energy and strength to the séance. Dorothy and Russell were also listed as "Music for the Season, Russell and Dorothy will be with us for most of the season" and as "being a welcome addition to our musical program." Although we have no information on what payment was received for their work or what terms and conditions were made by either party, accommodation and food may have been included, along with some remuneration for the services given.

43

Camp Silver Belle — 1960   Page 37

Music for 1960

The musical program for the season will be in charge of Olive Searles, pianist; and Marta Mallery and Ruth Hirst, soloists.

RUSSELL and DOROTHY FLEXER will be with us for most of the season and will be a welcome addition to our musical program.

A popular feature of the musical program is the fifteen minute concert played by Olive Searles before each service on the **Peggy Jefts Memorial Carillonic Chimes.**

Extract from the Camp Silver Belle Program for 1960.

The Camp closed, Monday, 5th September. It was thought that the lack of heating made the venue unsuitable for winter seminars. Ethel Post Parrish's dearest wish was that central heating could be installed to make the venue suitable for use throughout the year.

Though the small family was to leave Portsmouth VA for Florida, they continued to visit their relations in Pennsylvania for the rest of their lives. In 1946, Russell and Dorothy followed the road to the summer lands of Florida and the city of Tampa.

Many people are taught to believe that if they lean on the everlasting arms of Jesus everything will be fine. I think the true believers have found that if they depend on the truth and learn to cope with material things, they have learned a lot more than that. Because you understand truth and depend on that truth you know how to cope with and interpret material things.

Chapter Two

"And the voice I hear falling on my ear
The Son of God discloses."

Dorothy was to say in later life that Florida seemed a place of light and warmth compared to the cold and dark of Pennsylvania. The end of the Second World War saw the troops demobilizing and coming home. Russell was asked 'to stand aside' and give up his job to returning veterans at the Portsmouth Dockyard. To the young couple in their early 30s, Florida, with its ocean, beaches, shaded decks and blue skies, the fragrance of sweet Oleander trees and the fruit groves refulgent with oranges, must have been very appealing. And there was work to be had, Dorothy was to later say, "Russell needed work and we automatically came to the industrial city of Tampa."

The lifting of wartime travel restrictions had seen a flood of vacationers and people retiring to live in the warm, sunny climate. Florida was to become and remain a major holiday destination. The state saw an economic boom that was to last for thirty years. Once the most backward and least populated states of the old Southern Confederacy, land prices were set to rocket and the state to become, in terms of population the third largest in the Union. In 1930, the population was just below 1.5 million, by 1960 it had mushroomed to nearly 5 million, with a population today of close to 20 million.

Tampa boasted the historic Latin Quarter of Ybor City, which was renovated in the late 1940s and gave a cosmopolitan feel to the neighborhood. In 1946, land was still cheap. A building boom was to follow as building lots abandoned in

Franklin Street, Tampa by night in the 1940s.

the depressed 1930s were bought up. A race track, one of the largest in the USA, opened in 1947. Tampa was a large port city with military bases and airfields. Though many were to close, the MacDill Airfield became a permanent US base because of its good all-year-round weather. Tampa had a variety of light engineering industries servicing the ports, building, and military. Civil amenities such as utilities, education, medical and civil administration all fueled a steady growth of the city and of Florida in general.

By 1947, Russell and Dorothy were mature adults. Much work lay ahead of them, and a sense of the truth and a vocation to serve has been noted. It is possible to paint a pen portrait of the couple at this stage in their lives.

It would be wrong to think Reverend Dorothy was academic. There was a sharp mind, clarity of purpose and sense of someone who lived in the present. Dorothy when at home enjoyed listening to Mario Lanza, baking and watching *I Love Lucy*. The cover portrait of Dorothy to this book has a glamour that speaks of the happiness that Dorothy knew in the 1950s.

Mahatma Gandhi said, "The best way to find yourself is to lose yourself in service to others." Dorothy and Russell devoted their lives to serving others and found happiness in doing so. The couple had a sense of being attached to something greater than one's self. The Flexers were a caring couple. Caring for others built loyalty, and also created and sustained the foundations of their spiritual community. It was because Russell and Dorothy practiced compassion in their relationships with the community that

Eileen and Russell's favorite photograph of Dorothy, 1955.

they founded, that the Flexers were loved. Caring for others is a key aspect of the pastoral role. The pastoral role was expressed through accepting others' needs of body, mind, and soul. Pastoral care is an aspect of healing which was central to the Flexers' spiritual life and community practice. The Flexers enjoyed a spiritual life of great breadth which was a highly spiritually creative outlet. Dorothy and Russell were grateful for the benefits their work brought them, and they enjoyed their lives.

It has been noted that Dorothy, on occasion, could be, impatient, forthright if you were in need of correction, and a fool might not always be tolerated! Reverend Dorothy was resilient in adversity and proactive, energetic and positive in outlook. But Dorothy knew how to relax and restore her energies. There were family holidays in the Smoky Mountains of North Carolina and a cruise to the Bahamas.

Photographs of Dorothy show a woman who projected her personality. A very public person – yet also a woman who was quite private. There were few who got past that public persona. Counsel and confidence were taken with each other, with spirit and close friends. Their only child, Eileen, said that her parents were easy going, but there were rules to follow. Dorothy and Russell as parents didn't lose their temper with Eileen or with others.

Dorothy liked to watch baseball, game shows and also enjoyed eating out. It would be the custom after a morning service to have lunch with friends and relax before the evening service. Being a musical couple they enjoyed going to the shows. This was the era of Rogers and Hammerstein's great movies, and the sound of those shows would have filled the airwaves and cinema screens. Dorothy is fondly remembered for 'feeding the world' as Reverend Dorothy loved to bake, especially pies!

Russell was the more reserved of the couple. As noted, there was something about Russell that reminded Dorothy of her father. Slow to open up to strangers, he was a good friend when he got to know you. Russell was possessed of a sense of fun and enjoyed playing tricks on people.

Dr. Russell was the more academically minded of the two and his sermons show forethought in the structure and presentation. Whereas, Dorothy in a state of deep trance would allow the discarnate to give a discourse on spiritual topics, the structure of which, would show variation in form. The content was not being determined by Reverend Dorothy nor was the presentation. Dr. Russell, it was thought, was in an 'overshadowed' state, one that allowed some contribution by him. Such an over-shadowed state developed over a long period and varied in the degree of spirit influence and inspiration. Dr. Russell could go into a deep unconscious trance, in support of Dorothy, at the regular classes, more of which later.

As Einstein said, "The Intellect has little to do on the road to discovery. There comes a leap in consciousness, call it intuition or what you will, and the solution comes to you, and you don't know how or why."

A handwriting analysis of Dr. Russell's hand shows that he was decisive and the sizable script shows leadership. A vertical slant and rhythm show that Russell was enterprising in his search for knowledge. He was a visionary but able to see through illusion. Russell could become over involved with his work but was nevertheless imaginative and logical. He was able to focus on the physical aspects of life. He was protective of his relationships and careful to be sensitive to the needs of others. The analysis concludes by saying that Russell was musical and proud of his accomplishments.

Cyndy Mayer, the graphologist also had this to say of Reverend Dorothy's handwriting:

"An independent person who was straightforward and liked to keep things simple. It also indicates spiritual awareness. Dorothy was ready for work, dynamic, idealistic, capable and ambitious with long-range planning skills. Firmness in the handwriting shows that she was firm and decisive in decision making. There was in Dorothy's nature a stubborn streak and a need to be in control. That resolute side to Reverend Dorothy made her a good organizer and good administrator. A single letter H shows that Dorothy needed to stand out spiritually yet needed at times to be distant from other people. Nevertheless, a responsible attitude to others is shown an expressive and communicative person is indicated. Reverend Dorothy, was honest and rather protective and maternal in nature. Dorothy could keep a secret."

Margaret Hodge, an astrologer, contributed the following analysis of Dorothy's character, the full script and chart are given in the appendices.

"Dorothy was born under the sign of Scorpio. Scorpio and its ruling planet are associated with transformation through the 'evolutionary journey of the soul', psychological growth and emotional development, combined in Dorothy's chart, with mysticism, devotion, and profoundly deep emotional power. This was the foundation upon which Dorothy entered this earthly life. She harnessed and developed these inherent qualities with courage and determination to fulfill her destiny, which was related to the collective and universal mind," – i.e. Metaphysics.

It is right to pray, you are communicating and asking for strength to understand the things to do. Guidance to show the way to go. You are leaning on that experience and knowledge and that you also have a part to play, in order to bring about the right result.

Russell quickly found work as a welder at the American Can Company and worked split shifts, so there were times when he had to work on Friday evenings. The American Can Company grew during World War II to become the largest manufacturers of tin cans in the USA.

The contact address given for Reverend Dorothy in the 1949 program for Camp Silver Belle was 1010 E. New Orleans Avenue, Tampa, FL. You could telephone 5-4187 for services of Direct Voice, Lecturing, and Clairvoyance. This was likely the home address for the Flexer family. Dr. Russell set up a séance cabinet and a dark room for home practice and development of Dorothy's mediumship. Whether Russell took his place in the cabinet is not known.

Though we cannot regard the following as a definitive statement, *Hartman's International Directory of Psychic Science* in 1931 listed only three Spiritualist Churches in Florida, two in Miami and one in St. Petersburg. Independent churches may have existed. In December 1949, *Psychic Observer* listed twenty churches and Psychic Centers in Florida with four in Tampa and three in St. Petersburg. By Christmas 1961 the same journal listed twenty-eight Spiritualist, Metaphysical Churches and Psychic Centers (that offered Spiritualist services as well as occult studies) in Florida with eight in St Petersburg and six in Tampa. Listing in the bi-monthly may have been charged for; the journal says that churches were to write to enquire for inclusion. Therefore, we can't regard the lists as definitive.

Naturally, the couple soon found the local Spiritualist Church. This Church may have been the The Rose of Sharon at 21st Avenue, Tampa. Russell and Dorothy came from the background of Camp Silver Belle where the highest standards of mediumship were demonstrated. The advanced level of phenomena that the couple had witnessed and of which Reverend Dorothy Graff Flexer was also capable, it was not surprising that local church was found to be parochial.

Dorothy thought the locals to be 'sincere' and the organization to be 'struggling'. The people who led the Church were not trained in church Leadership. Nevertheless, they served

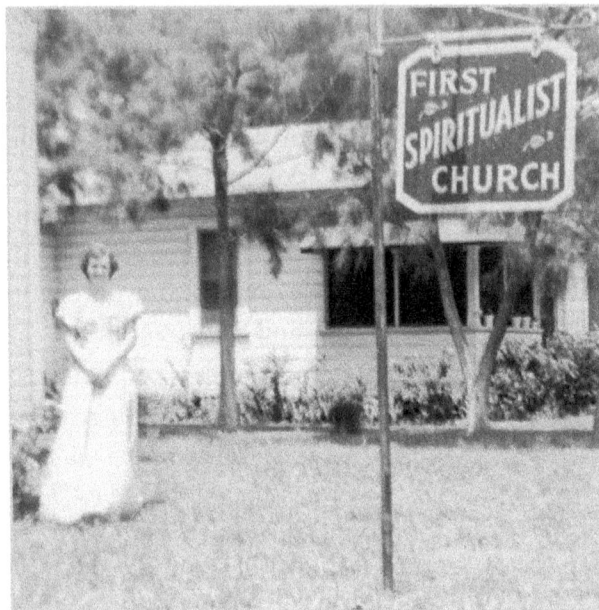

Dorothy outside the "First Spiritualist Church", Tampa, 1946.

for two years and without payment. But it became apparent to Russell and Dorothy that greater things were possible than had so far been dreamt by the local Church. The Church Members 'did not welcome change' which suggests that ideas were put forward but were rejected. Again, in 1947 Dorothy and Russell's followers asked the couple to set up a new church.

Dorothy commented, "We naturally named it The Shrine of the Master (Metaphysical Christianity)." The first meeting was held in a lady's home, and the Flexers began their search for a building. The first venue was a Union Hall where Sunday Services were held.

In order to acquire a building of their own, the Flexers and their supporters worked hard at fundraising. Dinners were cooked in their homes and transported by car to a civic club. Dorothy and the 'ladies' baked, raffle prizes were donated and chances sold (raffle tickets). Both Russell and Dorothy worked without pay and gave of their time freely to church activities. The dinners were good fundraisers. Their supporters were working-class, and Dorothy mentioned this to imply that church members didn't have much money to spare. As noted, Dorothy could earn money as a private spiritual counselor. One woman, who knew Dorothy and Russell from Camp Silver Belle offered to match dollar for dollar the money that was raised. In this way, a building fund was created. This may have been Katheryn Katz of New York, whom Dorothy names as helping The Shrine of the Master building fund to buy four lots on Memorial Highway. This highway was renamed Grand Central Avenue, and after 1963 Kennedy Boulevard.

With the land purchased, a salvaged army barracks was bought, transported and erected in the shape of a T. The center of the T formed the auditorium, there was a wing for the office and in the other wing was the kitchen. The main hall could seat up to two hundred people. There was also a room to the north of the main hall known as the Healing Shrine which was used for séance purposes or as they were known 'classes'.

Early 1950s with the original Flexer Hall.

The Tampa Shrine of the Master showing the original USAAF buildings.

In 1960, the Church was at 3416 Grand Central Avenue, Tampa with the first hall alongside being used as Fellowship Hall. The services were listed as Sunday school at 09.30 and worship at 10.30 and 7.30pm. Thursday

Services offered Prayer and Healing at 7.00 pm, with "All Messages Service 8.00 to 9.00pm."

Alda Madison Wade (1883-1956) and his wife Marianna were early supporters and experienced Spiritualists. Wade was the author of the 1953 book of *At the Shrine of the Master*. Alda refers to the Tampa Church as the Shrine of the Master, Spiritualist Episcopal Church. The Spiritualist Episcopal Church (SEC) was founded in 1941 by

The new Tampa Shrine of the Master built in 1956, alongside the original Hall.

Clifford Bias (1910-87), John Bunker (1893-1956) and Robert Chaney of the NAS. It was the intention of the founders to move away from Spiritualism's emphasis on proving survival and demonstrating phenomena. The word Episcopal was chosen to indicate governance by Bishops or in this case by Ministers. The teachings of spirit would be prominent and right living would be encouraged. The SEC held seminars known as Institutes at Camp Chesterfield. Dorothy and Russell agreed with the emphasis on the teaching of Metaphysics and affiliated to the SEC on 2nd January 1951. The Flexers would have visited Camp Chesterfield a number of times up to 1956.

Dr. Davis, Dorothy's Spirit Doctor and Redwing Dorothy's Doorkeeper guide, were key figures in Reverend Dorothy's spiritual life and mediumship. In their way these Spiritual helpers were as well-known to the sitters at the classes as to the medium herself.

Dr. Russell was ordained as an Associate Minister of The Shrine of the Master on Sunday, 2nd March 1952. The date is uncertain as to when Russell became a full-time minister of the Shrine, 1951 is possible, but after 1952 it is known that Russell gave up other forms of employment. Posterity has Redwing to thank for this, for it was Redwing's wish that a record of the day was kept. Another, Grace Kieb was ordained that day as a Minister. The administering minister that day was Reverend Clifford Bias of the SEC. Bias was described by Alda as an "Appellate Clergyman" this would have made him a senior figure in the SEC with the power to review and impose decisions on the church and laity. He was described as having abilities of Direct Voice, clairvoyance, clairaudience and of being 'of world renown'.

Dr. Russell during ordination by Rev. Clifford Bias, 2nd March 1952.

In stressing the importance of the steps taken that day by the two new ministers, seven candles were lit. These signified Attainment of Knowledge, the Worship of God, the Natural and Spiritual Worlds, Divine Law, Immortality, Communication with the Departed and Progression. Bias (himself a trumpet medium) described ordination as very ancient, its purpose was to set aside priests and to stand before God as the representative of the people and as God's witness. The body was spoken of as a temporary dwelling of the spirit. The purpose of which was to individualize part of the Universal Spirit.

Reverend Bias spoke at length of the role of ministership. He referred to the Direct Voice as a revelation of those who had gone before, that we are spirits. Bias then gave a prophecy saying, "as you go forth, you will be an example and instruction, to make life finer and sweeter as you give assurance that those that have gone before can and do come back to communicate with their loved ones in the flesh. It will be on this basis that you will do your part in bringing peace on earth and goodwill to men."

Russell Flexer became a Doctor of Metaphysics in 1955, studying Metaphysical Bible Interpretation at the College of Divine Metaphysics. This would likely to have been a correspondence course. The College records date from the early 1970s; earlier archives have vanished. The College was founded by Dr. Joseph Perry Green in 1918, and during the 1950s the College was based in Indianapolis. We will look closer at the story of the College and the Metaphysical movement in Chapter Three.

The Tampa Church was packed to the limits on that Sunday in 1952. Clifford Bias was well-known in the Spiritualist movement, as was his spirit helper, Sylvia. The certificates were handed out, and Reverend Bias was then blindfolded – "to shut out all light". Billets containing questions addressed to people in spirit were collected from the audience and psychometrized by Bias. Records show that – "In every case, the questioner and the spirit were fully identified by name. The questions were answered, and much additional information was added." We are not informed if there were celebrations afterward, but it is likely that refreshments and a party would have been held. Bias would have been paid for his work, but we don't know how much.

In the early years at Tampa, it was not unknown for other speakers to visit and serve the Church. On 2nd January 1952, the guest speaker was Reverend Lillian Dee Johnson of St Petersburg. We know that Lillian Dee served churches in the area and was pastor at a church in St Petersburg. Reverend Lillian Dee Johnson's mediumship had aspects of physical phenomena. On that occasion, the evening was concluded with Reverend Dorothy being blindfolded and giving "many messages which were to the point and highly interesting." A photograph of Reverend Lillian Dee Johnson's ordination with Reverend Dorothy and Clifford Bias in 1946 is reproduced below.

The ordination of Lillian Dee Johnson, 1946, with (L to R) Nellie Curry, Dorothy Flexer, Lillian Dee Johnson, John Bunker, another and Clifford Bias.

Sally Hayden von Conta, (of whom we shall hear again) remembered seeing a man serving on the platform at Tampa SOM. He was entranced and held a box which was full of filing cards and colored pencils, he covered the box, and people were called up, and they got a picture. This form of mediumship is known as precipitation. Twenty years later, Sandy, the friend who was with Sally, recognized a woman from that meeting on a street in Sarasota. The woman went into her purse and pulled out a picture that she had received that evening of her husband who died before the meeting.

Sally recalled, "…a big event up in Tampa SOM, there were many mediums in the large auditorium, there was a dim light, and there were materializations, this would have been around when I was fifteen years old, around 1955."

In praying, it's not just you doing nothing and just relying on Jesus and the God power and angels to do the rest. That is quite a different interpretation and you have come a long way in understanding the right way to live, the right things to do, the right conditions to create so that you may benefit more completely by your religion.

We know that Ethel Post Parrish's Church of the Beloved (NASC) was at St. Petersburg (25 miles away) and that Clifford Bias is listed as Pastor of the People's Spiritualist Church, St Petersburg. Other speakers from the Episcopal Church would have served at the Shrine. There is nothing to suggest that guest speakers served any of the Shrine Metaphysical Churches after 1956. And it was not until the early 21st century that visiting speakers became a feature of SOM life. However, Reverend Dorothy did on other occasions serve other churches. On 2nd December 1956, Dorothy gave a special Sunday service at the SEC Memorial Church at 10th Avenue, St Petersburg. Reverend Edith Maywald hosted, and Revered Dorothy gave a "Service with Messages" at 2. 30 pm and 7.30pm.

The American Metaphysical and Spiritualist Movement has shown a capacity for splintering, and not all was well with the Spiritualist Episcopal Church. In 1951, Robert Chaney left the group to start a Metaphysical publishing house in California. In 1956, a scandal broke out in the SEC when a charge of immorality was brought against a church elder who was a candidate for office. At the1956 SEC conference at Lancing, Michigan, the dispute became bitter and divisive. Conference hoped to dissuade the controversial medium from standing by removing him from office.

Dorothy proposed moving the SEC Institute (a summer training facility) from Camp Chesterfield. The Northern Institute in 1956, being held at Lancing, Michigan and the

Southern Institute at the Ritz Hotel, St Petersburg, Florida. 1957 saw both venues used again for training and ordination. Russell and Dorothy attended with their daughter Eileen. Dorothy and Russell were on the Advisory Board of the Institutes and teachers in 1956 and 1957. *Golden Rays*, the magazine of the Spiritualist Episcopal Church, in 1956 indicates that Dorothy was elected to succeed at the Lancing Conference as 'Presiding Clergyman' of the SEC. Dorothy was acting Presiding Clergyman, on behalf of Reverend John Bunker who died earlier that year. Dorothy would also have succeeded Clifford Bias as Head of the Institute after succeeding John Bunker. It was Reverend Dorothy, as Presiding Clergyman who is credited with moving the Institute from Camp Chesterfield. We know that Reverend

I will strive to become more aware of the presence of the angels in my own life and add my good thoughts to theirs, to create a "heaven on earth" daily.

Dorothy was on the Board of Clergy before the Conference of 1956. The President of the SEC Board was the Reverend Richard Berry of Lancing, Michigan.

The origin of a great deal of incorrect information is J. Stillson Judah in his 1967, *The History and Philosophy of Metaphysical Movements in America*. Appendix Two, 'Mrs Flexor' and the Chinese Whispers, examines more closely the actual events and resulting incorrect information in publications and on the internet. *The Encyclopaedia of American Religions*, (McGrath Pub. Co. 1978) follows J. Stillson Judah's lead and elaborates on the incorrect information on the SEC and Dorothy's role in that movement and Convention. It is commonly said that the HQ of the SEC was at Camp Chesterfield. This is not true, they were incorporated at the Mother Church in Eaton Rapids, Michigan 1941. The Mother Church, HQ was listed as being at Eaton Rapids by *Psychic Observer* in December 1949 and 1951, and it is still there.

Masthead of the official stationery of the Spiritualist Episcopal Church, 1955.

The Encyclopedia of American Religions states that "those who sided against Dorothy Flexer" – that is Clifford Bias and Lillian Dee Johnson – "left the SEC in 1956, and founded the Universal Spiritualist Association" (US Association, see the abbreviations for details). In February or March 1957, Dorothy also resigned the Presiding Clergyman role of the SEC and in 1961, Lillian Dee Johnson of St Petersburgh, and later Bradenton, was listed as President of US Association, and Bias was listed as vice-president."

Audience at Spiritualist Episocpal meeting, Camp Chesterfield in the 1950s.

The stress that Dorothy and Russell must have felt during the difficult days of the 1956 crisis of the SEC can be imagined. The long distance between Sarasota and Eaton Rapids, Michigan also made the carrying out of the roles of Presiding Clergyman and members of the advisory board difficult. The needs of their churches and their own congregations must have made growing demands on the couple's time.

The Encyclopedia named above writes that the Indiana Association of Spiritualists at Camp Chesterfield barred access to the Camp by SEC mediums, but this needs to be verified. If so, Russell and Dorothy shared the humiliation of being barred from serving at Camp Chesterfield and did not visit the Camp after 1956. The US Association took over the credential issuing seminary role at Camp Chesterfield, originally carried out by the SEC.

Clifford Bias who became President of the US Association is not referred to in any of the records of the SOM after 1956. Apparently, Russell and Dorothy and Bias, as head of the US Association, went their separate paths. Bias himself, in addition to his new Spiritualist role included mysticism and arcane knowledge as part of the Seminary teaching program for future ministers. He organized the Ancient Order of Seekers for student associate ministers. Bias wrote several books on occult topics.

The difference of opinion between the Flexers and Bias concerned fundamentals of approach to spiritual matters. Metaphysics is a spiritual approach that sought to emphasize the teachings of spirit and a way of life over the necessity of proving survival. Fundamentally, metaphysics is opposed to secret and elitist teachings.

Metaphysics is not a mystery school; it is an open exoteric movement dedicated to 'Everyman'. Dorothy and Russell taught by enlightening and empowering others. Metaphysics is not Freemasonry. The New Temple or New Jerusalem would be the open door of the Shrines of the Master. As Leo Tolstoy said: "There is no greatness where there is no simplicity, goodness, and Truth."

In April 1958, the Shrine of Master Churches disaffiliated from the Spiritualist Episcopal Church and the couple founded the Church of Metaphysical Christianity (CMC). This body was the governing authority that had a seminary role in creating Ministers and had ultimate control over the local boards of the Churches. This was a new movement and a new departure in spiritual organizations, though as we shall see in Chapter Four, not one without precedent.

In July 1960, accusations of fraud were brought against various well-known mediums. Some of whom were filmed by the editor of the *Psychic Observer*, Tom O'Neil (d.1965) on infra-red cameras infiltrating collaborators into the séance to impersonate departed spirits. The resulting scandal nearly brought the *Psychic Observer* to bankruptcy as Spiritualists and their organizations abandoned the newspaper. In the 1950/60s accusations of fraud were brought against many prominent mediums, including Peggy Barnes Jefts, Ethel Post Parrish and Arthur Ford.

The Flexers would have known Ford from the early 1940s and posterity does not record what the couple thought of these accusations. The summer of 1961 was to be Dorothy and Russell's last trip to Camp Silver Belle. Mediums whom Dorothy had respected, Peggy Barnes Jefts and Hugh Gordon Burroughs whom the Flexers had known for many years, almost certainly invited the couple to work. After 1961, except for rites of passage i.e. funerals, weddings, etc., it appears that Russell and Dorothy confined their services entirely to their own churches.

As Lincoln observed, "…you can't fool all the people all of the time." Conviction of the truth of spirit communication and phenomena was a matter of personal witness and experience. To witness levitation with a group of fellow sitters; to have the impression of the departed for oneself and to receive accurate information from speakers, who could not know of what they spoke, was highly persuasive of conviction.

Camp Silver Belle and Camp Chesterfield progressed from this period. Though CSB was to close its doors in the late 1980s, both Camps flourished, and Camp Chesterfield celebrated its Centenary in 1986. Notable materializing mediums that Dorothy and Russell would have known were Virginia Falls, Warren Smith, William Donnelly and Harold Ahearn. All worked at the Spiritualist Camps and in the churches of Florida.

No life is without its stresses, and such pressure can stimulate efforts and clarify thinking. No doubt there were rewards as well as sacrifices in the life that Russell and

Dorothy were drawn to. The life of mediumship requires a high demand on the physical, psychological and emotional energy of the mediumistic individual. As noted in chapter one, high standards of truth in mediumship require high standards of honesty in the individual who practices mediumship.

Notably, Reverend Dorothy was never accused of fraud. The majority of mediums were sincere and honest and suffered the mud-slingers who defamed their reputation. Dorothy spoke of Camp Silver Belle mediums, John Reese, Peggy Barnes Jefts, Hugh Gordon Burroughs, and "…they were fine mediums" because of the standards they

adhered to. The necessities of living did not come easily nor without effort; heavy demands on time, energy and patience were needed. Preparation and long hours in thought and awareness of mental processes are required. Mediumship cannot be rushed, relationships with the spirit world need time to develop. A mature mediumship is not arrived at till several years have passed. Dorothy would have known, as do all mediums that mediumship never stops developing. Such development requires patience, dedication, and love of the work.

The role of Pastor of her flock and President of the Board of the SOM and CMC needed forbearance and ability to deal with the emotional needs of others. People would have expected Dorothy's attention and to have their ideas listened to. Rejection of unwanted proposals might not always have been welcome.

There must have been times when Dorothy's life was not her own and the

Lena Barnes Jefts
Jefts
(Peggy Barnes)
Books on the Science,
Philosophy and Relig-
ion of Spiritualism
(for class work and the
Investigator)

❖

The Fundamentals
of Spiritualism
Psychic Facts
The Trinity
of Spiritualism
The Story of Healing
The Chemistry of Thought
The Christian Bible—Its Mediums and Prophets
Lo I Am With You Alway
Ancient and Modern Prophets and Religions
These eight books constitute four years of study
in class work.
Sold as a group — $10.00
Single copies — $2.00 each

The Way of Life	$2.00
Alone With God	$2.00
The Questionnaire	$2.00

Special rates on orders of one dozen or more
to Mediums and Churches.

❖

LENA BARNES JEFTS
Camp Silver Belle   Ephrata, Penna.

Lena Barnes Jefts acknowledged by Dorothy to be a fine medium. (Camp Silver Belle program 1960.)

telephone never stopped ringing. Nor was Dorothy's body entirely her own, as weekly, the spirit world under the guidance of Redwing took control. An emotionally draining session could leave Dorothy tired. Likewise, a joyful class could be exhilarating for all who attended, including Dorothy. Attendance at Classes was guarded as a disruptive sitter could damage and fatigue Dorothy. Screening by the spirit side, by Dorothy and those whom she trusted, would have eliminated sitters with emotional, psychic or psychological problems. Likewise, unresponsive sitters who would not speak up, and also overtaxed the medium's energy.

The psychic field is an area where any might set themselves up as channelers, mediums, fortune tellers, tarot and Qabalah readers. It was against this background of potential anarchy and disintegration that we must set the Flexers' life-long dedication to their Truth. This criterion meant that standards of mediumship, the procedure of practices, an excellence of teachings, respectful conduct, and aspiration to link with the highest, brightest and the best of spiritual life, would prevail. Such dedication to the Truth provided a 'Firewall' against lower standards gaining entry to the Shrines of the Master. The values of the SOM were underlined by the teachings of the spirit world. These teachings were received through Reverend Dorothy's trumpet mediumship and heard by the sitters in the classes. The sermons of a Sunday also gave ethical, principled and spiritual instruction; this gave Dorothy and Russell a moral position as Senior Pastors of their flock. The Dalai Lama expresses this moral position as: "Knowing we represent the truth renders us calm and strong with time and justice on our side."

The stress that Dorothy and Russell must have felt with problems within Spiritualist organizations, accusations of fraud, the possible immortality of Ministers, differences of opinions, approaches to teachings and the stresses and demands of running two churches sixty miles apart must have been great. These were all to contribute to Reverend Dorothy Graff Flexer and Dr. Russell going their own way in June 1958 and starting the Church of Metaphysical Christianity. Russell and Dorothy would have agreed with the motto of the *Psychic Observer* newspaper: "Truth for Authority, not Authority for Truth."

And there was music, Russell and Dorothy made a great team, and the couple harmonized beautifully.

> "Thou preparest a table before me in the presence of mine enemies;
> Thou anoints my head with oil,
> My cup runneth over.
> Surely goodness and mercy shall follow me all days
> and I will dwell in the House of the Lord forever."

Alda Madison Wade's comment on Sunday 21st January 1952 regarding the Flexers says about Dorothy, "as a soprano soloist, she is peer to the best … her rendition of the 23rd Psalm was most impressive." And on Russell who contributed a violin solo which "was well received, as was his solo baritone."

Classes were held in the winter months November through to April. In the Florida of the 1940s to 1970s there was no air-conditioning, and the muggy atmosphere of a darkened séance room would have been unbearable. Though electric fans were common, such could not be used in a dark séance because of the noise and the use of electricity would have interfered with the mediumship.

Alda Madison Wade had this to say of Reverend Dorothy's mediumship in late 1951: "Those who attend at the Shrine of the Master do so as a rule, out of a high regard for the medium and the words of wisdom which are transmitted through her voice organs from the spirit world."

Here Wade is telling us that Dorothy is in trance, speaking inspirationally without paper or notes of any kind. Also the author goes on to write of the trumpet mediumship of Reverend Dorothy at séance or class. It is thought that the physical phenomenon of Trumpet Mediumship developed in 1948 when Dorothy was thirty-five. Trumpet Mediumship is a form of 'direct voice' in which an ectoplasmic tube is formed that allows the levitation of the trumpet and the amplification of spirit voices. A voice box is created within the trumpet to allow the spirits to speak independently.

"The spirit voices which conveyed the information were entirely independent of the voice organs of the medium and were amplified by a megaphone-like instrument known as a trumpet. The room was in total darkness. Once under control of the spirit entity (that is Dorothy was in a trance state and unconscious of what was happening) this trumpet was levitated to the ceiling of the séance room, from whence came the voice of the entity speaking."

The sitter had a direct conversation with the spirit person who spoke. Because the voices were projected through the mediumship of Reverend Dorothy and the trumpet the voice did not necessarily sound like their earthly voice, nevertheless, the gender of each speaker was quite distinct and no one listening to Dr. Davis or another frequent visitor, Dr. Josiah Royce, could mistake the voice for that of a woman.

In a Spiritual sense, songs are not sung so much for their meaning as for the vibration they produce. Very few people pay any attention to the thought contained when they are elevated into the higher vibration of the spiritual.... any popular folk song would bring about the same result as a hymn.

By the early 1960s, Dorothy's trumpet mediumship had developed to the degree that a cabinet was no longer necessary for the phenomenon to occur. Reverend Dorothy could sit at the head of the room, and the chairs would be in a circle formation around her. Dr. Russell, whom Dorothy regarded as a battery or source of energy would also go into trance.

"Good evening, everybody," the slightly high pitched voice of Redwing would say, "There is no time to lose, here is your Doctor."

"Class, this is Dr. Davis speaking." The doctor always spoke through the trumpet with Redwing opening proceedings via Reverend Dorothy's voice. The Classes were conducted on Christian Spiritualist principles. The class would commence with the *Lord's Prayer* being said. There is an idea that the same songs were sung throughout the class's duration. This is not literally true. Spontaneous choice of songs did occur. *In the Garden* was nearly always sung at the beginning of the class, as it was Dorothy's favorite hymn. Others, such as *There is a Land fairer than Day, It's a Long, Long Trail, In Ole Virginia* and many others were sung. Procedures no doubt remained constant, yet changed imperceptibly over the years. *Ad hoc* singing was needed when the energy seemed low. On one occasion in 1952, Dr. Davis said, "In your singing don't forget that religious songs are not essential to the creation of vibration. For that reason, I suggest that any lively popular song will have the desired result."

Dr. Davis, Dorothy's Spirit Doctor and Redwing, Dorothy's Doorkeeper guide, seldom gave personal information about themselves (see the Appendices for a classification of spirit guides and helpers). They were cautioned by the Doctor to regard the teachings as paramount over biography. However, in Alda Madison Wade's book Dr. Charles Davis does give the following information. He relates that he was born on the west coast, California and that by 1951 his town, no longer existed. The great immigration that occurred in 1849 was after his birth. He was trained as a medical doctor but the training was far different in his time and as a doctor of philosophy was now his main pursuit. However, Dr. Davis had been successful as a medical doctor. He was of English stock and born during the opening up of the area to European settlers. The area of Dr. Davis's birth is likely to have been northern Californian in the late 18th century.

Redwing, Dorothy's Joy Guide and Doorkeeper.

Of Redwing, almost nothing biographical can be said beyond, her personality. She was a young girl with a high pitched voice. Dr. Davis, of whom there are many recordings, has a deep masculine voice. Redwing would announce herself as "Redwing" and referred to Reverend Dorothy as her "Medi". Redwing would sometimes refer to people of whom she fond as "Uncle" or "Aunt". Of one thing we can be confident; on 13th May 1952, Redwing had this to say about her picture, the same, reproduced above, "then you have seen my picture. How do you like it?"

"You're a pretty gal," answered one of the inquisitors.

Redwing continued, "You wouldn't say anything else in my presence would you?"

"Nor behind your back," answered the sitter.

"Are you sure that it's a good picture asked another?"

Redwing replied, "It's a perfect likeness, as I look at myself in the mirror or better, as I see myself reflected in the water."

Dr. Russell's spirit helpers are less well known. However, Dr. Thomas, Russell's spirit Doctor, worked with Russell and said through the trumpet early 1952 "…we have come a long way together."

Further development work was to be undertaken and spirit artwork to be perused. Dr. Thomas worked closely with Dr. Russell in the sermons and preachings. Some of these sermons are presented in the appendices. There was no doubt that as a medium and pastor that Russell devoted himself to development work. Love of sitting in 'home circle' (sometimes referred to as 'sitting in the power') would have been natural. This personal communion with spirit is fundamental to attunement and development of mediumship.

Snowdrop, Dr. Russell's Joy Guide.

Dr. Russell's other principle guide was Snowdrop, whose picture is reproduced here. Snowdrop also has little biography beyond the Indian heritage that was shared with Redwing. Snowdrop would often tell stories with a moral point to them.

The earliest 'Class' of which there is a record took place at 6 pm on Tuesday, 13th November 1951. Dorothy's mid-week séances were always referred to as classes as they were teaching occasions. The pattern of procedure was well established by 1951 and was almost certain to have been running for several years before that. For at least forty-eight years from 1948 to 1996 Reverend Dorothy Graff Flexer was to demonstrate trumpet mediumship in the service of the spirit world and its teachings of Metaphysics.

Dr. Russell acted as 'Circle Leader' or Master of Ceremonies. The classes were regarded as 'advanced' and attendance was always by invitation only. Once admitted to the class, attendance was automatic and expected. The classes seldom involved personal communication from known departed spirits. These weekly occasions were given over, half to lecture work and half to question and answers, usually with Dr. Davis answering them. An attitude of inquiry was encouraged; none were expected to accept without appeal to individual reason.

The practice of open inquiry was encouraged and had its origin in John 4:1 who had warned: "Beloved, do not believe every spirit, but test the spirits to see whether they are from God."

Faith and trust were to be stimulated in questions that were difficult to a sitter's comprehension, and faith was the Christian background of most sitters. Nevertheless, the practice of the tenet 'prove all things' was also encouraged. Selection of sitters was intended to weed out unsuitable, closed-minded, bigoted people and individuals who could not abide the claustrophobia of sitting in the dark. The atmosphere, as is apparent on the recordings, is one of joy and almost party like. There is an adrenalin buzz that accompanied those occasions that afterward left people hungry for the next occasion. As always, throughout Dorothy's life, these classes made frequent references to the Truth.

> *Dr Davis speaking on, "It is better to give than to receive."*
>
> *"The seed that you plant and the more the attention that you give to the seed the better the flower. The more you give of yourself the more you receive. That it involves the emotions and the feelings in a positive way. If you give only out of the sense of guilt or of negative emotion, you create that vibration."*

Redwing was not, if necessary, above telling people off. For example, in 1952 Redwing said, "Dr. Russell you didn't do a very good job of shutting out the light. I can see it coming through in several places, and I don't mean spirit lights. Whatever you do, stop them, remember not to stumble over my medium, for that might result in injury to her." Séance procedures require darkness as the energy of spirit is light sensitive; this is especially true during the development phase. Dr. Davis also might express himself forcibly. "Russell, I am telling you, no!" was the response when Dr. Flexer asked why the séance cabinet at their home could not be used for a class.

"Russell, it is my desire that a cabinet be formed by curtaining one corner of this room as a means of producing the phenomenon known as etheralization for our next meeting." Russell was proven right, and the circumstances were thought more suitable for their home séance room. Dr. Davis was to say that he did not want Dorothy to be thought of as an apport medium. A red light was needed, as when Dorothy was in the cabinet and apports came through the trumpet which was levitated in the air some distance away from the medium, a red light would help the objects to be caught and seen. Apports were thought to require more energy than direct voice mediumship.

Nevertheless, while not common, Reverend Dorothy's mediumship did produce apports, several of which are kept in private collections.

As we saw in Chapter One, Ruth, Dorothy's much-loved sister was to continue to be close in spirit and to work as a helper. On Sunday, 2nd March 1952, Alda Madison Wade wrote "…there came this sweet feminine voice which said, "This is Ruth." Alda went on … "Her present work is that of a guide, always ready to manifest whenever desirable."

Ruth was to say, "Dr. Davis finds it advisable that I take over to complete the message that he has thus far started." Ruth then went on to give a discourse on the observances of Lent and concluded with:

"Learn to master your thoughts and your deeds. Live not for yourself alone but let your life be a shining example to others, that others, seeing your good works, will pattern after you and benefit accordingly. Perform your mission on Earth through kindly and friendly acts, remembering that in doing so you are giving to God and that which you measure; it shall be measured back to you."

Alda wrote, "The voice of Ruth Graff (Madison Wade was unaware of Ruth's marriage) as she transmitted the words of Dr. Davis, echoed and re-echoed and the Shrine of the Master became a Cathedral to the living God."

A seldom-mentioned aspect of these classes was the provision of pens, crayons and writing pads. The purpose being that spirit visitors who were manifested but not necessarily visible could write their names on the pads. It is believed that quite a few departed friends did do so. On 20th May 1952, Wade noted the following:

"When the lights were turned on, it was observed that two names were written on the pad which had been left on the table. One, written in large script was that of Elmer, brother of Marianna (Alda Madison Wade's wife) the other written in very small script, was Mary." (Alda Madison Wade's previous wife who had died in 1932).

Alda Madison Wade who wrote a book about Dorothy's mediumship is shown with spirit faces in the background.

In Reverend Dorothy's Classes, there were many spirit visitors who spoke through the trumpet, these were often elevated souls with a mission to help and enlighten humanity. St Francis of Assisi was a particularly favorite throughout Dorothy's career as a medium, and the garden at Sarasota has a statute of him. Other religious figures that made their presence known included Mahatma Gandhi, Martin Luther and John Wesley. It was the habit to regard the discourse as more important than the name or title, as such cannot be proven. No doubt some were impressed by the names despite the lack of credentials. However, the quality of what was said could not be gainsaid. But not all figures were from the spiritual field.

Some returning souls from the great diaspora of the departed might be statesmen. On Wednesday, 29th April 1952, Franklin Delano Roosevelt materialized his voice through the trumpet and gave a talk that lasted for an hour of the hour and a half session. It was an occasion to ask political questions of the day and space does not allow here for a full report of what was said. However, topics that were mentioned included the conferences at Yalta and Potsdam, the Alger Hiss communist spy trial, and the fear of a Third World War, FDR was reassuring on the latter point.

The former President spoke of corruption in public life and the limitations of the Presidential office. As was the late President's familiarity with spiritualism and mediumship. It is known that FDR consulted the sleeping prophet Edgar Cayce in 1943 and that his wife, Eleanor Roosevelt sat with Clifford Bias. The late President also spoke of meetings with other deceased presidents to discuss matters of mutual interest. Finally, and remarkably the President then endorsed Republican Dwight D. Eisenhower for the Presidential election of November 1952. However, as *Glimpses of Immortality* was not published until 1953, the vote for the Democrat Party candidate Adlai Stevenson would not have been influenced. Roosevelt was, of course, endorsing across his party's choice. However, Eisenhower won by a landslide, with Stevenson taking only the Democrat 'Solid South' but not Florida.

Dr. Davis opened the class of 6th May 1952 with this, "I return to you again from the Land of Spirit to express my deep appreciation for the fine work of this class, and the excellent interest you, its members, are taking in the work we are attempting to do, and the basic ideas we are hoping to establish."

On that evening another US President made his presence known. As Dorothy Parker once said of Calvin Coolidge's death, "How can you tell?" Coolidge (1872-1933) was a reserved man known in some circles as 'Silent Cal', his voice was once again heard on 6th May 1952. Without any introduction, a voice spoke, "This is Calvin Coolidge speaking." Coolidge was to warn the class that the current President Truman 'effort' at raising the wages of labor would thereby bring about inflation in the economy and devaluation of the currency. He went on to encourage the citizens of Florida to vote with the north and elect a President who would bring harmony, guard the constitution which was the "rock of Liberty and would be in defiance of tyranny." The late President is referring to the 'Solid South' which voted Democrat as a block. The old Confederacy was referred to by Coolidge as "I love Florida and the entire south and I am sorry to note that there is still a division which precludes a harmonious balance of the nation." By implication, the late President is deploring the racial segregation that lingered in the dark corners of the old southern states.

Finally, Coolidge once again appealed to them, "to be ever on alert to guard against subversive elements in our government," and as "good citizens to vote intelligently and at all elections." He followed on with, "…that you urge and support courses in patriotic training in every school and college in the United States of America."

It is relatively rare for the departed to express themselves on more than spiritual topics in séances or classes. It underlines the troubled times and fear of Communism of the early 1950s that political figures should come forward and express themselves on matters of current interest.

Dr. Davis continued:
"We want you to be of a giving and generous nature and the more you will have. It is a positive process, if you give only to receive in turn that is a poisonous process. If you give out unhappiness and frustration, then your life is not enhanced."

In the appendices, I have reprinted a class in which spiritual leaders of the past spoke and gave their opinions on spiritual topics. That excerpt from the Alda Madison Wade book will give a fuller impression of the conduct of these weekly classes.

Other speakers included – British psychic researcher Frederick Myers, whose important work *Beyond Human Personality* had inspired many with the evidence for human survival of death. The spirit 'Doctors' connected to the sitters would also speak to their physical friends. At the first class in the New Year, it was the custom for each sitter to receive a spirit messenger and message for themselves. Only rarely was this pattern broken and then because of urgent need. Personal messages were reserved for platform work on a Sunday service. A personal, that is private, spiritual consultation might involve the direct voice but only if the sitter was well known to Dorothy as a high degree of trust was needed on Dorothy's part to be entranced and alone with a sitter.

Scientists, doctors of philosophy, psychiatry and medicine, artist and achievers and nobodies with something to say, from all walks of life, once again found a voice in this world through Dorothy's remarkable mediumship. Andrew Jackson Davis regarded as the pioneer Spiritualist, spoke on a number of occasions and his motto serves as a guide to the attitude that prevailed in the conduct of the classes, "In all circumstances keep an open mind, keep an even mind." Nothing had to be accepted that did not appeal to the reason of the individual.

Dr. Davis would end a class with "Goodnight and God Bless." It was the custom to end the classes with a chorus of *God be with you. Till we meet again.* Redwing would open the class and also close the class, often breaking in to interrupt the singing with her cheery voice saying something like, "Don't start that until I say good night to everybody." Redwing would then go around the circle thanking everyone by name. The trumpet would 'crash' to the floor. Russell would customarily give the Hebrew "Mizpah Benediction." This blessing is thought to be thousands of years old. It marked the bond between individuals as witnessed by God. The word Mizpah has come to have many meanings e.g. May the Lord watch over you and me when we are absent one from the other. A verse from the Mizpah, Genesis 31.49

"Go thou thy way, and I go mine,
Apart, yet not afar;
Only a thin veil hangs between
The pathways where we are.
And "God keep watch 'tween thee and me";
This is my prayer;
He looks thy way, He looketh mine,
And keeps us near."

Dorothy would be asked if she were awake, and if the answer was in the affirmative, the class would be asked to shield their eyes against the glare and the light would be switched on. The writing pad would be checked to see if any spirit writing had occurred.

Alda Madison Wade concluded his account of the classes between November 1951 and June 1952 in his book *At the Shrine of the Master* by saying, "Those of us who have experienced the joy of sitting at the feet of teachers who have progressed to the high degrees of attainment in the spirit world, there comes a thrill of satisfaction that cannot help but glorify one's earthly existence."

The US 49 highway from Tampa to Sarasota (now US 94) was a basic one track south and one track north, skirting the eastern side of Tampa Bay. In the 1940s, Florida's roads had not seen any improvement as all road building had been halted during the war years.

The average automobile of the 1940/50s weighed two tons. Power assisted steering and air-conditioning were gradually introduced for upmarket models from the mid-1950s and didn't become standard until the mid-1960s. The 120-mile round trip between the two Shrines of the Master must have seen Dorothy and, after 1951, Russell spending a lot of their lives driving.

Dorothy wrote about the late 1940s and early 50s, "We traveled from Tampa to Sarasota each Friday. Russell was still working as a welder…on split shifts, so there were times he had to work on Friday nights. Since we were not fortunate to have two cars, I traveled with Eileen and my mother. I held the Sarasota service and drove back to Tampa where we would find Russell sitting on the curb waiting for us to pick him up."

The route gradually improved with Eisenhower's interstate upgrade initiatives of the mid-1950s. The first bridge across the entrance to Tampa opened in 1954 with two lanes in either direction. This bridge was improved by the Howard Frankland Bridge which opened in 1960. This acquired the nickname of 'the Frankenstein Bridge' because of the high number of accidents that occurred on its spans. Extra barriers were introduced to prevent vehicles plunging off into the bay. Traffic jams became so common that local wits called it 'The Car-Strangled Spanner.'

Main Street, Sarasota in the 1940s.

As Jesse Owen remarked, "We all have dreams. But in order to make dreams come into reality, it takes an awful lot of determination, dedication, self-discipline and effort."

Such perseverance, commitment, and love on the part of the Flexers would lead to the founding of a new Shrine of the Master at Browning and Tuttle Avenue, Sarasota.

Right: May 1955. Dorothy and Russell Flexer outside the new Sarasota Church immediately before the Dedication.

Below: Shrine of the Master, Sarasota in the 1950s, (Tampa and Sarasota Churches had the same architecture).

Chapter Three

*"And the melody that He gave to me
Within my heart is ringing."*

*"I shall not commit the fashionable stupidity of regarding
everything I cannot explain as a fraud." - C.G. Jung*

The influence of the Spiritualist Movement and Ethel Post on Dorothy was noted in Chapter One. There was the life-altering meeting of the Graff family, with Dorothy's deceased materialized father, Otto. There was also a methodology in communication that was repeatable and Dorothy and Russell had, as did others, a gift that could be trained. There was the realization by the Flexers that in Gershwin's phrase the "things that you're liable to read in the Bible: it ain't necessarily so." The young couple were grounded in the scriptures, and their experiences had created in the young Dorothy and Russell a conviction and a passion for 'The Truth'. Nevertheless, the CMC was rooted in the teachings of the Master Jesus. As the Master Teacher had said in John 14:6, "I am the way and the truth and the life." A system, a 'Science' could be applied to interpreting the Bible in a positive, intuitive life-affirming way. Use was made of Charles Fillmore's *Metaphysical Bible Dictionary* and the method of interpretation owed little or nothing to historic Christian usage in the Bible.

In the Christian Metaphysics, Metaphysical thought was referred to as a 'Science'. Such thought was the practice of investigation that sought to understand the invisible, spiritual nature of life which transcended the physical plane. Religion as 'Science' stresses the primacy of Spiritual Law and man's harmony or otherwise with it as a means of personal salvation. God, as we shall see was regarded as impersonal, as a 'First Principle' infinite and unchanging. The Science of the understanding of Spiritual and Psychic Laws would realize health, prosperity and inner peace. The truth of the revealed science was verifiable by results. We will look again at this topic shortly. The enhanced consciousness would connect the metaphysician to the spirit world, teachers and ultimately, God. There could be no negative outcome from a relationship to the Divine. If there was disharmony in life, the key was to understand what the nature of the error was. We will look again at these ideas in the discussion of the Spiritual Laws.

An ideal of what the Truth was, would lead the couple, and in particular, Russell to come up with their own religious truth based on a number of influences. Inspiration other than Spiritualism contributed to the creation of the Church of Metaphysical Christianity. The Flexers were not given to reminiscing on the past and though occasional references were made, they were few. This chapter will look at how other influences impacted on Dorothy and Russell and will summarize the Christian metaphysics that Dorothy and Russell synthesized. Also, the chapter will look at how the teachings impacted on the practice of healing. The Flexers absorbed ideas and experiences from a number of sources, and their ideal was 'Truth for Authority' or as Dr. Davis said, "Let the Truth be your watchword," and it was the motto by which Dorothy and Russell lived their lives.

The Church that Dorothy and Russell founded was a 'stand alone' organization owing allegiance to no other organization. As we shall see the move away from Spiritualism was promoted by Russell and Dr. Davis, and came about through a higher vision of what religion could be. That vision was one that placed the teaching of wisdom above communication with the loved deceased. It was mediumship in the service of religious truth; the provision of a channel to bring the higher teachings to those that would listen.

The vision also foresaw a community of like-minded people living a moral life, supporting each other's personal spiritual practice. Dr. Russell was a 'Free and Accepted Mason' and may have been immersed in Masonic ritual and thereby had a keen devotional side to his religious

I hold that all orthodox religious denominations are a menace to correct thinking. For the most part they retain their members through a doctrine of fear.

character. This devotional aspect is something that Dr. Russell may have wished to emphasize in Christian Metaphysics. In Chapter Four the inspiration for the new church is credited to Dr. Russell and Dr. Davis, of course, with Reverend Dorothy's wholehearted endorsement.

As noted in the introduction, this book is written for those who knew the Flexers, and also those unacquainted with their lives and ideas. To non-American readers, the use of terms such as Metaphysical and New Thought (NT) will be unusual and require some explanation. To Europeans, a metaphysical church sounds like bad marketing, the word may appear difficult or abstruse. The ideas and terms in Europe are known but not used to the same extent, nor were there movements associated with these terms.

The New Thought movement dates from the early 19th century, and Phineas Quimby (1802-1866) is credited as the Father of the movement. In common with Andrew Jackson Davis, Quimby was initially a Mesmerist or Hypnotist. The key insight of Quimby's is the effect the individual has on his own mental well-being. Health and illness were a matter of the mind. The mind can thus be influenced positively or negatively by one's outlook on life.

Phineas P. Quimby.

Quimby initially practiced hypnotic healing on his patients and began curing people of their ailments when orthodox doctors had given up hope. Quimby later formulated a purely mental theory of ill health, which is, the capacity of the mind to affect the body for good or ill. Nevertheless, the inspiration for Quimby's methods was credited by him to God. For Quimby, disease was real, and its cure was a matter of a change of opinion. This approach to healing is based on the Law of Attraction in so far as we attract positive or negative influences to health. Nothing of Quimby's writings was published until the 1920s, though he had several followers who were influential in creating public opinion, belief, and various movements. We will look at the influence of Mary Baker Eddy's Christian Science and Charles Fillmore's Unity Church briefly later. The positive mental health and spiritual healing movements were highly influential in shaping the New Thought and complimented metaphysics. Such healing methods had grown into folklore practice in rural areas. As Reverend Dorothy wrote, in the book *In her Own Words*, on the early days in Pennsylvania – "the gift of healing has always been of interest to our family. Since I can remember our family believed in faith healing and prayer and that it was the source of our help. When sick our family often searched for a healer."

Vibrational Healing in the CMC was a central practice in the church's life. This view of healing is that the world of ideas is more real than matter. That spirit is the origin and destination of man, that the individual is spirit now and that to attune the self, positively to God would relieve all ills. Reverend Dorothy wrote, "If you have found that you have been lax in control of your thought powers or mind powers. It isn't too late to change."

Happiness begins within our inner being. Be good to yourself. Give your body and mind the rest they need and you will see a great difference as you return to work.

Quimby was a contemporary of Andrew Jackson Davis (1835-1910), who is regarded as the Father of the Spiritualist movement and himself a Mesmerist and later a medium. Quimby's thought on the transcendental nature of reality closely mirrors that of Davis's. Andrew Jackson Davis is credited as revealing the philosophy and metaphysics of Spiritualist thought without knowledge of the 18th century mystic Swedenborg, whose work it closely resembled.

Swedenborg was cited by A. J. Davis as a spiritual helper and as a source of his revelation. Andrew Jackson Davis's other lasting influence lay in his example as a medium, by which example Davis empowered individuals, especially women to speak on public platforms. The metaphysical reality of other dimensions of being were demonstrated publicly by individuals, often with little formal education, trusting that spiritual beings would pass on their identity and ideas. Authority to speak lay with the individual and the approval or not of the audience. Dorothy and Russell are heirs to the example of Davis's idea that metaphysics is the 'science' of bringing on oneself into harmony with the Laws of God, and thereby a means of personal salvation. The example Davis set as a public speaker and his metaphysics, empowered the individual, and created a tradition of on-going revelation. Reverend Dorothy and Dr. Russell understood that and no one leader could stake a final claim on the truth. In New Thought, as in metaphysics, it was assumed that the continuous witness of new revelation was God's intention to renew Man's

Andrew Jackson Davis.

understanding of Spiritual Law. Andrew Jackson Davis was the first 19th century metaphysician to expand on the idea of the Law of Attraction, and Davis coined the term "Like attracts Like." Christian Metaphysics in common with all metaphysical groups is heir to Andrew Jackson Davis.

Andrew Jackson Davis and Phineas Quimby were working in the early 19th century, a time when the young US republic was shaping an identity. Immigration was opening up the country. The mind that characterized the pioneer suited the atmosphere of liberty that relied on oneself and each other. This matched the mood of self-reliance that sought to put the democratic individual at the heart of the spiritual. Religious authority could be ignored, as could the hostility of the orthodox as the United States had no established religion and they had guaranteed freedom of religious worship. Therefore, the ground was fertile for a congregation focused approach whereby the audience could walk away if they were not satisfied.

A consumer orientated approach emerged, whereby the needs and thoughts of the person needed to be satisfied in order to retain the adherence and support of a congregation. Whereas Davis's trance discourses inspired imitators and admirers, Quimby stimulated others to take up the 'science' of mental health through positive mental attitudes, psychological reflection, positive affirmation, and the Divine as personal. The work of both is mirrored in the 18th-century work of Swedenborg whose trance discourses describe the spirit world in similar detail to that of the later Spiritualists. It is worth noting that as a young man, Davis was illiterate. Metaphysics meets New Thought in the following summary. The material world is an effect whose causes are spiritual and whose purpose is Divine. It follows then that as the man turns his mind to the Divine and works in his consciousness to eliminate the negative aspects of his personality, so God turns and is bidden enter in.

All religious movements partake of Metaphysics in explaining Man's relations to the Divine and thereby to reality. Indeed, the term, Spiritualist was originally an 18th-century European term for someone who was not a materialist.[1] What is different is that in the USA the New Thought movement gave rise to a diverse and influential movement. The US New Thought ideas were reflected in a wave of self-help organization, publications, and religions from the 1830s onward. New Thought empowered the individual, and women in particular, to study and develop themselves. A wealth of writings on mediumship, mental health, spiritual healing, hypnotism and positive thought became available that by-passed traditional creedal based authority models.

The tide of New Thought and Metaphysical ideas also germinated outside of the USA and was influential without producing movements that carry those names. The individual in the 19th century began to take authority for himself and to be self-reliant in matters of religion. A tradition of self-education as exemplified by Abraham Lincoln arose on both sides of the Atlantic. Educational institutes were created by trade unionists; religious groups and collectives were created to help educate the working man. British Spiritualist pioneer David Richmond exemplified the new spirit of the age, speaking in the mid-1860s

We must not forget to send out thoughts of love in words that vibrate to the good where otherwise evil would predominate. Jealousy, envy, hatred, covetousness, gossip and ideas of a like nature are negative. Great eras and great structures, have their origin and completion only in thoughts of the positive.

when challenged to state who had witnessed his alleged levitation, replied, "I was the witness." Stillson Judah described New Thought in *The History and Philosophy of the Metaphysical Movements in America* as "encompassing a practical spirituality that promotes fullness of all aspects of living, through positive thinking, affirmative prayer, meditation and other ways of realizing the presence of God."

In Great Britain, in the 19th century, where the dominance of orthodox religions was paramount the anonymous author 'Fritz' said, "...a man must, therefore be

---

1. See *Dead Men's Embers* by this author, for more on this topic.

independent, by reason of his poverty or by reason of his wealth, before he can defy the opinion of the world."

The metaphysics of Spiritualism, on both sides of the Atlantic, was being accepted amongst those who could afford to ignore the hostility of the orthodox. Nevertheless, in Britain and the USA hostility to the new religion and its implied self-reliance and empowerment of women was overt. American women mediums in the mid-19th century, such as, Cora Tappen Richmond, Lottie Fowler and Lizzie Dotten braved public antagonism in both Britain and the States, and gave public demonstrations of mediumship. Women in the USA and Britain who have been already mentioned in these pages all benefited from the struggles of their 19th century sisters. In an interview in 1974, Reverend Dorothy could say of being a woman and Pastor, "I was raised to believe that a person is a person and that what is important is the work to be done." Dorothy benefited directly from the women pioneers of the 19th century.

Emma Hardinge Britten, crossed the Atlantic to the USA in the 1850s, returning to England as a pioneer Spiritualist Medium. *The Seven Principles* which Emma channeled and which are the principles of the British Spiritualist National Union (SNU) are influenced by New Thought and Davis's metaphysics combined. The rise of Socialist thinkers such as Robert Owen promoted, on both sides of the ocean, the principles of mutual help and self-education for the working man. In Europe, metaphysical ideas became widely disseminated through such movements as the Quakers, Mesmerism, Swedenborg, Theosophy and Spiritualism. Hindu Yogis, Buddhists (Edwin Arnold, *The Light of Asia*) and others have all impacted on the European mind from an easterly direction. In the 20th century many US writers from the New Thought and metaphysical movements were widely influential on both sides of the Atlantic. To name a few, in America there was Ralph Waldo Trine, Charles Fillmore, Eric Butterworth, and in Britain, Emmet Fox (Irish), James Allen and Evelyn Underhill, all achieved great sales with their writings.

The metaphysical movement and the New Thought groups have diverged over the last one hundred years; whereas the Metaphysical religions all embrace New Thought not all NT is spiritual. New Thought, as a movement gave rise to many movements that are not necessarily spiritual. For example, Mindfulness techniques that originate in Eastern thought, dieting, yoga, self-education, the applied arts, and self-improvement of all kinds have all sprung from New Thought's emphasis on the individual self-help.

In Chapter Two, we saw that Russell had obtained his degree, probably through a correspondence course at the College of Divine Metaphysics, Indianapolis. The College started by Dr. Perry Joseph Green in 1918 was dedicated to a new vision of Man's understanding of the nature of ultimate reality, and the personal relationship with God.

The vision of the College was part of the New Thought movement. There are now some thirty-one colleges offering metaphysical studies in the USA. New Thought and Metaphysics have many offshoots, with at least twenty-two churches, often with the word Science in their title, such as Jewish Science or the Roanoke Metaphysical Chapel.

The New Thought movement gave rise to the metaphysical religious movement, the effects of which are still apparent. There are several metaphysical religious groups in the US. One of the largest is Unity, started by Charles and Myrtle Fillmore in Kansas City in 1889. Myrtle Fillmore had suffered tuberculosis and been cured of this by a spiritual healer. Unity started as a healing group, and healing continues to be important as part of its practice. The couple founded the Unity Village fifteen miles from Kansas City some time after 1918. The Church is Christian orientated, focusing on the power of positive thought or affirmations. Individual churches within Unity agree on core principles but vary in their practices. There is a seminary program for training pastors with numerous churches and a million members worldwide.

The writings of Charles Fillmore and Eric Butterworth, another respected Unity thinker, are to be found today at the Sarasota Centre of Light. Unity's *Metaphysical Dictionary* was known to be respected and consulted by Dorothy and Russell. The dictionary's importance lay in providing a ready definition of the inner meaning of words and scripture. The Art or Science lay in intuitively arriving at the meaning. The more difficult or irrelevant passages need not be included, and certain prophets such Ezekiel and Isiah may be preferred to other less relevant books of the Bible. The dictionary provided the key to a higher truth that explored the underlying meanings of scripture and pointed to a positive interpretation.

Camp Silver Belle — 1960   Page 25

Shrine of the Master
Metaphysical Christianity
3416 Grand Central Ave.   Tampa, Fla.

Pastors: Rev. Dorothy G. Flexer
Dr. Russell J. Flexer

Sunday Services
Sunday School .... 9:30 A.M.
Worship Services .... 10:30 A.M., 7:30 P.M.

Thursday Services
Prayer and Healing Service .... 7:00 to 8:00 P.M.
All-Message Service .... 8:00 to 9:00 P.M.

Notice in the Camp Silver Belle program 1960.

The formation of the Christian Metaphysical Church was influenced by other sources; we know of the previous affiliation to the Spiritualist Episcopal Church. This Church had been formed to include the teachings of Jesus in its remit and to practice a more Christian, church-like atmosphere. Whereas the National Association of Spiritualist Churches (NASC) taught that Jesus was a great spiritual teacher and that was all. Similarly, in Britain, Sir Arthur Conan Doyle had proposed a motion to the

Spiritualist National Union AGM in 1927 and again in 1928 that "…the Christian ideal be adopted as a principle of the SNU." The motion was defeated, though only after a heated debate.

The CMC bears a striking similarity to the British, Greater World Spiritualist Christian League, (GWSCL) (now known as an Association). It is similar in its loose Federation structure to the CMC. This church was established by Winifred Moyes in 1931, who spoke of Christian Spiritualism as a 'Higher Line' approach. By 1936, the church had over 500 churches in the UK and overseas, with many publications. The inspiration came from Moyes' spirit guide, Zodiac, who was said to have been a teacher in the temple at the time of Jesus. His purpose was to make the teachings of Christ central to the people within the Spiritualist movement. The aim was to develop understanding and work with the spirit world to spread the truth of Christian Spiritualism. The expressed aims and

> *If desire or faith, if you choose to call it that, is sufficiently strong, the patient without the assistance of a physician, a healer, spirit doctors or guides can accomplish his own healing.*

principles of the GWCL are very similar to that of the CMC. There is a relationship between Moyes' organization and the ideas that inspired the founding of the Spiritualist Episcopal Church in the USA in 1941, and which may have influenced Dorothy and Russell.

It is harder to assess what impact other mediums and speakers had on the Flexers. However, Dorothy and Russell knew everybody who was anybody in the Spiritualist movement up to 1961. Many names have been noted and to recap a few, E. Post-Parrish, John Bunker, Arthur Ford, Peggy Barnes, Clifford Bias and H Gordon Burroughs. In addition, the Flexers would have met and worked with leading British Spiritualists such as author and medium Horace Leaf, *Psychic News* and US *Psychic Observer* editor, Paul Miller and almost certainly attended lectures at Camp Silver Belle given by British editor, Maurice Barbanell.

The significance of these speakers lay in the standards that they set as workers for spirit. In addition, there was the example of the morals that the speakers observed in their lives. And

Tampa Center Opens

There is a new occult center in Tampa, Florida, located at 8806 Florida Avenue, where guest workers and mediums will be welcomed to serve during the winter months.

Regular Spiritualist services are held every Sunday at 8:00 P. M. under the direction of the Rev. Nellie Cherry through whose efforts, not only a Spiritualist church, but a school for students in occult science will be conducted.

Just recently, "the Mitchells," Phyllis and Fred, were visitors at the Rev. Cherry's church. Many noted mediums are scheduled to visit this center in the near future.

A new Tampa Church. Spiritualism grew rapidly in the 1950s.

there was the influence of the ethical values observed in the organizations in which the Flexers worked. For the young Dorothy and Russell, the speakers and mediums were exemplars to be emulated and lived up to. As mature and talented workers, the lives that these co-workers lived were also subtle pointers on how to conduct oneself as a public figure. There were no doubt differences of opinion, and we know that Dorothy did express fulsome appreciation (see Chapter One) for the example set by of many of them.

GANDY BRIDGE ACROSS TAMPA BAY. BY MOONLIGHT. ST. PETERSBURG. FLORIDA   THE SUNSHINE CITY   26

Gandy Bridge across Tampa Bay, by Moonlight.
Dorothy and Russell knew the bridge well.

Another influence and one admired, to some extent by Reverend Dorothy was the Christian Science organization founded by Mary Baker Eddy. The inspiration had originally come from Quimby whom Eddy knew, though Eddy claimed Divine revelation to be her source. Eddy's Christian Science is a set of beliefs and practices, which originally belonged to the metaphysical family of religious movements. Eddy became increasingly authoritarian and expelled women whom she felt threatened her authority. She further declared that the revelation had ended with herself. She believed Phineas Quimby had found the key to Jesus's healing methods, but after talking with him, she decided that Quimby's success lay chiefly in his charismatic personality and his positive approach to mental health. Mary Baker Eddy argued in her book, *Science and Health* (1875) that sickness is an illusion that can be corrected by prayer alone.

In the Christian Scientist view, ill health was viewed as a mental error rather than a physical disorder. The sick should be not treated by medicine, but by prayer. Reality and thereby ill-health were regarded as an illusion. Though the positive mental outlook remained a common feature, healing in the CMC was, as we shall see, to take a different approach from Christian Science. Reverend Dorothy expressed admiration for Mary Baker Eddy's positive attitudes to mental health and healing. Though Christian Science diverted from New Thought in its dogmatism. This aspect was not admired by the Flexers, nor would Reverend Dorothy put Russell through the suffering of a brain tumor without providing vibrational healing and the best medical treatment available.

Another direct influence on Dorothy and Russell was the example of existing Spiritualist communities. Communities based on specific ideas and ideals have been a feature of American life since the creation of the Republic. Examples such as the Shakers, the Utopian Socialists of Hopedale and New Harmony Ind, the Amish and the Spiritualists; there are many such communities in the USA. As noted in the first chapter, there are some twelve such Spiritualist camps still in existence with a residential core and most taking seasonal visitors. Silver Belle, Lily Dale, Chesterfield, and Cassadaga in Florida were the largest, with Silver Belle closing in 1988. Their importance lay in the fact that when the SOM was established at Sarasota in 1949, property lots became available around the Sanctuary that allowed for the creation of some seventeen homes. Such building effectively created a community of residents similar in most respects to the Spiritualist Camps. Such a project was never planned but occurred. We will look at the creation and purpose of these homes in the next chapter.

By your actions, by your thinking and I know that you have a lot more peace of mind, because just to believe in the "everlasting arm" leaves a lot to doubt if you are going to get results, when will you get results, is it now or in eternity? Isn't that true?

Russell would on occasion refer to 'Higher Thought'. This is a specific NT idea that promotes Deity as 'Infinite Intelligence' that the Great Spirit is the total of all that there is. Dorothy said once in a sermon "…we know that God is a spirit not a man and it is the power of God that creates." In Higher Thought Man himself partakes of the Divine nature and is perfectible in so far as he is willing to approach, in his own consciousness, the Divine assistance. Jesus had said in 'The Sermon on the Mount', "Be ye, therefore, perfect even as your Father which is in Heaven is perfect." It followed then that it is possible for Man to become Divinely perfect. Further, this in Metaphysics was regarded as an instruction to work at becoming perfect. The whole Sermon on the Mount, as interpreted by the influential Emmet Fox, is a guide to New Thought and metaphysical religion. The Sermon is an instruction in the nature of God, to lead a moral life and achieve spiritual completion. Man, in the metaphysical view, was not a miserable sinning creation of whom only some could be saved but rather one that had the potential to transcend the world and become at one with the Father.

The Flexers believed that there was no 'Redemption' of man in the vicarious sacrifice of an only son by a vengeful Deity. The Church of Metaphysical Christianity implicitly rejected the doctrine of Salvationism. Jesus had not died and 'atoned' for the sins of Man. But he had died and risen to prove the truth of eternal life for all. If eternal life was automatic and the promise for all that implied, the CMC, in common with other metaphysical groups rejected the old doctrine and dogma. The individual would live again but to do so well he would need to work out a personal salvation through working on a level of consciousness. Agreeing to some formulae of beliefs would, therefore, do nothing for you. The design for living in the next life was created by how this life was led.

Higher Thought taught that spiritual science was pragmatic and could be tested. The CMC did not ask members to believe but to demonstrate the principles of metaphysics in experience. The positive psychology of the CMC was optimistic in outlook. The teachings of the CMC achieved results and was underwritten by the phenomena of mediumship as religious experience. Meaning in life was found through investigation and experience, similar to undertaking education, the results would be found to be beneficial in living life. In metaphysics, God was demonstrated as being, and active, in the world and part of an individual's self-fulfillment.

Dorothy speaking in an interview with the *Sarasota Herald Tribune* in 1974 said, "The members are encouraged to develop themselves to be open to the voices of the angels. We accept this inter-communication as a way of life, and we approach God as spirit, love and natural Law. For us, heaven and hell exist only as states of consciousness, and we don't waste our energies being afraid or frightening others with the devil of orthodox religions."

Such pragmatism of approach also rejected Original Sin. In New Thought and Christian metaphysics, each child was viewed as born 'immaculate' and free from sin. Everyone including Jesus was viewed as sons and daughters of God. The Deity was not viewed as a medieval monarch or Lord; capricious and in need of supplication. Nor was God seen as an egotistical single parent of an extended dysfunctional human family. Eric Butterworth, the Unity writer, referred to the "Religion of Jesus not the religion about Jesus." The Master Jesus was viewed as the greatest of teachers, an instructor of

Rev. Dorothy Graff Flexer.

(a photograph often used in publications.)

morals, an inspiring miracle worker whose miracles were, in principle, repeatable. The Master instructors which included the great teachers of other faiths were sent by a loving God to help mankind. Worship in the context of the CMC was an understanding of, and obedience to the God Power and Spiritual Law.

In Metaphysical Christianity and in the New Thought movement, it was error and incorrect or false beliefs that kept Man from his potential greatness. As noted, the Calvinist doctrine of 'Grace' whereby man was seen as a fallen sinful being in need of redemption was rejected. God in the metaphysical view was imminent, always at hand to help his creation, unlike many Protestant groups that viewed God as remote, something distant, otherworldly. Evil and sin were errors of ignorance. Jesus had said, "They know not what they do." It followed that if the evil doers did know what they were doing, they would not carry out the evil. Wickedness and wrong thinking were done not in the name of evil but in the disguise of goodness. Dr. Davis through Reverend Dorothy's mediumship said, "Many clergy fail to realize that if they taught love and understanding, they would help and please their congregations far more than filling their minds with fear, negation, and doubt." There would be no Judgement hereafter.

In the metaphysical view, the individual was solely responsible for his actions. Man would flourish in so far as his actions were in accordance with the immutable Spiritual Law. Man had choice and options in life according to the circumstances in which he found himself. In effect, Jesus could do nothing for you, only the individual working at raising the level of consciousness could achieve union with the Divine. By extension, Man makes his own heaven and hell hereafter when confronted by his own entire, unavoidable conscience. By this we mean, an individual may make a hell on Earth which will be nothing compared to the hell he makes for himself hereafter. In the CMC where spirit communication was fundamental, the departed were understood to be inhabiting a spirit world of mind in which like attracted like. Heaven and hell were realms of thought created by the positive or negative habits and actions of the individual. The Law of Love, God's ultimate expression for his creation was the most creative of all forces in the universe. Man engaging that force of God through compassion and service would raise himself towards perfection.

Humanity was seen as a co-creator with God in so far as the God power was realized by the individual. If the individual sought a connection to the Divine, the God power would always respond positively. And God was always reaching out to those that sought a relationship with him. Reverend Dorothy said in a trance sermon, "Anything that opposes the Divine Law of goodness and right living is wrong, evil and destructive. When you allow something negative to become part of your life, you cannot survive in a happy, contented way."

For Russell, the conscious mind was reliant upon the Divine Mind. Deity deposited the divine aspiration to unity with the Father in the human mind. As there was only one God power, so there was only one Mind, of which the individual partook. Russell wrote, "We cannot think one thing and produce something different. For every effect, there is a corresponding cause. Our outside world, be it good or bad corresponds to our inside world." Thought was the parent of the deed. The effect of the deed would be good or bad according to the intention. 'Evil might reign a little day,' but could never prevail indefinitely. The informing mind of life ensured that all creation was moving upward toward perfection. Such bondage of wrong thinking could not endure forever. Russell quoted Ralph Waldo Emmerson who said, "If you do not like the image I project at the moment, I can improve it by altering the thought pattern."

The Divine was Spiritual Law and was part of nature and involved intelligence and processes. A key aspect of thought in Metaphysical Christianity and New Thought is the understanding of Spiritual Law. Dr. Russell taught that there is a Spiritual Law which cannot be broken by anyone. The CMC listed seven key Spiritual Laws (see some below). Spiritual Law was regarded as specific actions of the God Power that affect our spiritual being. Natural Law, however, has a wider implication such as the operations of the heavens and the life of nature. Both Spiritual and Natural Law are, in metaphysical thought, immutable. The Spiritual Law controls all human and angelic life, in both this world and the next. Spiritual Law operates on the basis of attraction.

When you believe as you believe that through your prayers, your knowledge you are asking for individual help of the angels and have the assurance that the angels are working right now. You have the benefit of their action and your action right now. You are not waiting for the angel Gabriel to blow the horn. You know that you are going to have results it's a combined power, a cooperation and a combination of power.

The Law of Attraction, the understanding of which corrects false beliefs and develops right thinking, through which our lives become healthier, happier and prosperous. Positive prayer or affirmation would draw to the individual that which they are! If prosperity without greed is how you think: you will attract prosperity and *vice versa*. Attraction brings to you, not what you want, but what you are. The Law of Attraction operates in all fields of human life. Metaphysical Christianity promoted the view that our personal lives attracted things and people that reflected ourselves. Fundamentally the individual should see the positive in people in order to attract the beneficial to themselves. A positive change of thought would alter material conditions for the practitioner.

In metaphysical thought, the Law of Attraction meant that compensation was an integral aspect of the process of attraction. "As ye shall sow, so shall ye reap." What you give positively or negatively comes back to you. What goes around, comes around – or in the Spirtitualist Seven Principles "Compensation for the good and evil deeds done on earth." Reverend Dorothy wrote, "The way to know the true nature of God is to put the Spiritual Law to work which fundamentally is this, whatever you think comes back to you. This basic Law of Compensation encourages you to do what is right and to love and understand others so that the good returns to you. This Truth is constant for everyone regardless of religious affiliation."

There was a Law of Freedom by which we understand that our will is paramount to the circumstances in which one finds oneself. As outlined above, the attitude to our situation controls our destiny even though we may be deprived of our freedom of action. Viktor E. Frankl expressed this idea in *Man's Search for Meaning*, "Forces beyond your control can take away everything you possess except one thing, your freedom to choose how you will respond to the situation."

Likewise, the Spiritual Law of Truth was of central concern to Dorothy and Russell. Living life in truth was a core value and created conditions for inner harmony. The Law of Truth was grounded, and truth made accessible by Jesus's promise (Matthew 7:7) "Ask, and it shall be given you; seek, and ye shall find; knock, and it shall be opened unto you." The Flexers believed that Truth would always prevail over non-truth. The word 'Truth' is repeated throughout their lives as ministers and mediums and is of central importance in understanding metaphysical thought.

The Flexers believed that there was a method, a 'science' in their system of metaphysical religion. From New Thought principles and the teachings of Jesus, Dorothy and Russell drew the idea that if the practitioner applied the principles of positive thinking, their lives must be enhanced. The science of metaphysical interpretation applied to scriptures must enrich the spiritual life of the individual. Essentially, the understanding mind was engaged and asked to reason in association with others, as to what the positive outcome should be? Likewise, an investigating student of mediumship would follow the discipline or science of psychic development to bring about communion with the spirit world and master teachers, who stood by to assist those that sought out their guidance. In metaphysical thought, belief and sincere application would bring about the desired results of understanding, spiritual enhancement and psychic awareness. Dr. Davis was to refer to the results of this science as 'knowledge'. Such knowing was a tool which would enhance the challenges of daily living. Such awareness both spiritual and psychic could be used to inform the metaphysician of the right course of action.

It was in association with others that the Flexers lived and in Reverend Dorothy's own words, "When the work of cleansing our mind is done, it is much easier to live in harmony with the God Power. Building a good reputation should be everyone's purpose in life." Victoria Woodhull, the 19th century US Spiritualist trance medium had said, "If you preach the doctrine, you must live the life." Woodhull meant that the teachers were called to live exemplary lives, the virtue of which would be apparent to observers. Woodhull's dictum was upheld by the Flexers. As we shall see in the next chapter, their lives, like the church they founded was, as Jesus said in Matthew 5:14, "Ye are the light of the world. A city that is set on a hill cannot be hid." The values of the Church of Metaphysical Christianity could not be, nor was intended to be, hidden.

The truth was verifiable by its positive or negative outcome in the life of the member, and spirit communication was verifiable by feedback from others. This 'science' was also a reality check to 'test the spirits to see if they be of God.' Jesus had warned, "Beware of false prophets, which come to you in sheep's clothing, but inwardly they are ravening wolves. Ye shall know them by their fruits. Do men gather grapes off thorns or figs off thistles?"

There were perils of false ideas, leaders and cults whose teachings would not withstand the Christian Metaphysical Science of Truth. Were the outcomes positive and beneficial to the self and others? Could others follow the same path and achieve the same results or would the false prophet be exposed? In other chapters, we see that Dorothy and Russell stood as bulwarks against false, fanciful or inadequate ideas. One theory that was

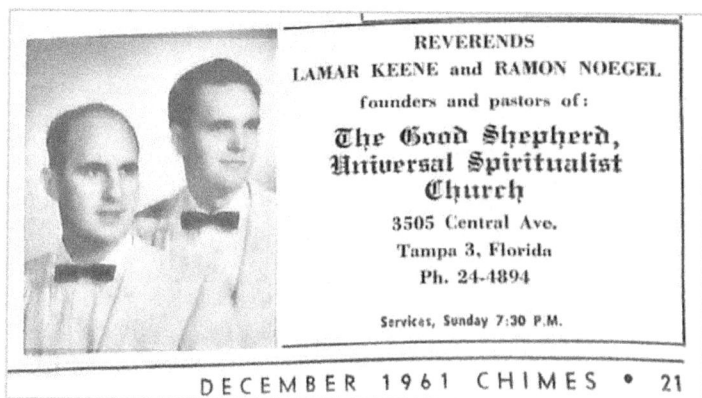

REVERENDS
LAMAR KEENE and RAMON NOEGEL
founders and pastors of:

The Good Shepherd,
Universal Spiritualist
Church

3505 Central Ave.
Tampa 3, Florida
Ph. 24-4894

Services, Sunday 7:30 P.M.

DECEMBER 1961 CHIMES • 21

Ramon Noegel, a minister of the early 1960s.
Later he broke away from the CMC.

rejected on the grounds that it was unprovable was reincarnation. In metaphysical terms, it was unscientific, unreliable and unprovable. Reincarnation in metaphysical discussion added an unquantifiable element that could not be verified. Acceptance could lead to delusional stories that may simply be fantastic. Such beliefs were a contradiction of the principle of metaphysics as a science of practice. Reverend Dorothy's attitude to reincarnation was similar to the use of crystals in healing when Dorothy said to Fern Bradburn, "You know that is a lot of nonsense."

There were no hidden agendas at Browning Street. Metaphysics asked for faith and belief from the practitioner, but it demonstrated the truth of change in the individual. It verified the reality of the paranormal, provided communication with the known deceased and with master teachers that sought to help the incarnate. These Truths were demonstrable, repeatable and available as an experience to the believer. As Reverend Dorothy said in *The Doorway called Death*, "Jesus developed his gifts to the point where he could cure the sick, restore sight to the blind, and give the sad and afflicted a new lease of life. Is it not our responsibility to do the same?" In the CMC, the metaphysical teaching, the development of mediumship, and positive living were a proven method and were the underwriters of the Dorothy and Russell's value system.

Shrine of the Master Healing Garden gateway and sign in the 1950s.

Dr. Davis speaking through the levitating trumpet said, "Attune to your guardian angels, and believe in Spiritual Law. Harmonize with the Law and let it become so much a part of your thinking and being that you form an invisible pact between yourself, the Law and the angels. As you bridge the gap between your lower self [earthly] and higher self, an inner peace grows that can continue throughout eternity, for there is no end to life."

In Metaphysical Christianity — the inner harmony of the individual, the vibration that a person has cultivated and the constructive process of thought all combined with the workings of Spiritual Law to create the organic processes and circumstance of being an individual in God's intended pattern. Metaphysical reality transcended the material plane of existence; its existence could be demonstrated in the phenomena of the séance room. Its teachings united and explained the worlds of being. The known dead spoke, objects levitated and appeared out of thin air. Therefore, the contemporary understanding of physics was demonstrated to be incomplete, and the Metaphysical was a demonstrable truth. As the Master Jesus said, "On Earth as it is in Heaven." Communication between the worlds, proved Jesus's words and demonstrated that there was a symmetry between this world and the spiritual worlds. Russell may have prayed in the manner of Upanishad, "Lead me from the unreal to the real. From darkness lead me to light. From death lead me to immortality."

Reverend Dorothy wrote, "Let us not fool ourselves that Metaphysical Christianity is a new religion." It was however, regarded as possessing a unique approach to the investigation and analysis of life on Earth and in Spirit. The practices of the church and its beliefs were regarded as ancient and rooted in the early Christian church. The new religion aimed to bring the highest and brightest thought to the individual. Dr. Russell was a mystic. The 'science' of metaphysics was a practical guide to union with ultimate reality. It was in Russell's and Dr. Davis synthesis of Spiritualist communication, New Thinking, Masonic ritual, and the appreciation of God and the Spiritual Law that lay at the heart of Metaphysical Christianity. We have noted that Russell and Dr. Davis were the inspiration for the new approach to religion and it was the mystical vision of Christ that was at the heart of Dr. Russell's vision.

For Dr. Russell, the mystical experience was absorption in the Christ Consciousness which was God in everyone. The man Jesus was separate, the Spirit Jesus showed the way. Russell's mind was to a greater or lesser extent in union with the Divine. Mysticism is defined by Evelyn Underhill as "...the art of union with reality." That reality for Russell was the imminent, innate, intrinsic and inborn. It was the metaphysical world that had created this temporary existence for us. Man was seen as Spirit having a physical experience. We noted in Chapter One that the absorption in the musical 'soundscapes' convey a language of God through our emotions that is beyond words and ideas. Union with the Divine was in St Paul's phrase, "In Him we move and have our being." Silence and inner harmony with the Spiritual Law were the objective.

Jesus had said in John 14:6 "No one comes to the Father except through me." By which the metaphysician understood that Christ was a state of consciousness, which if achieved would unite the individual to the Divine. Russell wrote, "Christ is the perfect inner self... this perfect inner man knows nothing of a negative nature because it is a God spirit. Therefore, we must resolve to become at one with God through the Christ consciousness." Absorption in the Christ Consciousness, the realization of our inner Divine Spark had for Russell a silent devotional aspect; that of Union with the Divine. For Russell, the Divine Mind was part of the individual and the spark that lit the fire for union with the Divine. Dr. Russell Flexer was what Ralph Waldo Trine called 'In tune with the Infinite.'

Dr. Russell Flexer.
(a photograph often used in publications.)

Those who knew Russell speak of him as Sally Hayden von Conta did, in July 2015, "He was a very dear man, very good with everyone and had a great sense of humor. He had a sweetness and humanness about him." I will look again at this quotation in another chapter. Russell's daughter, Eileen, added that her father would spend many hours drafting sermons in his study and he did not like to be disturbed while doing so. This involved, as any writer will tell you, much silence and thought. Dr. Flexer, it is thought did not have a private meditation practice. However, he did have a large library where he would sit, contemplate and write one of his sermons, *On Christ Consciousness* is reproduced in the appendices.

Dr. Russell took ill in the early 1970s with headaches and nausea and was diagnosed with a tumor in the brain. Healing was a principle religious and spiritual activity of the CMC and Russell was the beneficiary of such ministry. In the metaphysical church anyone could train as a healer though there were protocols (see the appendices); there was an application to join and a practice of healing to be followed. The process of using the healing energy was known as 'Vibrational Healing' and was regarded as a natural force, manifesting at a different vibratory rate. This energy was analogous to electricity, invisible but real. Healing, the removal or relieving of illness was achieved through patient and healer harmonizing with the Divine power. The energy was part of the God power, the healer was the instrument, and the angels were there to assist in directing the power.

For healing to occur at any level, faith was required, and the healer would bring relief and care according to the Law of Attraction. Healing was another aspect of the 'science' of the CMC religious way of life, in that proper application of the principles of healing must have a beneficial result. Medical diagnosis was forbidden, and the healing process was viewed as being complementary to the medical profession. Healers were instructed in the care of their own bodies through good living and healthy eating habits.

Healing was regarded as ancient, having been practiced by the early Christians as well as a feature in all cultures. In Luke 4.23 Jesus is quoted as saying "physician heal thyself" by which it was understood that healing started with the self and one's attitudes. In John 14:10, Jesus is recorded as saying, "... the Father who dwells in me and who carries out his work." The individual requiring healing had the spark of God within him, it was that essence that was affected by the healing which in turn altered the physical. Other theories which were compatible with the CMC approach to healing spoke of the etheric body which was thought of as an overcoat of several layers. Physical mediumship or psychic surgery is seen as literally operating on the etheric level which in turn created change in the physical body.

Shrine of the Master Healing Garden Fountain in the 1950s.

Healing was a regular and central feature of life at the sanctuary and the weekly members' development class always started with healing. Wednesday evenings were given over to a Healing and Prayer Service and were led by Dr. Russell until his death. Healing was also an integral part of the Sunday evening service and is now a part of the morning service too. Reverend Dorothy speaking in an interview with the Herald Tribune in 1974, "Many come for our Healing service and stay because they find peace in the metaphysical concept."

Karen Turner speaking in July 2015, commented that there were Tuesday afternoon healing sessions, largely attended by women and Karen's parents both became healers. Karen added, "There were so many people that it would overrun by an hour. Attending the healing cost 3 dollars and Reverend Dorothy also taught the healing classes. A book report on the student progress was introduced and in Dorothy's day the process was shorter than today."

Patients would contribute letters of commendation to students whom they felt had made a difference. Healing varied with individuals and some were regarded as better healers than others. Dorothy insisted on a dress code that has been dropped since her passing. Women were to wear white dresses and the men suits and bow ties. Fern Bradburn recalled being "chewed up" by Reverend Dorothy. Fern said, "One night, I wore a dress that had lavender and pale blue in the hem. Dorothy said 'you know that you are supposed to wear white.' I said, 'I am wearing white,' and Reverend Dorothy replied, 'You got color!'" Fern added affectionately, "Dorothy could be hard task master but could be fun too."

The Healing service was very popular and a beautiful occasion. Lori Rohrbach, writing in 1997, tells the story of her mother who was taken seriously ill with cancer of the tongue and was very frightened. Dorothy talked to the lady on the telephone who decided to attend the Healing service on the Wednesday evening. Reverend Dorothy explained that there was to be a special healing service. Rohrbach's mother was seated in front of the congregation. Dorothy lit the candles and led the special service. "As everyone concentrated in sending healing energy to my mother in the glow of the candlelight, I could see Reverend Dorothy's love and energy radiating to this frightened woman she barely knew. And as the magnificent energy vibrated I saw the fear starting to diminish in my mother's eyes."

Lori's mother underwent major surgery and made a complete recovery. Lori added, "The gift of her complete recovery is one I am eternally grateful for. I owe it all to the loving help and guidance received from a lady I believe to be true Earth Angel, Reverend Dorothy Flexer."

Another member, Livia Raynes in 1991, underwent a mastectomy; for ten days she had a dangerously high fever, and Livia realized that she was dying. Remembering Reverend Dorothy, Livia rang her, saying, "Please pray with me," and Dorothy replied, "I will call some people, and we will all pray for you, and by 3 pm you should feel better." At 3 pm the doctor and nurse called and Livia's temperature had gone down. Within an hour she was allowed to go home. Livia added, "I gave testimony of this miracle at the Wednesday night service."

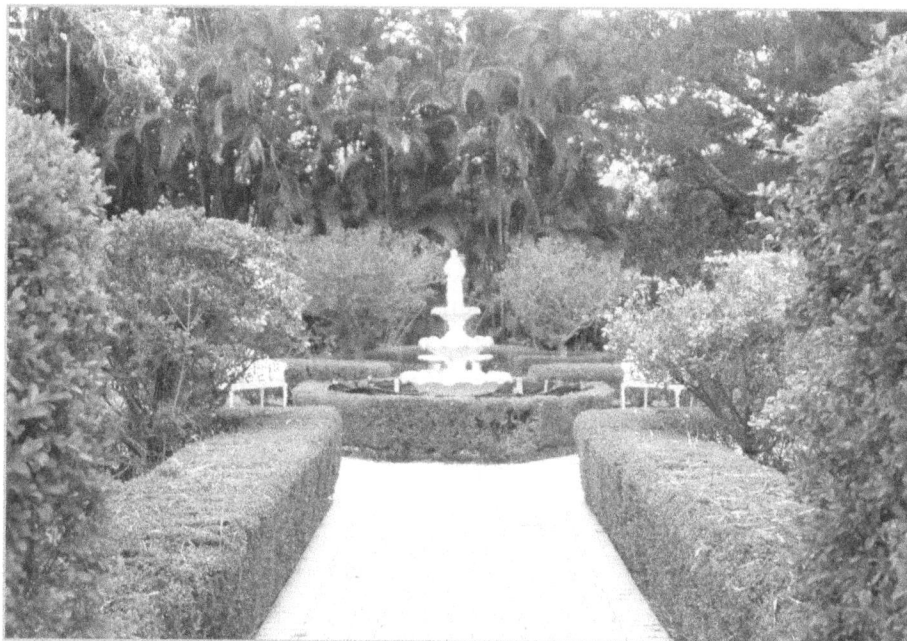

Sarasota Center of Light Healing Garden with the Saint Francis Fountain.

The Rowe family became very involved in all aspects of the church's life. Kenneth Rowe, Marie's husband, was President of the CMC. Marie Rowe's mother was also President of the Board of the church. Dr. Russell also taught the healing practice and Marie was as a student of Russell's. Chairs were placed in the Sanctuary for the patients to sit on and the healers would line up behind them and in meditative state would perform 'the laying on of hands'. Marie would often attend the Sunday service and not stay for the messages from the departed.

Karen Strauss reports that a little-known aspect of Reverend Dorothy's life was that Dorothy would take Chelation Therapy. Chelation therapy is a chemical process in which a synthetic solution, is injected into the bloodstream to remove heavy metals and/or minerals from the body. The therapy remains controversial and is said to be unproven.

It is possible that Reverend Dorothy took up the therapy as a result of Dr. Russell's illness. Russell was also said to have trained as a reflexologist.

In the Church of Metaphysical Christianity's Science, ill-health and death were a part of Natural Law. Good living and the avoidance of bad habits such as smoking and the cultivation of healthy mental habits would enhance the life of the metaphysician. Inherited illness such as heart conditions, viral infections, for example meningitis, or infectious disease such as the influenza epidemic of 1918 were all regarded as part of the Natural Law or occurring in nature. Ill-health was not a moral judgment on those who were ill; for the metaphysician, compassion for them was the correct response.

Kenneth & Marie's Wedding,
7th February 1960.

Whereas, at its most extreme, Christian Science denied the reality of illness. For the Christian Scientist, this world of matter was the illusion and its apparent realness was as a result of the error of Man's mortal mind. Therefore, ill-health and disease were an illusion. It is thought that in modern Christian Science practice its followers may have recourse to conventional medical treatment. Nevertheless, the more extreme the belief, the greater the degree of passion required to believe it. The US court system has since 1887 seen over fifty prosecutions for preventable deaths of adults and children. Mary Baker Eddy had declared that her husband Asa Eddy (1817-1882) had died of "arsenical poisoning mentally administered"; the autopsy declared that Asa Eddy had died of 'distinctly developed' heart disease.

Metaphysical Christianity was rooted in faith and practice and accepted that illness was real. When Dr. Russell took ill, there was a story that his seizures were as a result of repeatedly inhaling industrial paint in the shipyards in the 1940s where he has worked as a welder. This story, the family state, is not true. It is true that he was exposed to lead paint that was used to seal the cans in the American Can Company, but whether this was a factor in his death twenty-six years later is doubtful. Russell's illness did progress, and he had to give up traveling to Tampa to take the Sunday service. Dr. Russell gradually lost the ability to drive, and Marie Rowe and a number of others traveled to serve the Sunday congregation at Tampa. In July of 2015, Darryl Ritchie spoke of Dr. Russell as being "very approachable and jolly" and Marie Rowe added, "...he was a huggy bear." Florence Strauss recalled that in 1974, the gravity of Russell's illness caused fears that he would die. Spirit, however, said that this was incorrect and with vibrational healing that "he would live another three years," which he did. It was understood that only God knew the timing of anyone's death, but with surgery, hospital care and nursing it is believed that Russell's life was prolonged.

The minutes for the AGM of January 1977, noted that Reverend Dorothy "thanked everyone for the wonderful prayers, cards, calls and general support of Dr. Russell and her, during Dr. Russell's recent operation and recovery." The operation caused the cancellation of the Esoteric School (see the next chapter). 1977 saw the deaths of the president of the CMC, Charles Pixley who died on the 16th December as did Mary Flexer, Russell's mother who had moved back to Pennsylvania to be with her daughter Virginia. The AGM of 1978, noted these deaths and added "the absence of their physical presence is deeply felt but we know they are continuing to help in every possible way from the realm of Spirit."

The way through ill health and to Heaven had not proved easy for Russell Flexer. The Flexers loved the old hymn, *Amazing Grace* which aptly expresses the mortal struggle, "through many dangers, toils and snares, I have already come: 'tis grace has brought me safe thus far, and grace will lead me home."

Concerning health; if one holds to the proper mental attitude, one can cure oneself. It all hinges on the power of concentration, the matter of desire and one's stick-to-itiveness, whether the desired result may be obtained. The medical profession has been established for people who have not these qualities. If there is any question in your mind that you have not the determination to carry through to a positive healthy conclusion, then call on a physician by all means.

Russell let go of this life on the 22nd July 1977 aged 62. Death, when it occurs, is always a shock; it's never today, and Dr. Russell was gone, as if ... "in the mists of day."

The eyes of this world see no further than this life, but Dr. Russell saw deep into eternity. There was the science of religion in Dr. Russell's practice; a soul-realization of the self, that became an intuitive knowing of God. In Dr. Russell's thought, there was a mystery in the union of Man and the Divine that cannot be explained, nor should be. The happiest people are those that share their lives and love those with whom they live. In turn, Russell was, a much-loved man, a mystic and a thinker. Russell wrote, "To love God is to live in Harmony with the Divine Law and the Laws of Nature."

Dorothy would go on for another nineteen years without her soul mate. The dedication and vocation that motivated the Flexers would sustain Dorothy in the strength needed to build the community and the Church at Sarasota.

Reverend Dorothy, January 1978, shortly after the passing of Dr. Russsell.

Meeting the departed. And when he saw Aeneas heading towards him over the grass he stretched out both his hands eagerly, his face streaming with tears, and a cry issued from his lips, 'Have you come at last, and has the loyalty your father expected conquered the harsh road? Is it granted me to see your face my son, and hear and speak in familiar tones?

From Virgil: Aeneid Book VI. Translation by Seamus Heaney

Chapter Four

"He speaks, and the sound of His voice,
Is so sweet the birds hush their singing,"

"Dorothy Graff Flexer is a petite woman who radiates a serenity and a convincing inner strength. As co-Pastor and co-founder of the Shrine of the Master in Sarasota, the Reverend Dorothy is a lady who has never allowed her ministerial work to be compromised by her sex. "Goodness no," she says, "I never thought being a woman was any problem. I was raised to believe that a person is a person and that what is important is the work to be done. One or two times in the past a man thought he couldn't respect a female minister, but that has been rare." Profiles of Dorothy when alive are few and the above from the *Sarasota Herald Tribune* for July 1974, give a good impression of the self-confidence and self-assurance that members fondly remember.

Dorothy spoke of a dream that occurred in 1946. In the dream, Dr. Davis suggests to the couple that they move to Sarasota and start a Shrine of the Master Spiritualist Church there.

The city of Sarasota was once a modest town, the area being known for its rich agricultural land, fishing, and hunting. The town has several islands (known as Keys) and bays which are part of the landscape of the city. The healthy climate attracted those unwell to take cures by the sea. The major areas of the city, are now key districts whereas once they had been agricultural land. Tuttle Avenue and Browning Street where the Shrine of the Master is situated are remembered as dirt roads on the edge of the town. The Spaniard Hernando de Soto first explored the area in 1539, twenty years after the conquest of Mexico. For many years an annual gala was held in his honor; the Sara de Sota parade. A backwater and lawless place the city started to grow in the in the 1880s and the Florida Mortgage Investment Company hired a Scotsman J. Hamilton Gillespie to lay out the streets of a new city. Gillespie laid out streets, built hotels, houses and businesses and in 1902, Gillespie became the first Mayor of Sarasota. Being a keen golfer and seeing a market Gillespie created the first golf course in the area. In 1921, Sarasota separated from Manatee to become Sarasota County.

Sara de Sota parade, 1949 (SHTC).

As we have seen, in 1948-1949 Reverend Dorothy had asked Ethel Post Parrish for her impression of Sarasota and when the reply was at length received, Ethel expressed her opinion of the locals as 'unreceptive' – "Others have tried and failed."

Nothing daunted Russell and Dorothy, as they felt that the move was being "guided by spirit". Dorothy remembered that there had been a couple by the surname of Bacon and that they had known Ethel Post Parrish. Taking a trip to Sarasota and finding a telephone book, Dorothy found the right couple and arranged to visit them. Mr. Bacon was away on a hunting trip. Mrs. Bacon sounded rather suspicious but became convinced of Dorothy's sincerity in wanting to start a Church. Mrs. Bacon then contacted the President of the local Woman's Club and arranged to rent the Hall. That first meeting was, Dorothy tells us, on 9th November 1949. According to Dorothy's own account, there were eleven members of the Church. It was, incidentally, Ruth's birthday. "We couldn't help but feel that she, Dorothy's sister, was being honored and every time we celebrated a Church birthday we celebrated Ruth's too."

The meetings were to continue in the rented accommodation for some years, as we find in March 1953 the following advert appeared, "Shrine of the Master, Spiritualist Episcopal Church, services Friday, 7.45 pm at the Sarasota Woman's Club. Public

Invited." Dorothy and Russell are described as 'co-Pastors'. We can imagine Dr. Russell sitting on the curbside waiting for Dorothy, Eileen and Mary to return to Tampa.

A regular attendance had been created, and in March 1953, the new Church was confident enough to have Reverend Clifford Bias a "nationally known lecturer and medium from Camp Chesterfield Indiana." The meeting was to commence at 7.30 pm at the Sarasota Woman's' Club, Palm and Park Avenues. A further advert for the event describes Bias as "Appellate Clergyman and Head of the Institute." Dorothy was to become the Presiding Clergyman and quite likely as head of the Institute at the SEC Conference at Lancing in 1956. We don't know of the financial arrangements or of the remunerations paid to Bias, but Clifford Bias would have earned a fee, the Flexers had rents to pay, and there were other expenses.

Lucille Bloodsworth whose family have been members of the SOM since the 1950s.

From 1949 to 1953 the new Church started to build a congregation and establish a presence in the city. Living memories of Russell's and Dorothy's early days in Sarasota are growing fewer, but there are some who still remember. Lucille Bloodsworth, a veteran of those days and a 'kid' in the early 1950s, remembers going to psychic readings with Dorothy on Palm and Park Avenue with her mother. There were stores on the Avenue (now all gone), and the readings were held upstairs. Lucille's parents were "all into that kind of thing and had Ouija boards, long before the Church." Another veteran remembered being taken as a twelve-year-old to classes and séances of Tuttle Avenue. "There was a dirt road and a house with a chicken coop, they had a building at the rear, and it would be dark, just like it was in the Chapel." Lucille grew up in that psychic environment, and Lucille's parents and grandparents were members of the SOM.

Florence Rye had an Aunt Ellen de Mollie who knew Dorothy well. In the early 1950s the aunt and uncle owned a grocery store on Osprey Avenue and Ringling, one day the Flexers went in and they got talking. Florence's aunt and uncle lived above the store, and they arranged to hold a séance upstairs. It was successful, and they decided to keep one room free for Dorothy. One day after school, Florence entered the room to find nothing except folding chairs, a card table and Florence's grandmother who did not believe or approve! At that moment in walked Grandma's daughter, Florence's mother. In her hand, the woman held an apport from Reverend Dorothy, a red rose, which she said was from Howard and Hannibal, who were the Grandma's brothers who died within a week of each of the Spanish Flu in 1918. According to Florence, "Grandmother just shut up after that."

The de Mollies helped Russell and Dorothy to start the Church. Florence's Aunt Ellen loved Dorothy and Russell and would follow every word that was said. The night Aunt Ellen died, sometime in the 1950s, Florence and her mother were having a séance with Dorothy when Dorothy spoke of the Aunt's passing.

George and Dottie Clary added, "The message Reverend Dorothy gave to us that evening was such an accurate description of our home in Norway and of the people in it, that we were convinced that those people were right there describing it all to her." Florence Rye tells of how in the 1960s, leaving her husband Lawrence on the porch, Florence went to the Sunday service. The message service was nearly over when suddenly Reverend Dorothy asked if anyone knew of a Lawrence. Dorothy went on to explain that this Lawrence was in a wheelchair and wants to say he is sorry. Florence went home, and her husband asked, "Well did you get a message?" Florence explained and her husband "turned white as a sheet". One of his colleagues (also named Lawrence) had severe rheumatoid arthritis, it was so bad that he was confined to a wheelchair, and he shot himself.

Dorothy wrote that at the time, 1949/50, "We were glad to have any place to meet." It was mostly Dorothy who pioneered the new venture in Sarasota as Russell was in full-time work at the American Can Company and studying for his doctorate in Metaphysics. Dorothy would hold her classes, seances and sittings wherever there was a welcome and Friday evening a service would be held at the Woman's Club.

While it is true that as light has the greatest influence on the exterior of the body and the vibrations of sound penetrate the entire being, there is one far greater influence in the life of a person than either and that is the element of love.

One advantage that Dorothy and Russell had in Sarasota was a lack of competition from other Metaphysical Churches and Spiritualist groups. Sarasota was growing rapidly, as was all of Florida, and provided an open field in the Metaphysical area for pioneering new ventures. Ethel Post Parrish's comment that the locals had "not proved receptive" would have been made increasingly irrelevant as the city attracted outsiders. However, in Tampa and St Petersburg there were several such groups. Congregations were not above vacating one Church for another, especially in a field where phenomena were available and where big names in the movement were present and would prove a draw on a congregation's loyalty.

In these early days of building a membership and finding venues to hold meetings, the need to find a permanent home became urgent. In 1954, a foothold had been made on Tuttle Avenue. Reverend Dorothy remarked that "One of our members, Ethel Crawford, told us about a tract of land of twelve lots on Tuttle Avenue belonging to an acquaintance who was willing to sell." The owner allowed the Church to make a down payment and to pay the balance as and when they could afford to do so. Dorothy and Russell signed the contract, probably late in 1953.

In February 1954, the following advertisement appeared in the local press, "Spiritualist Episcopal Church-Shrine of the Master, South Tuttle Ave, the Rev. Russell Flexer and the Rev. Dorothy G. Flexer. Sunday service 10 am. Friday service at the Woman's Club Palm and Park Ave."

Ellen Foulke Damilot, in whose home Reverend Dorothy gave private sittings in the late 1940s.

An advertisement for November 1955 advises that services at South Tuttle, are at 10 am and 7.30 pm. Early meetings at the property were held in the open. Services at the Woman's Club were discontinued shortly after this advert appeared. Another feature of 1955 was the introduction, in May of that year, of morning and evening services. The morning service being dedicated to the spiritual and healing and the evening service to include personal mediumistic messages.

A building fund was started, and many of the members and friends volunteered their time and labor over the next few years to clear the land of scrub, weeds and trees and as Dorothy said, "pour the foundations." The Vestry of the Church was the first to rise, and it was this building that was used for the dinners that were as Reverend Dorothy was to say "terrific fundraisers." Easter Dawn services would be held outdoors where the Healing Garden is now situated. The sanctuary (Church) was built by contractors and was dedicated on 19th June 1955. 1960 saw the installation of air-conditioning at the then extraordinary cost of $6,000.00, (now some $48.000.00 in 2016). In 1956 a parsonage was built at 2717 Browning Street, and the Flexers along with Bertie, Dorothy's mother, moved from Tampa to live permanently in Sarasota. We will look at the financing of the parsonage later. An office building followed in 1965. At the Tampa SOM, a side room was converted to a bedroom and either Dorothy or Russell would take the Sunday service, take readings on the Monday, and lead the development class on a Monday evening.

Also, advertised under Spiritualists for the early winter of 1955, was "the School and Church of Divine Law" run by Rev. Nina Ward Hughes, Sunday at 7.45 pm at the Woman's Club. Reverend Dorothy had moved out, and Reverend Ward Hughes had moved in, as had the competition. But it was to be short-lived, and the new Church quickly disappeared from the small ads.

Florence Strauss, remembers, as a young woman, services being held in the parking lot of the new Church, as the buildings were being put up. The chairs would be put out in the open and Reverend Dorothy and Russell would wear their white robes. Florence moved away for a time, and in 1975 visiting a sister who lived on Fruitvale Avenue they passed the Church. A signboard carried the quotation "He shall give Angels charge over thee," that spoke to Florence in a way that Orthodox churches didn't.

*Florence Strauss,
a long time member of the SOM.*

The sisters stopped and went in. Dr. Russell was on the platform with Marie Rowe and they were giving the evening messages as Reverend Dorothy was at the Tampa Church. The sisters went again, the following week. Dorothy was again on the platform, and Florence got a message, "Boy, you don't know if you are coming or going" – which was correct regarding her situation at the time. The sisters attended regularly after that. At one of the regular classes Florence spoke to her father who had died in 1975. Florence said to him "… so glad you came and come again." He replied, "What for, I ain't got nothing to talk about." Florence remarked, "That was my dad!"

In 1976, Florence and her sister joined the Church, and it was the custom for several people to be admitted to membership at a Sunday morning service. The organist would play, and the choir would sing a special selection as a welcome to the new members. Florence's husband was skeptical though, and Florence said, "Before you say anything, come along and find out." One day Reverend Dorothy gave Florence an envelope. It was Florence's husband's birthday, and Florence asked her husband what was in the envelope. He took out a membership card for the SOM. Florence's husband had been attending classes in private, going along after work. Dorothy called him the "Silent Partner."

We have seen that Reverend Dorothy resigned the Presiding Clergyman board role of the Spiritualist Episcopal Church in early 1957 and the SOM withdrew from the SEC in 1958. There were distances of geography, as well as of opinions. The Flexers were inspired to create a new religion and a new denomination of Christianity; that of the Church of Metaphysical Christianity (CMC). This new approach would empower the mediums as ministers. Marie Rowe adds that Dr. Davis spoke of this project as a "being a bridge between Orthodoxy and Spiritualism."

By 1958, the Flexers were looking to take their ministry and mediumship to a new level of Spiritual attainment. Sally Hayden von Conta wrote that the CMC was a definite plan on the part of Dr. Russell. The new CMC was also a part of the spiritual growth of the co-Pastors. Those who knew the couple at the time speak of the apparent spiritual flowering of the Flexers themselves. The new religion taught that through focusing on the presence of God, absorbing in faith the teachings, and doing the practical work in your own consciousness, Metaphysical Christianity could become a living religion. Natural Law meant that good existed through God's presence in the world and in God's intention for his children. In Metaphysical Christianity, the challenge was to make this 'good' manifest in our lives through our own realization of God as an active force. In this way, the believer realized the truth of Metaphysical Christianity as experience.

Sally Hayden von Conta, early SOM member and close family friend of the Flexer family.

Further, the Flexers had a vision of the Shrine of the Master that would empower the member. Through working at a level of consciousness, the member would grow both spiritually and psychically. Though Christ, as Master, could do anything, nevertheless the work of growth had to be done by the individual. Christ came, as Robert Louis Stevenson said, as a "Lamplighter" but the individual had to admit the Master to the house. The spirit world would then be engaged in helping the individual to grow. The congregation would achieve a new degree of spiritual enrichment, psychic empowerment and be led by a new breed of Pastors.

Reverend Dorothy said, "Our religion is based on the life, teachings and demonstration of the Master Jesus. Because we believe in communication with the

Angels and ask for the guidance in daily living, we believe in communication between the spirit world and this one."

The Thursday classes at Sarasota were for mediumship development of the members, and the Wednesday classes were for communications from Master teachers. The Master could be a personal teacher that was connected to an individual, and they could be evolved beings intended for all to learn from. Angels were regarded as spiritually evolved beings and any disembodied spirit who had passed on. The spiritual and psychic truth would be collectively and individually arrived at through their ministers, as mediums and Pastors. The Church of Metaphysical Christianity would be unique in that what the Master Jesus had demonstrated and taught would cease to be ancient myth and dogma, and would become, as it was meant to be, a way of life. The spirit world would be actively engaged in the life of the individual member and as act as a guiding force to the SOM. A new age would be born, death was proven to be a lie and the member who had faith would witness through Dorothy's mediumship the 'mountains move'. For as the Apostle Matthew 17:20 wrote, "Faith can move Mountains." Russell and Dorothy's unique vision was that the age of miracles was not a thing of the past but was a demonstrable living basis for a new way of life.

Post Card of Main Street, Sarasota 1940s.

It was accepted as fact that the Master Jesus was himself a wonder-working medium. It was also obvious that if the known departed could communicate with the people of Earth, so could the Master Teachers. These advanced beings could once again find expression and influence amongst those willing to listen. The contact between the worlds, therefore, demonstrated that there was a symmetry between this world and higher dimensions.

 The Shrine of the Master, at Sarasota, was the third Church to bear that title. The new denomination of Metaphysical Christianity would dedicate itself to the teachings of the Master and to those who were in that tradition, be they Christian, Hindu, Muslim or Indians. The Master had said there were "Many Mansions" and from those heavenly halls would come voices in harmony with the Master's teachings. The harmony of the teachings would bring the member into a way of life that reflected Natural Law. That immutable and unchanging order that God created, and which if we learn to understand and live by cannot fail to bring about the happiness and spiritual elevation of the individual. The Master Jesus had taught in 'The Sermon on the Mount': "Ye are the light of the world. A city that is set upon a hill cannot be hidden. Neither do men light a candle, and put it under a bushel, but on a candlestick: and it giveth light unto all that are in the house. Let your light so shine before men that they may see your good works, and glorify your Father which is in heaven."

 The Shrine of the Master was to be a "City set upon a hill". It was to be transparent in its teachings, open to seekers without distinction and of service to all. There was to be no fear, no punishment, no 'Dread Lord' in Metaphysics. The new denomination would see the truth when it set the members' minds towards the infinite. God was a loving presence in the life of all; we have only to realize that truth. It was Dr. Davis's dearest wish that a new approach to spiritual growth, a new religion be founded. Indeed, the new religion of Metaphysical Christianity and its Churches would follow in the Master's footsteps, accepting the old teachings and taking those teachings forward in new understanding.

 "Let your light so shine before men, that they may see your good works, and glorify your Father which is in heaven. Think not that I am come to destroy the law or the prophets: I am not come to destroy, but to fulfill."

 "Let your light so shine before men," was taken to mean that we should teach by our way of living, good works and by the example we set that others could emulate. It was regarded as Natural Law that as we speak and act to towards others so will others speak and act towards us. As the metaphysical author Emmet Fox put it "Whatever sort of conduct we give out, that we are inevitably bound to get back. Anything that we do to others will sooner or later be done to us by someone, somewhere. The good that we do to others shall we receive back in like measure."

The new religion was to be free of hidden teachings intended for an elite. There was nothing exclusive that forbade access to the suitable person, openness, honesty and the integrity of the new religion, would be guided by the greater world of spirit teachings. Metaphysical Christianity was intended to be a science in that any may follow the pattern and achieve the spiritual result. Similarly, the new approach to spiritual life was a philosophical understanding and a guide to living. Further, the highest spiritual teachings were the standards that Russell and Dorothy aspired to. Above all the emphasis the couple placed on 'the Truth' underwrote everything the Flexers aimed for in their religion.

In addition to the SOM activities, as we noted in Chapter One, Russell was a Freemason, known by the description of 'F and AM'. This meant that Russell was a 'Free and Accepted Mason', in other words, "in good standing and of regular attendance". Dorothy was part of the Order of the Eastern Star. This was a women's group for Masons that supported men's Free Masonry. Officially the Eastern Star are not Masons and membership was open to daughters, wives, and female relations. It is thought that the Flexers did not attend the Masons after they left Tampa in 1956. The Masons and Eastern Star accept the Bible but not as literal truth, books of other faiths are also respected. Some of the beliefs of the Eastern Star and Masons include Universalism (that all religions have elements of truth), salvation by works, the Brotherhood of Man, living a moral life, freedom of religious worship, equality for all, and, it is said, rituals.

The Eastern Star is dedicated to charitable and community works. We have no way of knowing how influential or how involved Dorothy and Russell were but we know that Masonic beliefs and ways of seeing the world, were in agreement with Metaphysical Christianity. Mozart's *Magic Flute* uses elements of Masonic imagery that tells us something of the atmosphere and attraction that Masonry had for Russell and Dorothy:

In these Hallowed Halls.

"Within these hallowed halls
One knows not revenge.
And should a person have fallen,
Love will guide him to duty.
Then wanders he on the hand of a friend
Cheerful and happy into a better land."

In 1958, there is a sense of energy being released in the congregation and co-Pastors. There is a feeling of optimism, and of direction, found through taking a step forward to independence. The sermons have a confident expression in the vision of the new foundation and its future. The Shrine of the Master and its new parent body the Church of Metaphysical Christianity came together in 1958 in a realization of the vision shared by Dr. Davis, Dr. Russell and the Reverend Dorothy Graff Flexer. The Flexers articulated a new view of what the spiritual life could mean for the individual involved in the SOM community. That community would be created through belonging and shared devotion. Happiness and love were built through dedication, hard work and, above all, joy in the life shared with others.

Remember that the unhappy person wastes time in resentment and rancor. The happy person enriches these hours with forgiveness and faith.

Anyone who has served on boards and committees knows that discussions and decisions are really taken informally behind the scenes and that the actual meetings are usually the pro forma. However, the minutes of such meetings do offer some insight into the 'noises off' and deliberations taking place off stage.

At a Board meeting on the 15th March 1958, Reverend Dorothy pointed out "We have received little or no help from our affiliation with the SEC and that membership has brought little prestige to our Church." The minutes noted the "possibility of forming a new name eliminating the term Spiritualist," new by-laws would be needed. The name, "Metaphysical Christianity" was approved by the board to be presented to a general membership meeting on the 18th March. "Reverend Dorothy expressed the opinion that withdrawing from the SEC would free the SOM to expand on concepts of organization, literature et cetera." Frank Bloodsworth motioned to the Board that a recommendation be made to the members to secede from the Spiritualist Episcopal Church, seconded by Frances Greene and the Board passed the motion unanimously.

Dorothy opened the members' meeting on the 18th March 1958 in prayer. It was thought appropriate that Reverend Dorothy should explain the background of the proposed secession from the SEC and the reasons for joining the newly formed CMC.

Dorothy stated that "latterly there were contrary teachings in Spiritualism and that though she held no ill feeling toward the Church, Spiritualism had come to represent something we, with our teachings of the highest and the best, would not care to become associated. The Spiritualist Episcopal Church shows little interest in the concerns and activities of its member churches in any other location than its northern branches and has failed in many instances to reply to correspondences. The new affiliation would entail many changes... for example, liturgy, ritual, and publications."

David Dower moved that the Shrine of the Master secede from the SEC. Sally Mitchell seconded the motion which was carried unanimously. Dolly Hayden moved that the SOM affiliate with the newly formed CMC, David Dower seconded and the motion was passed. The motion was given, in the phrase of the minutes "a rising vote of thanks," which meant that the members stood to vote.

The new National Headquarters, for the CMC, were to be in Sarasota at Browning Street. The new organization also elected a Board to govern the CMC and to regulate the churches. A number of other churches were said to be interested in affiliation. The first President of the CMC was a Roy Kaywood of Bradenton and Vice-President was Thomas Courtney, the Secretary was Mrs. Sally Mitchell, and Dr. Russell was Treasurer. Dorothy and Myrtle B. Faithful were trustees. Affiliating churches would be individually incorporated with the CMC, conducting annual Institutes with classes for prospective clergy and lay ministers. August 1958, was to be the first such teaching institute. The CMC created a publications department under Myrtle B. Faithful.

We know that in March 1958 at the time of the affiliation to the CMC, that the membership stood at 150 and that a sanctuary (Church), parsonage and a classroom had been built. Further, residential housing was planned and eventually a Chapel was dedicated in 1972. In 1958, ground breaking was underway to build a recreational building, and a garden of healing had been established. If Dorothy and Russell reflected upon the journey that had brought them to that day in March 1958, it must have seemed a long way from 'the blue remembered hills' of Pennsylvania.

Hatred is a consuming thing that raises and destroys. On the other hand, love is a constructive force that adorns and makes life beautiful. There can be no hatred nor jealousy nor strife where love is in control. And love must be in control if one is to reach his highest spiritual attainment.

A fourth Shrine of the Master was to affiliate with the Church of Metaphysical Christianity, that of Lakeland under Pastor Raymon Noegel. This Church was situated at 401 East Park Street. On Sunday, 2nd November 1958, this SOM celebrated its first anniversary with guest speaker Rev. Dorothy Graff Flexer giving a lecture while in trance. In the early 1960s, a fifth Church the Englewood Mission held services on Fridays at the American Legion Hall in Englewood. In addition, a sixth group under Myrtle B. Faithfull's leadership started in Bradenton. This group broke away from the CMC, and it is unclear what became of this venture.

The community was fostered around shared worship, labor to create the premises and the communal activity of providing food! Feeding people brought people together, created social occasions and was fun. The congregation over the years had many core activites of which a meal, often served buffet style was a key aspect. Many extra Church activities were undertaken just because they were enjoyable, such as baseball, and, as usual, food would be served. Dorothy was to often say that meals were "terrific fundraisers" and the profits all went to the Church.

Karen Strauss remembers a venture out on roller skates that the Church members took, to be followed by a picnic. Labor Day and Memorial Sunday would be held with a special service and a picnic. Reverend Tom Newman attended a Tampa Church Halloween party and buffet in 1962 in which Reverend Dorothy dressed as a witch. But that happened only once, it

Russell relaxing on a cruise to the Bahamas,1963.

was not Dorothy's style. Outdoor socials and get-togethers were accompanied by picnics. Dorothy loved Baseball and would watch it on TV; Karen Strauss remembers Dorothy playing baseball. Pancakes or full breakfasts would be served to the choir at Easter. Donuts and coffee would be served after services.

Lucille, whose husband Clifford Bloodsworth was Vice President in the 1960s, says that Dorothy would cook Christmas dinners at the parsonage. On these occasions, no one was allowed to help, and the house would be full of people. Marie Rowe who was a Church Secretary attended as did her husband Kenneth who was a Trustee. As a fundraiser 'Pot Luck Suppers' were popular, and everyone brought a dish to share. Members would sit outside on the picnic benches and Sally Hayden and members would make coffee, and a donation would be taken.

Some events on Saturdays were held purely as socials and would involve a meal. Dinners would on average cost $1.50 and 75cents for children, which rose to $5 by the 90s. In March 1962 one event was promoted as a 'Swiss steak dinner'. You could phone ahead for a reservation and the meal was served buffet style in the Davis Hall. Jean and Tom Courtney would sometimes be taking the bookings, at other times Dolly and Jack Hayden would officiate. Another occasion in 1962 a 'covered dish' meal was served. While another event might coincide with a members meeting, and afterward a 'Turkey Dinner' would be served at 6.30pm. For an anniversary of the founding of the SOM in November 1962, a 'roast beef dinner' was served 'country style'.

These activities were part of the life of the SOM for nearly forty years, often Jean Courtney (Eileen Courtney's future mother-in-law) or Reverend Dorothy would take turns to cook the dinners. These events were held twice a month and in the early years were assisted by groups made up mainly of women known as auxiliaries; they had names such "Redwing Circle" at Tampa SOM and "Sunshine Circle" in Sarasota. These teams had monthly meetings and family members of the SOM would sign up to have a special celebration meal prepared. If this was a birthday or an anniversary, it was the custom to donate a $1 for each year as a gift to the Church. The Sunshine Circle at Sarasota raised $1,619 in 1956/57 and some $14,288 in 2016. Also, active in these catering brigades were Bertie Graff, Dorothy's mother and Mary Flexer, Russell's mother. At the end of every summer a 'bake sale' would be held, and Reverend Dorothy loved to bake. Later an 'art sale' was added in which donated items were sold. This was supplemented with unwanted goods from the homes. Reverend Dorothy is remembered for not caring for second-hand goods.

*Pictured left: Bertie Graff, Reverend Dorothy's mother,
and pictured right: Mary Flexer, Dr Russell's mother.*

Though picnics were popular, Thanksgiving Day and Memorial Day would usually be accompanied with a Roast Turkey or Roast Beef dinner served buffet style. Mother's Day and Father's Day were also occasions for a meal, and in 1967 on Father's Day, Beef Stroganoff was served. Although 'feeding the folks' was a real priority and a joy to the

Flexers there are few photographs of Reverend Dorothy with food. Eileen Courtney has donated one picture of her mother, and it shows the pies that Dorothy loved to bake. The community that was built at the SOM Sarasota devoted their lives to others and those that cooked and cleaned also served. If love is a verb, an action; the Flexers gave a life of service for which they were in turn loved.

For most belonging to the Community of the Shrine of the Master was an important aspect of their lives. For some the heart of the SOM was the communal activities. Sharing and participation in the activities could take the form of service to others, which was a key idea in the development of the spiritual life. Faith combined with the experience of extraordinary mediumship could compensate in moments of doubt regarding complex metaphysics. To some, the 'Master Teachers' spoke, as in a Johnny Mercer's song, "From their vast, mysterious sky," not all members were highbrow, many simply wanted to be part of something bigger than themselves. Members could understand at their own level, witness the mediumship, focus on the needs others and leave the metaphysics to wiser heads. If teachings were a matter of faith and belief, for many the life shared in fellowship, fun, service, and community were enough to merit belonging to the life of the Shrine. And, at the end, when death came, the member may

1984 Typical Monthly dinner - Dorothy with the pies that she loved to bake.

have shrugged and agreed with Johnny Mercer's stoical phrase "we'll find out just as sure as we live."[1]

Another annual feature was the School of Esoteric Science; this was held in Lent or spring. The School had started in 1957 and would continue until Dr. Russell's passing in 1977. A whole week was dedicated to all aspects of spirituality. With special sessions in the mornings, afternoons and evening. Certificates were presented at the end of the week to students who had completed their studies. Topics in 1972 included, "Healing Arts, various types of healing their development and application." There was a course on "Metaphysical interpretation of the Bible." "Handwriting Analysis through which the student would learn to recognize traits in one's own handwriting that will help you in your daily associations." There were courses on "Psychic Development" as well as a course on "Basic Concepts of Metaphysical Christianity." These weeks were well attended, and there was competition to obtain a place. The charges in 1972 were, $20 for five daily classes, 09.30 to 3.30pm. Single classes could be attended for $1.50. During the School of Esoteric Science week, there were also "Special Night Classes" on offer for those in attendance. Such classes included apport and materialization sessions in red light; These were not on offer during the rest of the year.

Thoughts are things. We build according to our thoughts. Nasty thoughts build contemptible things. Words are things. Corrupt thoughts as expressed in dangerous words, go out in vibrations that echo and re-echo throughout the world. Only through thoughts of love, as sent out in contrasting vibrations, can there be brought conditions of security and peace.

One of the many aspects that drew people to Russell and Dorothy was their capacity to give inspirational sermons. In Dorothy's case every two or three months, there would be a demonstration of trance. Reverend Tom Newman tells, of Reverend Dorothy standing on the platform as the organist played some soft music. There would be a sharp intake of breath from Dorothy, her left hand would come up to her chest, the right arm would bend at the elbow, and two fingers and a thumb would point upwards in a teaching position. Dr. Davis would be in control and move Reverend Dorothy's body at will. Tom says that the posture was a sign of the presence of the Great White Brotherhood. The discourse would last exactly twenty minutes. Those who remember these addresses say that these were powerful occasions to have witnessed. The voice of Dr. Davis would change, he would speak in a different voice and open with "Friends of the Earth".

---

1. A line from the Johnny Mercer Lyric *"Something's Gotta Give."*

It was the habit to announce the title of sermons in advance and often these titles appeared in the community pages of the local press. The archives of the Sarasota Center of Light (SCOL) preserves many sermons. For advertising purposes Reverend Dorothy would announce the title of a sermon but they were never written down in advance. Dr. Russell would draft his sermons before the service and a number of these are given in the appendices. Dorothy's classes would involve a trance address given by Dr. Charles Davis and many have now been transcribed, and recordings on CD are available to buy from the SCOL.

Amongst Dorothy's sermons are titles such as *A Voice in the Temple, How little it Costs,* or *The Governance of God.* This work was the weekly labor of being a minister. There were also trance discourses, two of these are reproduced in the appendices. The text of two sermons by Dr. Russell are reproduced in the appendices, and others not reproduced in this book had the themes of *Liberty and Justice for All,* based upon Leviticus 25:10 and *Work – More Than Necessity,* being based on 2 Timothy 2:15-7.

One of Dorothy's greatest joys was the journal *Metaphysical Messenger*, the cover of the Memorial Edition is reproduced here. This Journal was almost wholly written and produced by Reverend Dorothy and can be seen as a vehicle for the Spiritual concerns and counsel that Dorothy wished to convey to the congregation. The *Messenger* was 'run off' in the offices by Dorothy and was issued monthly. There were other publications, and an editorial board worked at their creation and Dorothy wrote most of the literature. Most were printed as pamphlets; titles included, *Healing, Stand up and Be Counted* and *What is Metaphysical Christianity?*

In Chapter Two we mentioned *At the Shrine of the Master* which had been written by Alda Madison Wade on his experiences at the Tampa Church. Two further books were written based on the trance teachings of Dr. Davis and others, these are *Spirit Speaks* (1988) and *Teachings of Angels* (2013). As mentioned earlier, Dr. Russell had a large personal library which he read and consulted

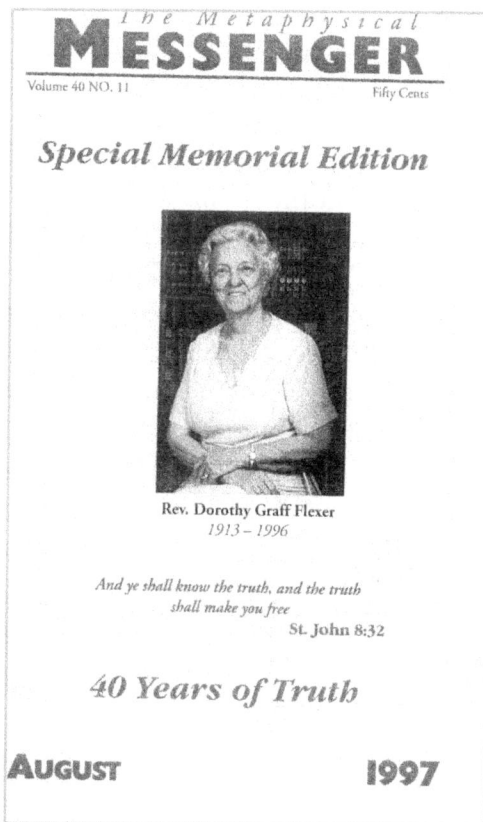

The Metaphysical **MESSENGER**

Volume 40 NO. 11   Fifty Cents

Special Memorial Edition

Rev. Dorothy Graff Flexer
1913 – 1996

And ye shall know the truth, and the truth shall make you free
St. John 8:32

40 Years of Truth

AUGUST   **1997**

Cover of the Memorial Edition of "The Metaphysical Messenger".

frequently. Whereas Dorothy was not known as a reader but gave inspired sermons and trance discourses every week. There is only one book that Dorothy is known to have consulted for sermons, which was *The Metaphysical Bible Dictionary* (1931) published by the Unity Church.

A regular feature and one that still continues was live music to accompany the Sunday service and other events at the SOM. There are records from the late 1950s of the organist Irene Spencer attending morning and evening service. At a double wedding in spring 1962, Irene Spencer played, and Reverend Dorothy sang a solo. The evening service in the 1960s was frequently held in candlelight. With Irene Spencer on the organ and either Reverend Dorothy or Dr. Russell leading the worship and giving the sermon. It was the custom for the organist to play an offertory selection while the collection was taken.

A choir is mentioned as early as 1963 and special programs of music would be arranged to suit the occasion, for example anthems (popular hymns) for Thanksgiving. On another occasion, an evening Vespers (a sung-service for the evening) was presented by candlelight, and attendance at the 7 pm Thursday rehearsal was obligatory. Christmas would see a performance of Bach's *Cantatas*, a sacred choral composition. Sally Hayden von Conta remarked that Dorothy sang beautifully and entities would sing through her. Reverend Dorothy would introduce a Sister Teresa who would then sing using Dorothy's vocal cords. Sister Teresa maybe the same spirit who would scatter rose petals around the room in the dark classes. Marie Rowe and Lucille Bloodsworth who were Church choir members recall the "Sun Rise" services at 6 am on Easter Sunday mornings. You had to dress and look the part in white gowns, and the event was followed by a complete breakfast served in the Davis Hall. Rehearsal would take place on the Thursday preceding the service, and you were expected to attend. Christmas, weddings and other special occasions would see the choir making their contribution. Veteran members all mentioned the choir with fondness, as the music contributed significantly to the spiritual atmosphere of the services.

A little-known aspect of SOM was the twice yearly practice of communion; the sharing of sacred bread. The service was held on Maundy Thursday and was not regarded as being literally the blood and body of Jesus

The Davis Hall, built in 1960.

Christ but the union of spirits through shared experience of communion. The practice was dropped when a congregational meeting in June 2006 decided that the service was no longer needed.

Christopher Moore said, "Children see magic because they look for it." The SOM would encourage the development of children through introducing them to the sacred scripture. Later, when of age and suitability the children would be invited to the evening séance classes. The magic of the world would not be lost with adulthood; the child member would grow spiritually and psychically.

The children are the future of any organization, and there was a need to provide facilities, nursery and Sunday schools that would allow for the parents to attend meetings and educate the next generation in the principles, beliefs and practices of the adults. Attendance also needed to be fun, with extra activities provided that would encourage participation of the families and promote membership. The SOM built community by catering for the family from the toddler to the elderly.

O Divine Master, grant that I may not so much seek to be consoled as to console; to be understood as to understand; to be loved as to love. For it is in giving that we receive; it is in pardoning that we are pardoned; and it is in dying that we are born to eternal life.

(Prayer of St Francis of Assisi)

Sally Hayden von Conta taught at the Sunday schools. These schools were intended for adults and children who were new to the SOM and served as induction class. The classes were held initially in the back room of the Davis Hall and later in the education center. Topics were taken mainly from the New Testament. A quotation would be chosen according to the age group, and the Metaphysical interpretation would be discussed. Sunday School was not about psychic development. Everything in the Bible would be discussed, especially, Isiah who was regarded by CMC as being a mediumistic prophet. The doctrine of 'Salvationism' being the blood sacrifice of Jesus was not taught as it was thought of as not being True. Neither was the Revelation of St John considered as relevant. In the early 1960s attendees at the Sunday School were graded and known as Cherubs, Primaries, Juniors, and Intermediates. For the very young a nursery was provided while the Sunday service took place. There were many events organized solely for the children. Halloween parties, Easter Egg hunts, special trips out to the parks and children's entertainers.

A Chapel with side entrance was built and dedicated on 2nd January 1972. The Chapel was designed by Summer Darling without windows to exclude all light from the room. Previously, the back of the Davis Hall had been used for classes, but from 5th January 1972 the Chapel was used for all of Dorothy's classes. The dedication of

the Chapel was conducted by Dr. Russell and Reverend Dorothy, with Russell singing the solo, *My Cathedral.* Dorothy opened the building in prayer and their daughter Eileen sang a solo, *Bless this House.* The Chapel was dedicated to, and still is " ... the God Spirit, and the Angels."

The classes have been closely looked at in Chapter Two but there are many personal accounts of classes held in Sarasota that are of interest. An activity for children that was by invitation only was that of attendance at the classes. These classes cost $1 to attend and were, as noted previously the séance events of the Shrine of the Master. Reverend Tom Newman and his mother first attended the Tampa Church in 1962. Tom's mother was invited to attend the class in 1963 and Tom who was eleven at the time was fascinated especially when his mother spoke of having spoken to her 'spirit doctor', Dr. Thornbird. Reverend Tom remarked that he and his sister were the youngest children ever to attend the darkened

With Summer Darling, designer of the new chapel, after the dedication, 1972.

classes. Redwing would come to call Reverend Tom in time "Uncle Tom", and on his first visit Redwing asked him if he had "ever spoken to a spirit person?" Before Tom could reply Redwing replied, "Well you have now."

Classes at Tampa were on Monday evenings. These were mediumship development classes, and the sitter would have a chance to speak to their spirit doctor. Reverend Tom Newman reports that sitters would speak to their spirit doctor every week and that you were always standing when working mediumistically.

Fern Bradburn was to recall taking her granddaughter to circle. Dorothy liked to allow in suitable children who would not be frightened by the dark so that they could get used to the conditions and the events that took place. Fern was to say also that because you attended frequently you became more trusting of the spirits and life became more fulfilled.

Marie Rowe who was a member of the Tampa Church and later of the Sarasota SOM became aware of the classes and wanted to join. Dorothy hesitated for a few moments and then gave permission. Marie came to realize that Reverend Dorothy customarily would mentally ask her guides for their opinion. Marie and her husband Kenneth, who was a board member, joined the classes on Mondays and got to know their spirit doctors. Marie added that sitters at these classes would watch the trumpets fly about the room on ectoplasmic rods and the voices were witnessed to move around the room.

Reverend Marie Rowe, long term member of the SOM and SCOL.

Virginia Bergeson writing in 1997 said, "Through her (sic) ability as a trumpet medium, we were fortunate enough to share in the wisdom of the Master Teachers and through Dr. Davis and Redwing we were able to meet our own loving Angel guides."

Sally Hayden, spoke of how natural the séance events were and how it was taken for granted and only later realized how rare the phenomena were that the sitters had experienced. Competition was keen to be included. Fern Bradburn reported that sitters would take in flowers and these would be scattered around the room by the spirit visitors. On those occasions when known loved ones spoke, their voices would be weaker and they didn't necessarily sound as they used to. Fern tells of how one lady replied to her departed husband "I don't want to speak to you, you didn't finish laying the floor."

Darryl Ritchie who attended classes in the 1960s said that the trumpet was levitated in the air in the darkened room and would stop in front of someone and would move to either side of the person's head. In other words, the trumpet was under intelligent guidance.

Darryl Ritchie, SOM member during the 1960s.

Karen Strauss who grew up in the SOM, in an interview in July 2015, recalled that Dorothy's mediumship was affected by bad weather. Classes would be canceled if electrical storms were predicted. Perfume was not to be worn and smoking before classes was frowned upon. Though we saw in Chapter

Two that Dr. Davis did not want Dorothy to be thought of as an apport medium, nevertheless apports did occur at specific classes for that phenomenon. Sally Hayden von Conta received a perfect round "sweet stone". Sally added that a rubber band was placed across the end of the trumpet to catch the items as the came down the tunnel from another world. One apport that Sally received was as long as the trumpet. Marie Rowe received a poignant apport. Marie's brother was killed in Vietnam in 1968. The young man had promised to bring a piece of Jade back from his tour of duty, but he was killed, and later Marie received a piece of Jade as an apport from him.

The usual routines were varied for special occasions such as Christmas and New Year. Florence and Karen Strauss recalled that the sitters would bring a little present for the spirit children. Tom Newman added that no battery toys were allowed because of the light that such toys would make. Dorothy would sit at the head of a table for the classes with the room in

Karin Strauss, virtually raised in the SOM and whose Mother is Florence.

darkness the spirit children would open the wrappings and play with the toys. When the lights went on the wrappings would be found in all parts of the room. Reverend Tom Newman remembers that sometimes the presents were not wrapped and were placed in the center of the table and, when the lights went up, they would be found all over the Chapel. The spirit children enjoyed playing with the toys which were chosen for the noise they would make when played. Drums would be banged, toy pianos played, bulbs were taken off the Christmas tree, and toy horns would be blown.

Several members remembered the Master of Bells at Christmas would give a talk and play the hand-held bells that were on a table in the corner of the room or Chapel. Doorkeepers of the sitters would materialize and play the musical instruments and the bells made a "terrific din". Reverend Tom Newman who sat with Dorothy in classes for nearly thirty-three years tells of how at New Year the Master of Light would come through and give personal messages as well as predictions for the future. These messages were about personal growth, and it was also an opportunity to ask questions about the state of the world.

In addition to other services, Dorothy (but it is thought not Russell) would offer private 'Spiritual Counseling' sessions. The charge for these sessions varied over the years, but on average would cost $5.00. Dorothy did sit for private trumpet and trance sittings but only to known people who had sat in the classes. This was an opportunity to speak directly to one's guides. Reverend Dorothy would occasionally give a sitting to non-Church people if she was asked to do so, though these sittings did not involve trance or trumpet mediumship.

Reverend Tom Newman referred to Dorothy as "the truth teller" meaning that Dorothy would "set you straight" and privately advise what would be best for your improvement. Such confidences would not be shared with others. No special day was set aside for such sessions but given as and when it was convenient. Karen Strauss said the same of Dr. Russell, and that he would draw you aside to talk privately regarding personal matters.

In 1977, Sally Newton wrote, "Reverend Dorothy once gave me the best private sitting I ever had; for it was, word for word, about my life." Another story also from 1997, this time from Livia Raynes who was facing terminal cancer and was very afraid of the ordeal said, "Upon entering the room I sat and faced Reverend Dorothy and all was calm. During the reading, she looked at me and said, 'there is a strong message that I am supposed to give you and it is this. You are going to live a long life.'" Livia added, "It was as if a dam had burst inside me and with those eight simple words my whole life had changed to one of hope."

Florence Strauss and family moved out into the countryside and tells the story that when family dogs went missing for five days, Florence telephoned Dorothy who called the name of the dog out loud, and the dog returned within two hours. Florence added, "Reverend Dorothy got the Angels after my dogs. That happened twice, I'll be darned."

Bells that were rung in Dorothy's classes, and are still in the chapel.

Florence's daughter Karen Strauss had a sitting at which Karen was put off marrying. Karen reported that "the hand went on the hip and Dorothy said, 'You are not marrying that man,' and that happened twice." Karen's friends were surprised by that and not a little put-out and thought Karen must be mad to be deterred by her Minister. But as Karen added, "They did not understand, she knew what she talking about. Reverend Dorothy had a short circuit to the other world."

It was possible to talk to your doorkeepers at the classes and maybe in the private consultations. Karen and others would ask, and Redwing would say, "Well, do you think that you deserve it? Let's see if there is time and it might be this week or the week after." This access to transcendental personal advice was a unique feature of Pastoral life at the SOM. Private spiritual counseling was a key aspect of the ministership and life of Reverend Dorothy.

10th Anniversary of the Sarasota Shrine of the Master, 1959.

Attendance at the SOM was keen, and membership noted as 150 in the 1960s rose to 200 in the 1980s. Seats at the weekly classes were also much sought after, and word of the phenomena that was occurring on a regular basis helped to fuel the interest in attendance at the services held at the SOM. There are many who remember the Flexers with affection, and many have joined since they passed away. Their legacy endures and still inspires those who have come later to reach for the spiritual highest and brightest. Florence Strauss, now in her mid-80s and a member since the earliest days, remarked with admiration and her usual directness, "Reverend Dorothy was nice, she was something else."

Chapter Five

"And He walks with me, and He talks with me,
And He tells me I am His own;
And the joy we share as we tarry there,
None other has ever known."

One day a journalist said to Mother Teresa of Calcutta, "I wouldn't do your job for a million dollars," and the Mother replied, "No, neither would I." For Dorothy and Russell, it was never about the money. We all want to be happy and the Flexers found their direction early in life through discovering 'the Truth', (see Chapter One). They fell in love, shared a sense of vocation to lead a spiritual life and above all, discovered Reverend Dorothy's extraordinary gifts of mediumship. Money was a tool of service; necessary in its place, but never an end in itself.

In the previous chapter, we saw that the Parsonage at Sarasota was built and occupied in 1956. Prior to that, Dorothy and Russell took turns to commute between their home at Tampa and the SOM in Sarasota. The creation of this home and its usage illustrates the above point that to Dorothy and Russell, money was of secondary importance. At a Board meeting in May 1956, member Virginia Dower motioned that "an efficiency apartment be built, complete with bathroom, and kitchen facilities." The design must have been basic as the minutes noted that "…an addition could later be built to the finished structure." Irby Stafford seconded the motion.

At a SOM Board meeting in May 1956, Reverend Dorothy discussed the usage of the Parsonage, Dorothy who became Presiding Clergyman in 1956, and the SOM, which was a member of the SEC, would need accommodation at the Parsonage for "visiting officials, their entertainment and room for guest workers." Dr. Russell commented, "If sufficient funds are not available, such extras as carpets and a porch could be added later." At the same meeting, Thomas Courtney motioned that "the Board be given the authority to build a Parsonage, with two bedrooms, a living room, bathroom, breezeway (a roofed passageway) and a kitchen with all conveniences."

However, there was not enough to pay for the new building and fundraising as well as mortgages were required. With the average cost of a house in 1955 being $22,000 ($194,889 in 2016) the mortgages, $325 each ($2,868) were sold as pledges to the members who would pay a regular amount to the bank to pay for the Parsonage. The building though remained the property of the church, in return the member received 3% interest, plus the capital was repaid at the end of the loan. In this manner, most, if not all of the buildings of the SOM were built. Nor was the Parsonage ever part of the estate of the Flexer family.

Note that Dr. Russell and Dorothy were making no demands and the Board were more than happy to help the pastors whom they respected. Significantly, in September 1956 with the roof nearing completion and the paint being bought, Dollie Hayden motioned that "the church be responsible for the furnishing of the Parsonage." The motion was passed unanimously. However, Dorothy and Russell would accept no blank check to spend what they wished and declined the offer with thanks, and suggested instead that a committee member accompany them to approve the purchases on behalf of the Board. A domestic consideration came to the fore later that year; a fence was needed for the new Parsonage to keep the dogs in the garden, the motion was granted by the Board.

"Let your light so shine before men, that they may see your good deeds and glorify your Father in heaven."(Matthew 5:16.) The Board and members of the SOM must have found in their pastors a lead they could follow, teachings they respected, and mediumship that inspired and awed them. Moreover, as noted in the introduction, why Dorothy and Russell were loved is a theme of this book and they were in part, loved and respected because they lived the values that they preached. The 'light' that was lit at the SOM, Browning Street, was not hidden. On the contrary it was reflected in the lives lived by Reverend Dorothy and Dr. Russell. As Lincoln observed, "you cannot fool all the people all the time." The motives of individuals become apparent, voluntary community cannot be built, nor last, on foundations of duplicity and greed. Conversely, respect and love are generated because the values of honesty, righteousness and morality are shared and recognized in others.

When permission was given by the Sarasota Zoning (building) committee for the construction of the Davis Recreational Hall, mortgages were issued and a collection of $1,105 ($9,043 in today's equivalent) had been taken with Dorothy and Russell contributing. The

TAMPA

SHRINE OF THE MASTER, Metaphysical Christianity, 3416 Grand Central Ave. Service Sun. 7:30 p.m. Rev. Dorothy Graff Flexer and Rev. Russell Flexer, Ministers.

FIRST SPIRITUALIST CHURCH of Tampa, U.C.M., 512 East Paris Street. Services Sun. 7:45 p.m. Class Mon. 7:30 p.m. Circles Thur. 1-4 p.m. at 9301 12th St. Rev. Hazel Fleckner, Pastor. Phone WE 5-6087, Rev. Dorothy Bragg, 1st Ass't Pastor.

FIRST CHURCH OF TRUTH, S.S. No. 220, 2010 Morrison, Cor. Albany. Unfoldment class Tue. 5:30 p.m. Church services Tue. 7:30 p.m. Rev. Arthur H. Laruelle, Pastor. Doris Hensel and Joseph Chaput, Assistants. Hazel Mao, organist and medium.

THE CHRIST SPIRITUALIST CHURCH OF TAMPA, 303 S. Brevard. Services Sun. 7:30 p.m. Wednesday 7:30. Healing period, half hour before above services. Rev. Dr. Lillian Frey, Pastor., Rev. Mary R. Dowling, Co-Pastor. Phone TAmpa 8-3505.

GOOD SHEPHERD, UNIVERSAL SPIRITUALIST CHURCH, 3505 Central Ave. Services: Rev. 7:30 p.m. Wed. 7:00 p.m. Ministers: Rev. Raymon Noegel and Rev. Lamar M. Keene.

CHURCH OF ETERNAL LIGHT, N.S.A.C. 1505 East Osborne Street. Services: Sun. 7:00 p.m. Healing; 7:30 Lecture and messages; Thurs. 8:00 p.m. Circle. Pastor: Mary P. Stephens. Phone WE 8-1544.

In 1961 Tampa listed 6 Spiritualist churches, with 27 in Florida State.

Davis Hall was completed in 1960. At a meeting of the members, Reverend Dorothy reported that previous loans had been met leaving only a debt of $11,675 ($95,550). The $11,000 was split between two mortgage issues. There is then a sense of confidence and trust in the future that SOM would grow and pay off these balances.

In Board meetings of 1960 and 1961 the committee approved, as various lots adjacent to the SOM property had become available, that they were bought up at an average of $3,000 each. The largest of the lots was 94 feet x 147 feet and was known as the Alhambra Court. The Board voted to buy the lots in November 1960. A picnic area adjacent to the Parsonage eventually, in 1972, became the chapel. Other lots formed the basis of the Featherstone Housing project, but more of this later. One idea that did not happen was the use of the new lots to form a small hospital for members.

Another source of income, though rare, was the leaving of bequests. One of the largest was that from Miss Ella Emmerson's estate. Reverend Dorothy gave the figure as $17,00, plus $3,000 in bonds, and there was a further $1,000 from the estate of Arthur Janusch; a total of $169,000 in 2016 values. Miss Emmerson had been active in the church in the early 1950s. To help with the building of the

Dr Davis speaking on when is it right to give:

"If it is offered at the right time it will be accepted. It is the way of giving of yourself and it is the opening to giving to others. It is wrong to not offer or think that others are not open to receiving. The spiritual law takes care of these things, why don't you try it? Everyone is able to financially to give, because that is the divine law. You can give graciously and accept graciously without feelings of obligation. Those that give happily and easily are not the losers."

Davis Hall $6,000 ($48,780) was drawn against the estate. Reverend Dorothy spoke of the new vestibule that was being built onto the Sanctuary, in which the library would be located. Dorothy also spoke of Dr. Davis and others from spirit having expressed the hope that a rest home, owned and operated by Metaphysicians may be located on the lot to the west of the present church property, which was in the process of being purchased. Reverend Dorothy added that "such a home would be the first of its kind and would help people mentally and spiritually as well as physically." For no known reason, nothing came of this project. And the areas spoken of were used for the creation of the Featherstone Housing complex that still exists.

The support and trust that the founding couple created in the members speak volumes in the figures that follow. A balance sheet for the Sarasota SOM, in November 1959, reveals just what had been achieved in the ten years since its foundation. The Church was valued at $19,308 ($158,997), the Parsonage $10, 016.79 ($81,991) whereas the Davis Hall, which was incomplete was valued at only $7,619 ($62,355). In total, the

Shrine of the Master in late 1959 was valued at $54, 488 ($445,946). In ten years Dr. Russell and Dorothy with the loyal support of the members and Board had created an estate worth, in today's prices, of nearly half a million dollars.

Dollie Hayden proposed in May 1955, that "a weekly salary be paid the pastors." The secretary explained that the Board of Directors had agreed a temporary salary of $25 per Sunday ($221.) We can assume that Russell and Dorothy received payment for the other services that they provided. The annual church returns for November 1959 gives the salary of the pastors as $2,565 ($20,998.). There may well have been additional payments for services ad hoc such as funerals, christenings, and private spiritual counselling. The salaries would grow over the years, and Dorothy and Russell enjoyed the fruits of their hard work. There were family holidays, and a cottage was bought in the Cashiers Mountains, N. Carolina as a retreat and holiday home. This was sold by the family after Reverend Dorothy's death in 1996.

Dorothy and Russell, July 1963.

Dorothy kept what was known as an "Emergency Assistance Fund". This was used in particular to help aging or senior members who were in need. Lorraine Krypel related a story of the use of this emergency fund. Lorraine had been called away from Florida to take care of her mother in New Jersey and subsequently to attend to the estate. "Reverend Dorothy reassured me that I was not alone." Lorraine became short of means and had to take a job. "Reverend Dorothy would call me to give me encouragement and upliftment. She would call me even during her vacation at her cottage in North Carolina. Dorothy always assured me that I could ring anytime. Later, during a conversation, Reverend Dorothy told me that the angels wanted me to stop working and take care of legal matters. It was a test of faith and scary to give up the income. Dorothy did not leave me in distress and sent me money. Later she called to say, 'Don't worry you can pay me back when you return to Florida.'" Lorraine added, "Reverend Dorothy eased me through the worst of this time, and I made it back to Florida. It was easy to pay back financial help, but I don't think I can ever repay the emotional help."

It is known that Dorothy kept every cent from the weekly classes and that the money was used to set up a benefit fund for Church members. Classes initially in the 1950s/60s cost a dollar to attend, by the time Karen Strauss was old enough to attend, perhaps in the 1980s, the cost had risen to $3. Likewise, $3 was the fee for private spiritual counseling. Private readings were a daily occurrence, and the demand was constant. However, charges varied over the years for classes and sittings.

Nor was this just a day job. The dedication to hard work needed an extraordinary vocation to sustain over fifty years the Pastoral life of Dorothy and Russell. You will recall that in Chapter One Dorothy herself said that there had been two things that interested her in life, one was religion and the other was music. In the growth of the Sarasota SOM, and from 1958 onwards, in the realization of a dream, a renewed sense of a calling is apparent in the building work and accounts. Sources closest to the couple and friends and family all say that, "they were on call all the time and there were no office hours." You will recall that Florence Strauss rang regarding her stray dogs. Dorothy was an 'agony aunt' at the end of the telephone for those in need of advice, though the counsel needed to be heeded, or there would be a rebuke! Florence Strauss recalled Reverend Dorothy saying from the platform, "I want you people to know that if you don't have money, you can come along to my church." Florence's husband said, "Well, I like her." Others recall that Dorothy once said from the platform, "The Church is here to help people, not to get rich."

Those who remember Russell and Dorothy, speak of their compassion for others. Money was forthcoming to those in genuine need. The loan had to be paid back, but not every cent was returned, and a few remember the shrug of the shoulders if a passing favor was needed. There was the confidence in the pastors that Dorothy and Russell could be discrete on delicate matters.

The pastoral role involved hospital visits for both members and non-members who were ill. Nancy Skalestski's son was in hospital, awaiting an eye operation which the surgeons and Reverend Dorothy had said was necessary. The doctors informed the boy Steve that he would still have to wear glasses. "No way," was his response, "Reverend Dorothy told me that I could get rid of these glasses." The eye surgeon advised Nancy and her husband to be realistic and to take responsibility for the situation and to talk to the boy, though Nancy believed Reverend Dorothy too. She said that after the surgery when Steve was resting, "Reverend Dorothy and Russell tiptoed into his room and started to give him healing. All of a sudden, Steve awoke and said, 'Mom, I know that Reverend Dorothy and Russell are here, I knew that they would be in the room.'" Six weeks later to the doctor's surprise, Steve could see better and never needed glasses again.

Dorothy could also be a quite private person, and one person who did get to know the Flexer family well is Sally Haydon von Conta. Sally and the Flexers' daughter,

Eileen, became friends and shared an apartment in New York. Dr. Davis advised Sally in a private sitting to go to NY and Sally left home, aged 20 with $50 in her pocket. Sally had a few sittings with local mediums but said, "Reverend Dorothy's standards were tremendously high and sitting with other mediums were not of the same caliber." One year in the 1960s Eileen, Sally, Dorothy and Russell all took a holiday at Cape Cod. Russell and Dorothy drove up from Florida. Sally remarked that Dorothy and Russell were a close couple and well balanced in temperament. Sally recalled how wonderful it had been to be with the Flexer family on holiday. "…we were just guys hanging out, no robes, no classes. Reverend Dorothy was totally approachable, and I was in awe of Dr. Russell, he could make Dorothy just melt."

Eileen Courtney, Russell and Dorothy's daughter.

Dr. Russell had a great sense of humor and was good tempered with everyone, and he took his time to get to know you. Whereas, Reverend Dorothy was, intelligent and in charge with a keen intuition about people. Dr. Russell is spoken of as having, as Sally Haydon von Conta said, "a sweetness and humanness about him." Russell's charm had its effect on Dorothy too, and Russell "could disarm Dorothy in a heartbeat, right there in front of everyone, and it would be hysterical and wonderful to watch." Jaya Coulson added, "Dr. Russell's influence was always a most positive one." Other sources report that Dr. Russell was attentive in the small considerations of married life, and if love is something you do, something you give, the dedication and vocation given to the work by Dorothy and Russell, is one reason why the pastors of the Shrine of the Master were loved.

Reverend Tom R. Courtney, Eileen Flexer's husband, son-in-law to Dorothy and Russell.

There were a number of close friends and families; perhaps the closest were, Jean and Tom Courtney (joined around 1950) whose son Tom (shown here) married Eileen Flexer. In the appendices, I consider the role of individuals, couples and families who were active on the Boards of the SOM and CMC. I include in the appendices a piece written by Reverend Jean and Reverend Tom Courtney. There were many people who gave their time and dedication to Reverend Dorothy and Russell's vision. Those supporters also gave a great deal of financial support to the young organisation. Sally Hayden's parents Dolly and Jack Hayden were close to Russell and Dorothy. In the early days, you could ring Dolly or Jack and book a place at one of the numerous dinners that were served at the SOM. Dolly smoked and Dorothy whose chest was not strong could not stand cigarette smoke or perfume, and Sally said, "Dorothy gave Dolly a tough time." The Haydens joined the Sarasota SOM in 1953. Dolly became a good medium and was respected by Dorothy and Russell. In 1967, Sally donated a large canvas painting of *Jesus, the Christ* and it hung in the Shrine till 2013. Sally also painted Dr. Russell's guide Snowdrop, which has been included in Chapter Two.

"Dr Davis, can you talk about giving too much?"
"Each individual needs to interpret the situation for themselves. There are some individuals who do want to be parasites and have feelings of dependency. They cripple themselves. The person that is doing the giving needs to help them to give them this extra boost sort this out and so that they can feel positive and stand alone. The giver can give too much in a short period of time, and some people enjoy being a crutch for other people. So don't ever become that crutch for others. And at the same time everyone needs to be given a helping hand at some time. Even though you may feel unappreciated."

Many remember that Dorothy could have an incisive manner. Marie Rowe recalled that one day when cutting roses for a dinner, Dorothy said, "You don't know how to cut 'em right." On another occasion potatoes were being peeled for a meal and too much skin was being removed, the peeler was rebuked with "… there's only one way to peel potatoes." Dorothy could be brusque; when some aspiring executives were getting above themselves, they were told to "go start your own group." Darryl Ritchie said, in an interview in 2015, that Dorothy was always very punctual, and very articulate when giving sermons. Reverend Dorothy would take off her glasses and would hold your attention, "You couldn't take your eyes off her."

Susan Carter Courtney writing in 1997 said, "Reverend Dorothy's life was a shining example of what a strong, intelligent, professional and hard working woman can accomplish…here was a professional woman up in front of our congregation each Sunday." There clearly was something indefinable that Dorothy projected. Sally Newton wrote, "I could plainly see the love, peace, and harmony that seemed to radiate within her. Though the sermons were addressed to the whole congregation, it seemed like that she was talking to me."

Karen Turner in July 2015 reported that Dorothy had said Karen was ready to give messages but that she had not felt confident in doing so. Reverend Dorothy was disappointed as Dorothy was always right. Karen added, "Dorothy could be quite bossy, and strong, but in a good way." Florence Strauss said "She loved the men. Dorothy was maybe five three or five four and always wore heels, I never saw her dressed down, always a dress on, smart. And if you were ill, Reverend Dorothy was at the hospital." Florence added. "Once I had a situation where I had to call her late at night and she replied, 'Don't worry about the time, I was up watching the end of the World Series.' She was always there for me and my family."

That inner radiance that so many report was expressed by Susanne Upfield "She gave us strength and hope for tomorrow; she gave help, kindness, and love. She taught that we could achieve anything with the angels at our side. Blessings will surely follow us and all those we come in contact with."

Helen Blakeslee added, "I always remember the cheery good morning expression that she had whenever I called upon her. She always had a special smile for me that uplifted my day."

As we saw in the previous chapter, the Reverend Tom Newman, who became one of Dorothy's closest friends, spoke of Reverend Dorothy as "a truth teller", and advice was given for your improvement. Tom remembers that Dorothy was compassionate but put up with no nonsense. You were encouraged to take responsibility for your own life, to work hard on areas that needed improvement. The attendance at the classes brought individuals into contact with teachers and guides from the other side of the veil. Such communication enriched the spiritual life and raised many people closer to the greater world of spirit that surrounds and uplifts them. Reverend Dorothy herself wrote, "I dedicate my life to doing worthwhile things, saying uplifting and comforting words and most of all, to being an example of true discipleship."

I hold that the Master Jesus was a savior because He provided a new leadership; a leadership away from the old ruts which had been started by Moses and cut deep in the years since his time. It was a leadership into a new method of thinking, harmonious to the world of change into which the people of the time were gradually advancing. Instead of the doctrine of an eye for an eye and a tooth for a tooth His doctrine was of love.

Other close friends were Adah and Wallace (Wally) Heth. The couple were childless and had made their career running the Green Gardens horticultural nursery. They built their own Featherstone house on Browning Street so as to be close to the church. Adah died first, and Wally developed cancer. Dorothy was widowed as was Wally and he asked Dorothy to marry him and Dorothy was then known as Flexer-Heth. The motive was that he could pass on his estate without taxes. There was no question that they would live together without being married. Wallace needed caring for, and Reverend Dorothy fulfilled that role. Wally died and after Reverend Dorothy's passing it was revealed that all the Heth estate money had been placed in the Flexer-Heth trust funds, with two beneficiaries the CMC and the SOM with strict instructions as to how the funds were to be used for charitable usages.

Money was a tool of service, important in its place and to be respected, but for Dorothy and Russell Flexer it was a tool of service. We have noted that the SOM bought a number of plots in Browning Street and later in adjacent Bay Street. Initial hopes of founding a healing and rest home for elderly members had not come to fruition. The decision was taken to allow members over fifty-five to build a house on SOM land and live in the house until their deaths, at which time the property would revert to the church who would sell it to another older member. The housing was known as the "Featherstone Housing" (after the building method of the same name) and the legal arrangement was called a "Life Estate". There were originally nine homes built between 1970/79. SCOL still owns six of them and, in addition, other non-Featherstone homes were acquired and let out for rental. Marie Rowe believed that there may have been up to seventeen homes in the scheme. Occasionally, after owners died, there was no interest in buying the houses, and they were rented out. A number were sold off in the early 21st century.

Fern Bradburn, who was a Board Member and Trustee, stated in 2013 that the properties provided a good income for the church. Housing was an important aspect of the SOM community. SOM Secretary Ida Daisley and Marie Hurley both had houses and worked in a voluntary capacity in the SOM offices. Fern also recalled that Adah and Wally Heth had a house built on Browning Street which they occupied until Adah died of cancer and Wally married Dorothy.

The first lots were bought in 1961, and the first house was built to the west of what is now the Chapel parking lot. The houses spread along the length of Browning Street on both sides, and further houses were built to the north in Bay Street. Marie Rowe's mother had a house built at 2673 Browning Street which was occupied in 1971, and Marie's mother is thought to have been the first member to pass away in 1978 and have the property revert to church ownership. After, Reverend Dorothy's passing in 1996, the Parsonage did not survive as uncaring tenants did not look after the property, black fungus developed and became so bad that it caused the house to be demolished.

The Graff and Flexer families were close-knit and supportive. The reader will recall Dorothy's mother, Bertie traveling with the daughter Eileen to Sarasota on a Friday to help to establish the SOM. As the Featherstone housing complex developed a house was built for Bertie Graff. Bertie shared the house with Russell's mother Mary, until Bertie passed away in April 1972. Dorothy and Bertie were very close and Bertie had moved

Helen Divine, Dorothy's sister, an active member of the SOM, 1983.

to Tampa to be with her family, and followed them when they moved to Sarasota. Mary Flexer and Bertie Graff were both active in church life and were part of the 'auxiliaries' that helped with fundraising, catering and committee activities. Mary Flexer passed away in April 1977, the same year as Russell, and had by then moved back to Pennsylvania to live with her daughter, Virginia. Dorothy also had an older sister Helen, who moved to Sarasota with her husband, Charlie. Helen, who passed away in the mid-1980s was active in the church and taught Sunday School.

As noted, Dorothy had three brothers none of whom were Spiritualists. Dorothy remained in touch with her brothers and visited them. Paul Graff was the eldest born in 1910. He lived all his life in Reading PA., and worked as a bookkeeper. It is thought that Dorothy was closer to her younger brothers as they lived at home with Dorothy and Bertie after Dorothy's father died. The second eldest, James, was born in 1917. He lived most of his life in South Carolina, working in news/magazines becoming vice-president of the company. He died in 1968; he and his wife had no children. James Graff and his wife would visit Florida and the family there, and the Flexers visited with him often on the way to North Carolina and Pennsylvania. Eileen and Tom R. were close to Dorothy's youngest brother Richard Graff. Richard was born in 1922, married with two children he lived all his life in Lancaster PA where he was vice-president of a flooring company. The families visited each other often, and Richard Graff and his family took vacations in Florida and would visit his relations in Sarasota. Richard is well remembered for his sense of humor and Eileen remained close to her uncle until his death in 2007.

Our reward will always be in exact proportion to our service. Each of us is given the same land to plant; as we sow, so shall we reap.

Russell's illness in the mid-1970s meant that other members of the SOM took on some of the Pastoral roles at the Tampa SOM. From 1972, with occasional visits by Reverend Dorothy, Marie Rowe took this on with up to five others also helping out. There would be times when it was difficult to fill the pastoral role as members died and the congregation began to dwindle. The Board tried to fill the pastoral vacancy by creating new ministers. On one occasion Marie drove Dr. Russell to Tampa to take the service. The passing of Russell also brought about the introduction of trainee ministers at Sarasota. This change would lead to the training of future pastors and re-create a seminary role at the SOM which had fallen into disuse.

We will look at the ordination process in the next chapter.

In a Board meeting of January 1978, Reverend Dorothy said, "The Tampa Church has voted to sell their church and property and are planning to relocate in the north-east part of Tampa." If they needed to borrow money, all agreed that it would be "a good thing to lend them an amount to tide them over, after all, it is our sister church." Reverend Tom

Shrine of the Master, Tampa 1981.

Newman, who was President of the Board at Tampa in the early 1970s said that the church was always smaller than the Sarasota SOM. It is believed that the initial location of the Tampa Church had become untenable after the area had seen an increase in office buildings and shopping malls. This had also increased traffic and made the area less residential in feeling. The original church building which was, as you will recall a reused air force hut had been replaced with a modern building of the same design as the church at Sarasota. Both the land and the church at Kennedy Avenue were sold. The original church building was re-erected on Himes Avenue and stood until the Board of the church decided to close it in the early 1990s.

One of the joys of Pastoral work was the conducting of weddings. Personal counseling and consultation were a fundamental part of the marriage process and the Flexers both conducted marriages. One of the most joyous occasions was Reverend Dorothy officiating at her daughter's wedding on Saturday 15th of June 1968. In 1962, Eileen Louise Flexer graduated from the local High School, and then majored in 'Voice' at Memphis State University and was a member of the University Chorale. In December 1967, Eileen gave a recital at the SOM and the evening was presented by Eileen's voice coach Miss Minaperie Taylor and Mrs. Jo Ann Franz played the accompaniment.

For the occasion of Eileen's wedding, the members of the church SOM were invited to attend the service. Tom R., the son of Jean and Tom Courtney married Eileen at 3 pm that Saturday in 1968. Sally Hayden and Jill Van Scykle were bridesmaids and Eileen's cousin Carol Divine was maid of honor. A reception was held at the Davis hall afterward and the newly married Courtneys took a honeymoon in the North Carolina Highlands.

Another notable wedding occasion occurred when Russell acted as best man and Dorothy performed the marriage service for the Reverend Lillian Dee to Colonel John Johnson (retired) at the Tampa Church. There is a photograph in Chapter Two, from 1946, showing the ordination of Lillian Dee Johnson which John Bunker took as Presiding Clergyman.

The wedding was conducted according to the rites of the SEC. The church being decorated with gladioli, chrysanthemums and asters. The grainy newspaper picture (not shown here) shows a couple well into later life.

Reverend Tom Newman's wedding to Nancy in 1978 is shown here, as is the christening of their daughter, Anne Marie in 1981. There were many christening services, amongst them is the Rowe family christening of 21st November 1993. The photographs are reproduced with the family's kind permission and speak for themselves. They show these happy events as a key part of the personal and public life of the SOM.

Above: The Marriage of Tom and Nancy Newman,1978.

Right: Christening of Tom and Nancy Newman's daughter, Anne Marie, 1981.

Left: Dorothy with Tom and Karen Turner at their wedding, September 1988.

Below: Harvest Home and the Turner family Christening 1993.

HARVEST HOME * THANKSGIVING SUNDAY
November 21, 1993

Our love and blessings to Kenneth "Kenny"
George Turner as he is christened this morning
Proud parents, Karen and Tom and sisters Lisa
and Nicole are congratulated, as are godparents
Angie and Michael Holland and Mack Clary

Another frequent and largely unrecorded service was that of funerals. The first recorded funeral at the SOM Sarasota was in January 1954 for Homer Simpkins, referred to in the notes as 'one of the newer members'. The service which was noted as being the first of its kind was led by Reverend Dorothy. "A beautiful message of love and inspiration was given to all the friends who assembled to pay their respects and give power to the progress of our member as he entered the heavenly Kingdom of Spirit." Reverend Dorothy and Dr. Russell sang Homer's favorite hymn *In the Garden*, accompanied by organist Irene Sowter.

However, these pastoral roles, leave little in the way of written records. There are no photographs of funeral services but the Flexers led the ceremonies for many people at the SOM church. These key rites of passage are memorable to the participants, and Dorothy and Russell presided at them. It was these rites of passage that form part of the pastoral function. Much of the role went unrecorded and often was confidential.

The fact that Dorothy and Russell are well remembered is because they were not controlled by money and were motivated to serve the community that they had founded. That role of service was often an everyday event of compassion and provision of help. The headline teachings and classes were backed up by the weekly pastoral round of hospital visits, listening to the member in need, 24-hour-a-day telephone calls, money loaned and discrete favors for others. Those were the everyday tasks, commonly given, as it were 'laundry and cleaning' that was largely taken for granted. Cumulatively, the service given was noticed, and Dorothy and Russell were respected and loved because of their service.

Dorothy and Russell's lives were an example demonstrated to others, showing what living spiritually could be. The love, courage and inner balance that Dorothy carried with her was not something that set her apart but something that others could emulate; something that others could become. When today, people who knew them speak of the couple, they speak in tones of gladness and gratitude; they speak of how their lives were changed and remember the sense of communion that they shared together. Those that knew them speak of the unusual phenomena that demonstrated the teachings of the spirit world and of the certainty of the continuance of life that Dorothy and Russell demonstrated. The legacy of the Flexers is in the foundation that they created in the Shrine of the Master at

Re-dedication of the Healing Garden, May 1995 .

Browning Street, Sarasota. The flexibility that was built into their thinking about the Metaphysics of Spirituality allowed the present to redefine that Shrine as a Center of Light. Above all, the vision that Reverend Dorothy and Dr. Russell had was of the spiritually enriched individual working in a psychically empowered community.

*Healing Garden Gate
at the
Sarasota Center of Light.*

Chapter Six

"I'd stay in the garden with Him
Though the night around me be falling,
But He bids me go; through the voice of woe
His voice to me is calling."

Those that remained or came along after Reverend Dorothy and Dr Russell had passed away, were challenged to rise to the level of the founders' curriculum vita, this, it was acknowledged was to be, near impossible. There was a desire in the SOM community to keep the Church working, to preserve the teachings and to move forward with a living legacy.

Ordinations had not been frequent at the SOM, but assistant ministers had been introduced during Dr. Russell's illness. As Reverend Dorothy gradually gave up traveling, the innovation was made to help with the Sunday services at the Tampa SOM. In Sarasota on 12th February 1989, Jean and Tom Courtney were ordained by Reverend Dorothy. The Ordination service was pro forma and the next occasion that we have details was the Ordination service for Tom Newman on the 23rd April 1995.

The morning and Ordination service commenced with a "Welcome to all" by Reverend Dorothy who said, "Praise and thanksgiving will be part of my whole being forever and ever." Lex Beaton accompanied the service on the organ and the Call to Worship was led by a reading of the 91st Psalm. The healing part of the service opened with a processional hymn followed by an invocation and prayer. An Anthem, (a popular church song) was sung, *With a Voice of Singing* followed by the Ordination service. Reverend Dorothy asked the Candidate, to come forward. Dorothy took an unlit golden candle and addressed Tom in the following way, "I present you with an unlit candle symbolic of your present state, before the angel of light, the Divine Spirit and these assembled. Within the candle are certain latent powers, which when properly used, will guide your steps out of the darkness of ignorance and misunderstanding. I will give you the candle to keep. It may sometimes be your rescue and safety. In time of affliction or moments of distress, you must be ready to give yourself in service."

Tom then took the candle and touched each flame of the candelabra, representing Deity, Worship, Universe, Divine Law, Immortality, Communion, and Progression.

The Candidate then knelt facing the congregation and recited a prayer of commitment. Reverend Dorothy came to join Tom and placed a stole around his shoulders. Dorothy then offered a prayer of blessing of which the following is an excerpt: "May you ever be mindful of the spiritual attributes that remain as guideposts in your service to God and Mankind." Finally, Reverend Dorothy placed her hand on his head and said "By the authority vested in me, I declare you to be a minister of the Church of Metaphysical Christianity. God Bless you." After the service, the congregation and the new minister were invited to attend a celebration in the Davis Hall.

Ordination of Reverend Tom Newman by Reverend Dorothy,1995.

At that time, in 1995, there were other ministers, but Dorothy was the sole Pastor of SOM. At Reverend Dorothy's last Board meeting on 8th July 1996, there was no suggestion of Dorothy being ill. However, it is reported that Reverend Dorothy's health had been poor for some time. It was known that Reverend Dorothy's chest was weak and that cigarette smoke and strong perfumes were intolerable to her. Karin Strauss spoke of Dolly Hayden being a smoker, and that Reverend Dorothy "gave her a tough time." Dolly Hayden's daughter, Sally Hayden von Conta said in 2015, that "Reverend Dorothy respected my mother who was a good medium and who had been trained by Reverend Dorothy."

Reverend Dorothy was working in all areas, right up to the end and giving physically demanding classes. It is thought that the Trumpet work took its toll on Reverend Dorothy's health, especially on the lungs. Entering hospital with a virus infection, the condition turned to pneumonia. Florence Strauss, interviewed in 2015, said when Reverend Dorothy was taken ill she had wanted no visitors. On the evening before Reverend Dorothy's passing, Dorothy appeared to be getting better, and Eileen went home to get a change of clothes and take care of other matters, planning to return the next day. On the morning of 26th August 1996, the telephone rang from the hospital to say that Reverend Dorothy had suffered a heart attack and that they should hurry back. However, upon arrival, the family were told that Eileen's mother had died.

The funeral was held at the Sanctuary of the Shrine of the Master to which Dorothy and Russell had given their lives. On 31st August 1996 at 11 am, Reverend Tom Courtney (senior) and the Reverend Tom Newman led the memorial service. Reverend Dorothy's favorite poem was recited, *The Rose Still Grows Beyond the Wall* by A. L. Frink of which the following is an excerpt: -

> "Shall claim of death cause us to grieve,
> and make our courage faint or fall?
> Nay, let us faith and hope receive,
> the rose still grows beyond the wall."

The Church was packed, and extra chairs had to be found. Reverend Dorothy's ashes lie amongst the roses of the Healing Garden.

Dorothy and Russell's leadership is looked back upon as a high summer, a period of growth and confidence.

> "Shall I compare Thee to a summer's day?
> Thou art more lovely and more temperate:
> Rough winds do shake the darling buds of May,
> and summer's lease hath all too short a date."

Shakespeare's sonnet illustrates that the past and those that live there are easy to love, that their contribution seems to dwarf our efforts. The 'Rough winds' that followed at the SOM and CMC make that 'Summer's day' seem more appealing. Reverend Dorothy's remarkable mediumship, combined with Dr. Russell's devotion to the teachings of spirit; seemed to be magnified by their passing away.

Yet the 'buds of May' however shaken bear the flowers of another summer. Authority may seek to guarantee the future and secure the succession, but its power is spent when the office passes to the next generation. After Dorothy, the Boards of the SOM and CMC were faced with the dilemma of how to keep in step with Dr. Russell and Reverend Dorothy's vision, and yet update and make relevant that vision for new members and new congregations.

It appears, aside from the introduction of SOM ministers that little had been prepared by Reverend Dorothy to create an orderly succession. Life at the SOM would continue much as it had when Dorothy was present because the structures were in place to ensure continuity. Constitutional arrangements to handle everyday issues of administration and overall governance had been agreed. As stated in the introduction, the present seldom takes thought of tomorrow, and in the case of the SOM and CMC, the present was left to work out its own future. The priorities for the immediate future were defined at a special Board of Directors meeting called by the President, Tom R. Courtney (junior), held on the 2nd September 1996. Reverend Tom Courtney (senior) presented a draft proposal for the Board to "review the leadership of the Church and promotion of the teachings and psychic phenomena." A membership meeting was arranged for the 7th September. The subject of the Senior Pastor role was discussed, as was the idea of looking for a Trance medium. It was decided that Tom and Jean Courtney and Tom Newman would serve jointly as Pastors until the annual February members' meeting was held. The pastors were to meet to work out the platform schedule and other duties.

Reverends Jean and Tom Courtney , early members and close friends of Reverend Dorothy and Dr. Russell.

A further Board of Directors meeting was called by Tom R. Courtney on the 9th September. Spencer Rouse opened in prayer. Genevieve Hannon was thanked for the letters and flowers that had been sent in gratitude for the celebration of her 100th birthday. Eileen and Tom R Courtney gave a verbal thank you for the flowers, reception and all that was done for Reverend Dorothy's memorial. The need to establish a search committee was discussed which was to be made up of Board and congregation members. The task of the sub-committee would be to locate and screen candidates, guest speakers and especially, a trance medium. Spencer Rouse was appointed as head of the committee, and there was, it was felt a need also to define the appropriate criteria for the interview process.

In 1997, the committee approved the appointment of Reverend Donald A. Dugar. Don was a big man standing 6 feet 5 inches tall and weighed heavily. Don had the ability as a medium to manifest the phenomenon of trumpet mediumship and to also give billet readings. There was then a range of phenomena in his mediumship similar to that of Reverend Dorothy. Don had trained and been ordained at Camp Chesterfield, Indiana, by the Indiana Association of Spiritualists. In 1996, Reverend Don was teaching at the College of Metaphysical Studies in Clearwater, near Tampa. Similar to the Metaphysical College where Dr. Russell had studied in the 1950s, the Clearwater College, founded in 1986, was different in that it included in its syllabus, subjects that are now considered to be New Age rather than New Thought.

Born in Tonopah, Arizona on 22nd December 1940, Don was a heavy smoker. Upon his being appointed in 1997 to take the classes at the SOM he moved into a Featherstone house at 2714 Bay Street. It is known that he later moved to 3717 Browning Street. Don was invited to give a demonstration at the Chapel for the appointment committee which was effective and

Reverend Don Dugar, Trumpet Medium and Pastor at the SOM.

impressive. Don had a number of spirit helpers, one guide was known as Golden Arrow and there was a Dr. Josiah Royce who served as his 'Spirit Doctor' and there was another angel helper, his 'Doorkeeper', known as White Lily. Unlike Reverend Dorothy's spirit helpers, Don's guides would openly criticize their medium. White Lily is quoted as saying, "I am not responsible for his mouth; I am not responsible for him." Don Dugar is credited with widening the teachings and introducing non-Christian perspectives. Reverend Don is also credited with the idea of bringing in other teachers and mediums from out of the area. Karin Strauss said that her mother Florence received an apport through Reverend Don's mediumship. Don's Spirit Doctor, Dr. Royce said that he had a special gift, a heart-shaped stone. Florence's husband, Karin's father, came through and spoke through the trumpet, "I am waiting for your mother and I guess that I am going to have to shoot her or hit her with a two-by-four." Some twelve years later Florence in her mid-80s is still going strong.

With the Courtneys and Tom Newman taking the services, Don was booked to take the Classes that Reverend Dorothy had taken. Later, Don Dugar was asked to help with the Sunday evening services when messages from Spirit would be given. Don was particularly effective in giving billet readings.

There were a number of constitutional changes at the SOM during Reverend Dugar's time there. Membership rules were tightened; to qualify a member must attend two services in twelve months. Attendance at three night-classes was required, covering

Rev. Don Dugar and Rev. Tom Newman in their Pastoral robes.

topics such as principles, history and metaphysics of the SOM. The revised by-laws on membership were added to the constitution and presented to the board and members and were eventually passed. In 2002, Don Dugar was made co-pastor with Tom Newman. Reverend Dugar remained a divisive figure whose character to some, was not appealing. Reverend Dorothy's shoes were not an easy fit, and in January 2005, his appointment, with the agreement of the members, was terminated. Those who remember him, say that he was insecure, worried about money and of advancing age. Witnesses also speak of his devotion to spirit and his remarkable mediumship. Don only lived another two years, moving to Brookline Drive, Sarasota and died, probably of lung cancer, in April 2007. However difficult his time at the Shrine of the Master, he served and gave his best and is given a place in these pages.

Dorothy and Russell had accepted that revelation and mediumship were an on-going process. Jesus had said, "Truly I tell you, whoever believes in me will do the works I have been doing, and they will do even greater things than these because I am going to the Father." (John 14:12-14.) In Metaphysical Christianity, it was understood that the work that Jesus had performed was through the power of the Divine. Therefore, what others had done; you too could do. The essence of the legacy of SOM lay in the provision of a community to belong to and the ongoing development of the member through Spiritual growth and psychic empowerment. It was the capacity and strength of the SOM to offer the individual a system, a 'science of self-development'. The flexibility that the SOM demonstrated through the renewal of understanding and the redefinition of core beliefs complimented the system of personal development. The process of redefinition in itself that followed in 2011, ensured the renewal of SOM. Members found confidence in the renewal of understanding, and growth of membership and participation was encouraged because 'The Truth' was found in the openness of debate and the questioning of belief.

The Shrine of the Master congregation met in June of 2011 to ask the question, "Does the term Metaphysical Christianity properly describe our teachings?" The answer was no, as it was thought that the teachings went beyond those of just one Master Teacher. The teachings of the instructional classes started to reflect a less Biblical emphasis, in keeping with the new generation's less Christian background. Dorothy and Russell had always accepted the Universalist position that there was truth in all religions. It was thought that Metaphysical Spirituality reflected the teachings of spiritual truth as taught by all Master Teachers of mankind's history. A change to a more inclusive name it was felt, would be beneficial in opening the doors to all backgrounds and beliefs. Christianity was a specific approach to religion that did not reflect the 'Metaphysical Spirituality' that was being practiced. The congregation believed that the term Metaphysical Spirituality would be more inclusive of people from other backgrounds and would broaden the SOM's appeal. As well as more accurately reflecting the teachings and

It is not my intention to enter into a possibly debatable question as to the how or when of the birth of Christ, whom we class as the Son of God. It is just as easy to class him as a brother, for indeed, are we not all Children of God, and as such, sons and daughters of the Great Universal Intelligence? While I agree that he was a savior, I do not interpret the word in the same sense that Christians generally do – as one who saves from sin.

beliefs of the Church. Browning Street sanctuary library continues to provide many books on Christian Metaphysics as well as other masters' writings. With the redefining of the Church's philosophy, the name of the Church was also changed in 2012, to the Sarasota Center of Light (SCOL.)

After Dorothy, there may have been fears of the loss of the familiar SOM life and uncertainty for the future. The SOM had always been about community, belonging and participation. These narratives have sought to emphasize that it was the life lived with others that was important to Dorothy and Russell. Chapter Five, looked at the pastoral role that the ministers undertook as a love and service to their community, as noted "it was never about the money." After Dorothy, that sense of community remained important to the members. There were communal activities which were at the core of the SOM and provided a structure to people's everyday life. Belonging to the SOM community, you might say was as normal as Tuesday, because of the importance of mutual support and shared belief that gave the member a sense of belonging to something bigger than oneself. After Dorothy had gone to the Father, the legacy of Metaphysical Christianity began to develop and grow in new ways.

The tradition of Metaphysical Christianity would go on. In 2003, the Center for Metaphysical Fellowship was established by Reverend Jean and Tom Courtney at 2044 Bispham Road, Sarasota, FL. Reverend Jean became Senior Pastor and after the passing of her husband Tom in 2009, her son Tom R. became Assistant Senior Pastor. Services of worship are held every Sunday with music, Spiritual healing and spirit messages. In addition, there are workshops and classes that welcome anyone who has an interest in all things Spiritual, including healing. The education of future lay speakers is encouraged, psychic development is taught and the giving of messages is demonstrated. A 'Prayer Out Reach Program' co-ordinates a group of volunteers who daily pray and meditate, and offer prayers for seven days in a row for those whose names are entered in the 'Request for Healing' book.

"Consciously or unconsciously we have in our life this feeling of the Truth which is ever larger than its appearance; for our life is facing the infinite, and it is in movement. Its aspirations are therefore infinitely more than its achievement and as it goes on it finds that no realization of truth ever leaves it stranded."
Rabindranath Tagore

Reverend Jean Courtney at 96, is still active in 2016. In October 2015, Reverend Jean was made Emeritus Pastor of the Fellowship in acknowledgment of fifty years of service and of being a veteran Metaphysician. Jean was presented with a certificate, and a reception was held to celebrate the occasion. Reverend Jean may have reflected upon the long friendship with Dorothy and Russell Flexer. Long years of devoted service to the work of spirit, the communities that were served, the cooking, the building repairs, the committees and boards and the love of the Divine and the cause of Metaphysical Christianity, Reverend Jean Courtney has many achievements to look back upon.

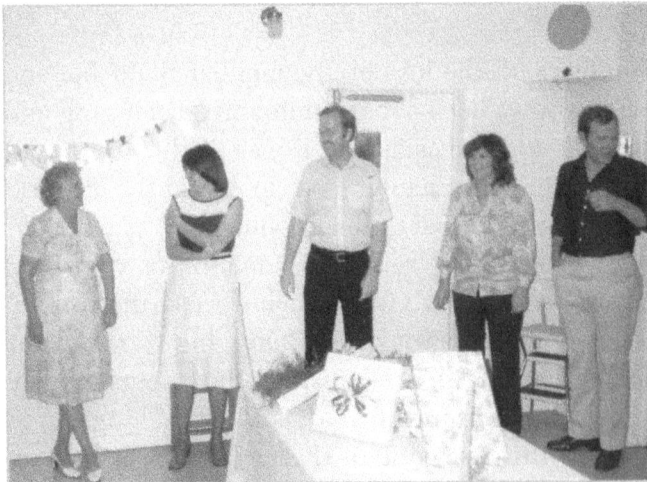

Sarasota SOM Party, 1981. Dorothy with Tom and Nancy Newman, Carolyn and Bob Loftus.

The Shrine of the Master continued with Reverend Tom Newman as Senior Pastor and sole Senior Pastor from 2005, retiring from the role in 2013. The SOM underwent gradual change.

Reverend Tom formulated a "Declaration of Principles"

which does not mention Jesus but does include Master Teachers, of whom Jesus is regarded as paramount. The ten principles are reproduced in Appendix 10. The Christian emphasis of metaphysics was broadened to include Universalist ideas so that Metaphysical Spirituality was seen to embrace Metaphysical Christianity. The latter is still taught alongside a wider conception of metaphysics. Dr. Russell's seven Spiritual Laws have been updated and there are now eight Spiritual Laws. The original Laws were Abundance, Attraction, Balance, Cause and Effect, Compensation and Freedom. These are now amended as follows, Law of Life (our relationship to God), the Law of Truth, Compensation, Attraction, Abundance, the Law of Freedom (will power, choice and responsibility), the Law of Love and the Law of Perfection being the inherent perfectibility of the individual as an aspect of the Divine within.

Tradition continues to be honored and spirit teachings and messages from the platform are given on a Sunday morning and evening as they were in Reverend Dorothy's day. Now with a new Pastor at the helm. The current serving Pastor of the Sarasota Center of Light is Reverend Jim Toole. Born in Sarasota, Jim trained for eleven years at the Shrine of the Master and was certified as a healer. Minister Jim has devoted over thirty-five years to working with people in their exploration and discovery of their own pathway in life. As Senior Pastor, Jim ministers to the spiritual needs of members and friends. The duties are extensive and include teaching classes, workshops, conducting healing and message services. The Pastoral role includes presenting community events and in common with the tradition of Dorothy, Jim offers private counseling, healing and mediumship.

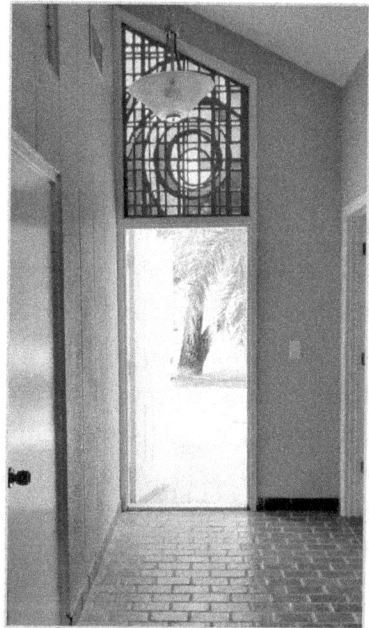

Entry way to the chapel, facing Browning St.

In keeping with the Universalist tradition of Dr. Russell and Metaphysical Christianity, Reverend Jim studied and is familiar with a full spectrum of religions, philosophies, doctrines including the metaphysical interpretation of the New Testament. Reverend Jim's family were Catholic, which introduced him to Christian beliefs. Throughout life, Jim chose to learn lessons 'the hard way' by coming face-to-face with life's challenges and finding ways to learn from them.

Eventually, in 1997, spirit led him to the Shrine of the Master. The religion that Reverend Jim found there, Metaphysical Christianity, blended with what Reverend Jim, as a child and adult, had come to understand. At the SOM, Jim would embark upon his personal transformation, which changed his direction in life.

I like that song "leaning on the everlasting arms" but I just wanted to interpret it as the everlasting arms of truth, and of the angels and of knowledge and love. – Don't doubt.

Not only did Jim find answers along the way, he also discovered a yearning to help others, out of gratitude for the changes that occurred in his life. Reverend Jim was drawn to the healing curriculum and the spiritual counseling program. Here he would begin to share what he had learned about helping others with a deeper connection to spirit; Jim's mediumship would begin to fully develop. Reverend Jim went on to complete the Associate Minister's program and eventually be ordained. He continued his development of his ministry, serving others through his connection to Spirit as a Minister of the Shrine of the Master.

Late in 2015, an opening was created for him to return to his spiritual home, the Shrine of the Master, now named Sarasota Center of Light. After being accepted as the new Pastor by the congregation on the 1st June 2016, a unique opportunity allowed him to begin to blend what he had learned during his eleven years at the SOM, and what he had come to understand in the years since, not just for himself, but as the expression of the Sarasota Center of Light.

A visiting medium gave a spirit message to Reverend Jim, "You have one foot in the past and one foot in the future, you are here to bring these together in balance." This made perfect sense to Jim. Knowing in his heart that the foundation of truth, established by Rev. Dorothy and Dr. Russell would be maintained and the expression of the Center would be widened to include the evolving spirituality of today. As Pastor of the SCOL, Reverend Jim Toole aims to be guided by Spirit, to blend the beliefs established by the founders with an ever-expanding reflection of the Center as a place of Love and Light.

Reverend Jim Toole.

The future of Metaphysical Spirituality and the Sarasota Center of Light is the combined training, experience and evolution of the members. Service to the community was Dorothy and Russell's purpose, and their pathway of spiritual and psychic development was their vision for that community. What was true in Russell's and Dorothy's day, remains the truth today and tomorrow. Reverend Jim's leadership will update and make relevant the

SCOL mission, and the Shrine of the Master will continue as the Center of Light to emit its radiance to seekers.

Perhaps one of the greatest innovations of the last twelve years, has been the gradual introduction of guest speakers. As noted Russell and Dorothy's Church was a stand-alone organization that developed their own speakers. None of whom could compare to Reverend Dorothy. However, the past of the SOM had illustrated that out of town speakers could offer a welcome addition to SOM life. Up to 1958, the Flexers had served on many other platforms, other speakers had visited their SOMs and the minutes of committee meetings often reflected the anticipation of outside speakers being invited. All that changed with the founding of the CMC in 1958, after which there is no evidence to suggest that non-CMC speakers were used.

Following on from Don Dugar's lead, the Board of the SOM developed links with external speakers who could bring a variety of experience and mediumistic gifts to the life of the Shrine. The list is long and changes over the years, but to give a brief resumé of current workers, Karen Cook from Albuquerque has worked as a 'transdimensional channel' for over three decades, channeling Benu.

David Thompson, physical
Medium through whom
Dr. Russell materialized.

Physical mediumship returned to the Chapel at the SOM with the invitation to British born medium David Thompson (b.1963) to give séances in November 2009. Of the four séances, the first given on 6th November, was the beginning of a successful relationship between the SOM and the medium. On the 12th November, the demonstration of spirit's power to move objects and to materialize was brought forcibly to the attention of the approximately thirty sitters. A wide range of phenomena is reported, the events were recorded, and there were known spirit visitors, among whom was Dr. Russell.

The four evenings usually started with William Caldwell, David's Spirit friend, introducing himself. The evenings proceeded with William answering questions on spiritual topics. The spirit of Caldwell explained that he manifested a hand that was larger than the average and bigger than David Thompson's, as David's hands are unusually small; thus emphasizing the difference between the two beings. William could be heard shuffling across the room, asking permission to touch and then touching the sitter. This was invariably met with exclamations of delight and pleasure. The Chapel at Sarasota has some twenty-four hand bells, some of which came from the Tampa Church. Materializing in the dark, William and Timothy Booth (Timmy, a young English lad and David's joy guide) at different times would pick up many of these bells and ring them vigorously. The figures in the dark are felt to pass the individual sitters, and intensely cold air fills the séance room.

On the 6th November 2009, Timmy picked up a Ping-Pong ball that had been covered in luminous paint and went around the circle so that the sitters could clearly see the tiny, childish fingers illuminated on the ball. Sometimes, Timmy would make a 'racket' playing on a drum. Timmy's role is to raise the energy by making everyone laugh, in which capacity he acts as Master of Ceremonies to facilitate the phenomena.

Accompanied by the music of *River Dance*, illuminated by strips of luminous tape, conical shaped 'trumpets' fly around the room, sometimes abruptly stopping in front of a sitter's face and then tapping him or her on the head. The trumpets then fly at speed around the room, accompanied by the gasps of the sitters. Occasionally, one trumpet will tuck itself inside of the other and both trumpets will fly around the room together.

Writing on the cabinet side through the mediumship of David Thompson at SCOL.

Plywood is laid on the floor of the circle so that the materialized forms can prove that they are fully materialized by stamping their feet. Many spirits stamp on this board but none more vigorously than Louis Armstrong. The late Jazz master is a regular at David Thompson séances. Louis will materialize while *What a Wonderful World* or *Hello Dolly* is being played, sing along and then pick up a mouth organ accompany himself by playing it. Louis has been known to break off singing to his own recording to have a conversation with a known sitter.

Reverend Don Dugar materialized in November 2011. He came in with a greeting to all who knew him. He admitted that he had made mistakes when he was in the physical and apologized for them. He brought a specific message from Reverend Dorothy and Dr. Russell to the Church community on an issue that the Board of Directors had been

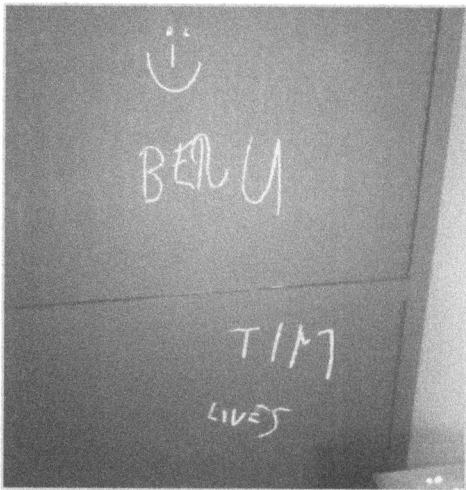

Cabinet Wall Chalk Drawings by Spirit at a David Thompson Seance 2011 in the SCOL Chapel.

working on for three years. This issue it is believed, was the change of the Center's name to that of the Center of Light?

Known people who are loved by the sitters appear at the Sarasota séances of David Thompson, Famous people can seldom prove their identities but at SOM the following list was recorded in 2011. Quentin Crisp, the well-known English personality is a regular visitor, Albert Stewart doorkeeper and guide to the Scottish medium Helen Duncan put in an appearance as did Helen Duncan (1897-1956) herself, who spoke to her granddaughter Maggie Hahn, now living in Chattanooga. Other notables of the Spiritualist world that visited were Dr. Henry Slade (1835-1905) the 19th century US medium, Harry Edwards (1893-1976) the British Healer, Admiral Usborne Moore (1850--1918) a writer on Spiritualist topics, and Andrew Jackson Davis (1826-1910).

On 6th November, Freddy Mercury spoke "...don't forget my lyrics, where are the boys? I have communicated before but not through a physical medium. I hear that you sing my songs here, I will try to sing through the ectoplasm, I will need the energy." Freddy sang a few bars from *Love of my Life*. Freddy then said, "I would appreciate it, if you would tell them that I came. And remember that it is the world that we create together."

The famous bring a glamour to these occasions, but those whom we have loved are special, and none was more welcome than the appearance Dr. Russell on 12th November 2009. In Chapter Five, we noted that in the *Memorial Metaphysical Messenger* August 1997, Nancy Skaletski expressed her gratitude of the late Reverend Dorothy and Dr. Russell for the hospital visits and healing given to her son Steve when undergoing a major eye operation. Twelve years later on 12th November, and some thirty-two years after his death, the materialized Dr. Russell was heard to say, without any introduction, "Nancy, how are you?" And Nancy replied, "Oh Dr. Russell, I will never forget how you came to see Steve when he was in hospital."

Russell is recorded as saying, "Lots of friends here, it is great to be here, it's been a long time." The responses are not, for the sake of brevity included here but there was a great deal of appreciative welcoming! Dr. Russell continued, "I can speak through that

Looking back: A Phenomena group at Camp Chesterfield, the author was told that 'it was all Physical mediumship then'. (CCC, date unknown)

Cabinet in the SCOL Chapel for physical seances today.

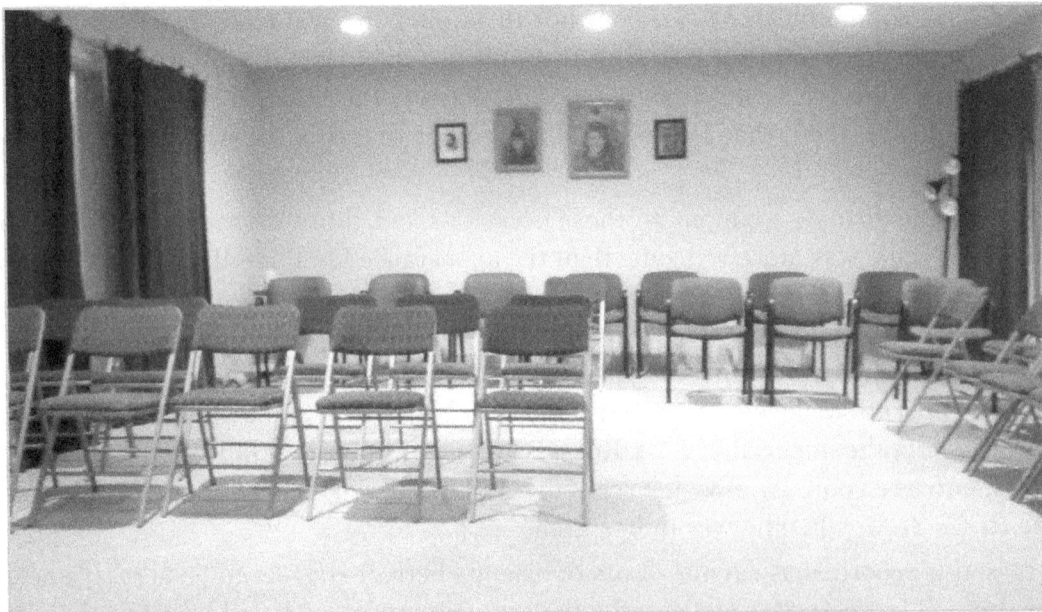

Interior of the SCOL Chapel today.

young fella, can you hear me? Dorothy will try and speak too." Dr. Russell expressed his own and Dorothy's happiness with the Church's direction and said, "I say to you all, what you must do is to preserve the good nature of the Church. Always, open the doors to everyone that may come. Dorothy and I decided that the Church of Metaphysical Christianity was the best way forward. There was just too much arguing and too much being vague and not understanding the true nature of spirit. That's why there should never be any discrimination at all. It doesn't matter the color of your skin or who you are, as long as you love each other. Always hold close those that are dear to you. And remember this, every time you have your service Reverend Dorothy and I are usually there with you, we often inspire Reverend Tom. God Bless every one of you. We can see right through a person's heart, and we are always close by. Oh, and Tom, my legs are much better now, no pain in them anymore." Reverend Tom Newman has confirmed that Dr. Russell had suffered from pain in his legs when in the body.

Reverend Tom Newman then asked Dr. Russell if he and Dorothy would be agreeable to having a picture of them put up in the Chapel, to which Russell replied. "…agreeable, we would be happy to." Dr. Russell prepared to depart saying "Goodnight, my gallant friends. This is only the beginning of our communication."

But Dr. Russell was not finished. "I will get him (Virginia's husband) for you now." The shuffling of feet can be heard and Russell saying, "Where is she, where are you, my dear?" A voice in the audience is heard to say "Dr. Russell, that was my foot." The séance circle all laughed as the good Doctor had trodden on someone's foot. A voice asked, "Are you looking for Virginia?" Russell replied, "Of course I am looking for Virginia." Virginia spoke up, "Hello, Dr. Russell, just being here tonight is wonderful."

In the *Memorial Metaphysical Messenger* for August 1997, Virginia Bergeson who had not known Russell wrote of her appreciation of Reverend Dorothy. "Thank you God, for placing Reverend Dorothy on my spiritual path. Through her ability as a trumpet medium we were fortunate to share in the wisdom of the Master Teachers. Everyone invited into her classes, we were given a priceless gift and met our own loving angel guides. I will always remember Reverend Dorothy as my friend and mentor. She will always be in my thoughts and prayers until we meet again."

Russell said, speaking to Virginia Bergeson in 2009, "I tell you that husband of yours, where do you think he is, right now? He is with us and he is going to come and speak with you. You wait there and I will get him for you." Gene, Virginia's husband speaks and some had initial difficulty in getting his wife to respond. "Virginia where are you? Why won't you talk to me?" Virginia replied, "How are you?" Gene continued, "Do you know who it is? It's Gene, why aren't you speaking to me? I am standing here and I am shorter than you." (Virginia, who died in 2016, was a tiny woman.) This comment provoked a lot of laughter in the audience as Gene in life was much taller than his wife Virginia. However, materialized forms use physical energy and are sometimes only partly manifested and on this occasion Gene was shorter than Virginia in order to save the medium's energy. Virginia's husband continued, "You are still as pretty as a picture. How is everybody? You know I miss you terribly." Most of Virginia's replies are not included here, though she said, "Tell Patrick I love him and take care of Charlie too. I miss you too." Her husband Gene, can then be heard kissing her three times we are told, on the forehead. This private family ritual of daily kisses Gene did when leaving for work in thanks for the three children that she bore him! Gene Bergeson then said again to his wife "pretty as picture." To which Virginia replied, "I look at your picture all the time."

That evening another member, Lori Marshall, spoke to her grandfather. After Gene Bergeson had vanished, Reverend Dorothy spoke briefly, "Can you hear me? It's Reverend Dorothy, I was waiting so that I could come. May I speak to Tom?" Tom said, "Yes, Reverend Dorothy." Dorothy replied, "You place that trumpet on the wall, you take good care of it. I am never far away. My heart is in this Church; ... [will] always be in this Church. I am everywhere…" Dorothy's voice broke off suddenly, and the voice of William Caldwell, David's doorkeeper came forward and said, "Good evening once more, it is unfortunate that Reverend Dorothy, you call her Reverend Dorothy is unable to use the last of the ectoplasm."

Since that first trip in 2009 David has become a regular, indeed almost annual visitor to the Sarasota Center of Light. Other speakers have become regulars too and have helped to take forward both the spiritual development and experience of the SCOL members.

An inheritance of bricks and mortar was left by the founders that still houses and provides an income for their spiritual foundation. Music and healing remain core practices at the SCOL. The current pianist, Rosemary Erbeck, and Russell would understand the sentiment of the English author Arnold Bennett who said, "Music is a language which the soul alone understands, but which the soul can never translate."

What can be done about the mess you on the earth are in? There can be no relief until people in their daily lives, through initiation and example, send out emanations of love and not of hate.

Community was at the heart of the Shrine of the Master, it could compensate in moment of doubts. The member can still understand at their own level, witness the mediumship, focus on others needs and leave the metaphysics to wiser heads. The practice of communal service, fellowship, fun and activity remains a cornerstone of belonging at Sarasota Center of Light.

Russell and Dorothy left a subtle legacy to the members, that of seeking and sensing a universal truth behind the appearance of reality. Rabindranath Tagore expressed this as: "We see the truth when we set our minds towards the infinite. The ideal of truth is not in the narrow present, not in our immediate sensations, but in the consciousness of the whole which gives us a taste of what we should have."

In so far as our thoughts, actions and organizations are in error and do not match that subtle reality; so will they fail.

"And the soul of Enoch was wrapped up in the instructions of the Lord, in knowledge and in understanding and he wisely retired from the sons of men, and secreted from them for many days." Jasher 3.2

The old truths and needs of the members remain same. Among which are, personal support by developed souls on the path of spiritual growth and understanding. The need to learn charity, practice service and have compassion for one's fellows. The growth of the spirit through attuning to higher vibrations in healing and meditation. There is the urge to unity with the Divine and the necessity to experience the transcendent nature of this existence. Dorothy and Russell knew that these eternal certainties were universal in character. The couple understood that each age brought forward its own interpretation and revelation, only the message and messenger changed, but the sense of Truth remained the same.

The legacy left by Russell and Dorothy has been renewed, with the introduction of new perspectives in metaphysics. Each generation revives its understanding through on-going redefinition and experience of metaphysics. The use of language changes. Styles become old-fashioned and no longer speak the truth in ways that people can appreciate. 'The Truth' needs to be spoken in language the people understand.

Sarasota Center of Light Education Center.

Perspectives change, and spirituality renovates itself with each new turn of the world's cycle. Dorothy and Russell knew that the underlying 'Truth' was found in many a tradition and those other traditions have found a greater voice in the years after their passing.

The metaphysical approach to spirituality was shown to be a flexible, living tradition. The search of the individual for guidance on the path of living and for inner unity with the Divine can be facilitated at the Sarasota Center of Light now, as it was in Dorothy and Russell's day. Yesterday has gone, its achievements were great, and its truths were taken and understood. The living heritage has been renewed today as it will be renewed again tomorrow. The member is invited to work at their own progress in union with this community. The member can enrich him/herself spiritually and develop that psychic aspect of themselves that will outlast this day – as the eternal soul.

The Last Word

Reverend Dorothy Graff Flexer

"Wherever I may be; I may not know the people who will brush past me this day. But I will never forget that they too, are creatures of the same God Spirit as I and deserve prayers of healing, abundance, understanding, love and peace. I dedicate my life to doing worthwhile things, saying uplifting and comforting words and most of all, to being an example of true discipleship."

Reverend Dorothy Graff Flexer in later life.

The Rose Still Grows Beyond the Wall

Near a shady wall a rose once grew,
Budded and blossomed in God's free light.
Watered and fed by morning dew,
Shedding its sweetness day and night.

As it grew and blossomed fair and tall,
Slowly rising to loftier height.
It came to a crevice in the wall,
Through which there shone a beam of light.

Onward it crept with added strength,
With never a thought of fear or pride.
It followed the light through the crevice-length
And unfolded itself on the other side.

The light, the dew, the broadening view,
Were found the same as they were before.
And it lost itself in beauties new,
Breathing its fragrance more and more.

Shall claim of death cause us to grieve,
And make our courage faint or fall?
Nay, let us faith and hope receive,
The rose still grows beyond the wall.

Scattering fragrance far and wide,
Just as it did in days of yore,
Just as it did on the other side,
Just as it will forever more.

A. L. Frink

*This poem was known to be dear to Reverend Dorothy
and was recited at her funeral in 1996*

Saint Francis Healing Garden SOM, 30th January 2011 at Noon
via phone camera - untouched photo.
(Note the light around the statue.)

Appendix One

An Appreciation of the many who served
and helped to build the Shrine of the Master.

As John Donne observed "No Man is an Island", and the building of the Shrine of the Master, took many hands and many years to accomplish and the story is not yet complete. The accounts that are given in this book, have emerged from the records, memories, and published materials that have come to light in the research. Nevertheless, there are many names that have not gotten the coverage they deserved as they were not part of these narratives. There is a saying, "Those who make the tea (it's an English saying) also serve." I am confident that Dorothy and Russell understood that the quiet background worker was a vital part of the life of the SOM. Or as Mahatma Gandhi put it, "The best way to find yourself is to lose yourself in the service of others." Community has been a key theme in this book, and serving the community could bring a sense of joy and belonging to the member.

There are also, the bigger players who often gave years of devoted service on boards, committees and kitchens and whose names pop up throughout the records, but whose names have not left stories connected to them. That means that the narratives are constructed from stories that illustrate a point or a theme. In the negative that is to say, that while 'so and so' was on this and that board they remain names and not accounts.

It is the purpose of this appendix to mention those that warranted greater coverage but of whom there was little to say. Another objective is to rebalance the accounts and say that these members were involved and to give where possible, dates and roles and offices held. It is impossible to mention everyone and if a member is absent from the records they are, as it says on the War Cenotaphs, 'Known to God'.

No names are more connected to Reverend Dorothy and Dr. Russell than those of Reverend Jean Courtney and her husband Reverend Tom Courtney. Many times was I told that the 'Courtneys' really built the SOM. And there is something of literal truth in the statement in that Tom Courtney was instrumental in helping the organization of the buildings themselves, and he certainly worked on maintenance of the structures.

This appendix includes the piece written by Reverend Jean for the memorial edition of 1997, in tribute to the close relationship of the Courtneys and the Flexers.

By Reverends Jean and Tom Courtney:

We have known the Reverend Dorothy Flexer since November 1950 when we first met her and Dr. Russell at the Woman's Club on a Friday night. We used to bring our boys, aged 3, 2, and 6 months old. We were very impressed by her sermons which were always given inspirationally and occasionally in trance. Tom said it was the first time he was able to stay awake during a sermon.

We first attended a séance in the small building on Tuttle Avenue almost across from where the Church is now. She was an outstanding medium, able to bring in apports and wonderful materializations. Her messages were of the highest calibre and so evidential.

She and Dr. Russell were always determined to present only the highest and best. She was always there for us at a moment's notice to help with any problems that we had. Our boys loved her and thought of her as a mother, and one of them became her son-in-law. We miss her, but know that she and Russell are continuing to work and inspire from the realm of spirit, to bring Truth to all who ask. We surround them both with our love and admiration.

The passage of time has left many names out of the record and there were many members who were regulars who left no name in the records. We are lucky that the names of the founder or Charter Members from 1949/50 are known. Some of the records for the earliest years at Sarasota are extant, whereas the records of membership for the Tampa Church have not come to light. We know that Reverend Tom Newman was President at Tampa in the early 1970s and that Marie and Kenneth Rowe were members at Tampa, and we have a little on the Redwing Circle. However, the following accounts mostly reflect the Sarasota Church.

In 1949, the following were listed as Charter Members, Dorothy and Russell Flexer, J.C Vick, Jonneye Vick, Tom Dalliot, Ellen Damillot, Adelaide Maltby, Alice Strattton, Gracie Newhall, Bra Brausa, Alma Abbott, Bea Marshlick, Bessie Ridenour, Arthur Bullen, Mae Bullen, Phillip Albritton, Charlie Albritton, Wade Koplin, (Florist) Daisy Koplin, Evelyn and Maurice Roberts and Mary Vossick.

The list of members grew every year and this account mentions only prominent members. 1952, saw Jean and Tom Courtney (a future Reverend, Sunday School Superintendent and President) join. Also in 1952, Dolly and Jack Hayden became members and the following year 1953, Sally (Hayden von Conta) and Sandra Hayden joined. Dolly served as Secretary for a number of years in the 1950s and was a member up to her death in the 1990s. Ethel and Joan Crawford joined in 1951 and Ethel was listed as a Board member in 1961 responsible for membership issues. In November 1953, Fay, Carlyn and Frank Bloodsworth were admitted to membership as was Patricia Hayden. In March 1954, future President and Reverends Myrtle and Roy Kaywood joined. Most of the names listed here were prominent in the life of the SOM, and a few have contributed their memoirs, such as Sally Hayden von Conta and Lucille Bloodsworth whose parents were among the early members.

The first Board meeting, date unknown but probably 1953, had Roy Kaywood as President, Myrtle (his wife) as secretary, Dorothy and Russell, Wade Koplin, Tom Courtney and Frank Bloodsworth all serving on the Board at that time. It is worth noting that Dorothy and Russell held permanent places on all Boards and Committees and that in addition the couple would stand for election to specific offices.

Wally and Adeh Heth, who became close friends of Dorothy and Russell, were also early members, at the latest in 1955. Wally took care of the gardens for some years. Another key player was Irene Spencer who was the resident organist at $5 per night from 1955 onwards. Irene had succeeded Harry Vincent Lee who died in 1960 after a long illness. Also listed for 1955, was Ella May Emmerson who in 1960 was to leave a large bequest to the SOM, as was Helen Clark who was listed as a Vice-President. Also in 1955, the minutes noted the SOM had 28 members whereas forty years later the membership was closer to 200. Other members who were listed included Cecil Vick, who stood for President, (Dr. Russell was elected.) In that same year, Glenn and Thelma Baldwin (who worked on the Boards) Virginia Downer President of the Sunshine Circle or auxiliary committee for catering as did Irby Stafford, all became members. The years rolled along, the old names continued and new members joined. David Downer acted as auditor in 1957 with Tom Courtney and Dolly Hayden. Jean Courtney took over as President of the Sunshine Circle in 1957 and Jean Schmidt served as Secretary.

The landmark Board SOM meeting of March 1958, shows the group that were closest to Dorothy and Russell. The following was noted in the minutes "a group of interested people gathered to form a new organization to be known as The Church of Metaphysical Christianity." Frank Bloodwsorth recommended Roy Kaywood and Dorothy and Russell Flexer formulate plans for the group. The following were assigned as officers: "President: Mr Roy Kaywood, Vice-Pres: Tom Courtney, Treasurer: Rev. Russell Flexer, Secretary: Sally Mitchell and Trustee: Rev. Dorothy Flexer: Publicity: Myrtle Faithful." The titles are as given in the original drafting. While the names given re-occur throughout the 1950s there were others who were close but not necessarily serving on the various Boards.

We know a few of the names from the Redwing Circle that worked at the catering for the Tampa church. Both Mary Flexer and Bertie Graff were involved and were close members of the family. Also, Isla Lippincote, Ruth MacMillan and Mrs Wally Drake, and Eva Hewitt served as secretary. In 1960, the name Charles and his wife Ilo Pixley make an entry in the Members' Meeting minutes and Charles Pixley was to be President and served as a Board member, dying in the same year as Dr. Russell, 1977. Other names to appear in the records that year were Charles Case, Hazel Hinckley, Reginald Giles (Church usher) and Harold Mitchell all of whom were on the Boards of the SOM and CMC.

In 1961, the SOM listed 84 members, including Roger and Jon Courtney (Reverend Jean Courtney's other two sons), the Willis family – Sara, Franklin, Charles and Lawrence. Also, Marguerite Brightman and Frances Greene who served on the Boards. Sally Mitchell, a former Secretary, was listed that year as being responsible for Publications. Jean Courtney was listed for so many roles over the years that there is scarcely an office that Reverend Jean did not fulfil. 1961, saw the role of publicity and advertising being assigned to Reverend Jean.

Our knowledge for the 1960s comes mainly from local newspaper records, the earliest of which that has come to light is for 1964. Many names of the veterans are present, Tom Courtney was elected President, Clifford Bloodsworth was VP, Dolly Hayden was secretary and Ralph Magee and others were Trustees. In 1964/5, the auxiliary committee or Sunshine Circle had as President Mrs DeGraw and as Secretary Arawanna Kemp, Lucille Lawrence as Treasurer with Mrs Chase and Adeh Heth as trustees. In addition, Mrs Ed Kemp, Mr and Mrs Bingham and Hazel Armstrong are known to have served on the auxiliary Board. An account from 1966, gives the elected executive for the Church of Metaphysical Christianity Board. There are a number of new names, William Stockford, Charles Murray, Cele Broad and Carol Divine. Others referred to were Jean Giles, Lillian Grantland, Maxine Ross and Charles Hand. There is a gap in the records which end in January 1973 with the following limited listing for the Shrine of the Master, President Tom Courtney, VP Harold Fultz, Secretary Marie Rowe, and Board members Pauline Dorneyer, Summer Darling and William Reid. It is worth noting that Kenneth Rowe served as President and worked on the various Boards from the late 1960s until the 1990s. The auxiliary for that year also listed new names, Mrs Leon Christy and Mrs Marvin.

Many have worked to keep the doors of the SOM and its successor SCOL open. There is a story of hard work and dedication to be written about the many people who have given their lives and labor over the past 40 years to the Church and ideas pioneered by Dorothy and Russell at Browning Street and Tuttle Avenue.

Appendix Two

'Mrs Flexor' and the Chinese Whispers –
Setting the story straight. The origins of the errors
and the facts with references.

It is true that a truth repeated by sufficient people will become untrue. Stories grow in the telling and when those are repeated over several decades, publications and later the internet, the truth begins to disappear. This is what has happened to the story of 1956, Spiritualist Episcopal Church (SEC) Conference, and Reverend Dorothy's role in those events. We shall start by looking at the errors and their origins and then shall give the true picture with evidence.

But to re-state the fanciful story:

....according to which account you are reading, the President or Presiding Chairman Dorothy Flexor (sic) of the Spiritualist Episcopal Church at their HQ at Camp Chesterfield, objected to the selection for office of a "prominent" clergyman (all agree it was a man) when the individual had been placed on a "morals charge". Uproar ensued at the Annual Convention with the conference splitting pro Reverend Dorothy and anti-Clergyman. The President or Presiding Officer Flexor (sic) decided that the best action to calm the conference, was to move the HQ out of Chesterfield to Florida. The Conference divided with Clifford Bias and Lillian Dee Johnson leading a faction of some 26 churches out of the SEC. Bias and Johnson then founded a new Church in 1956, the Universal Spiritualist Association (USA.) Leaving Dorothy in charge of the rump of the SEC from which the Flexors resigned in March 1958 when they founded their own CMC.

The originator of this tale is J. Stillson Juddah in his 1967, *The History and Philosophy of Metaphysical Movements in America*. Ironically, in its main brief the book is an excellent and indeed a landmark study of the impact of Metaphysical Thought on American society. However, the author is almost certainly quoting an interview with Reverend Dorothy Flexer from 1957/58. The author gives quotations as being directly spoken to him i.e.

"Dorothy Flexor said" or "Mrs Flexor explained...". Stillson Juddah calls Reverend Dorothy 'Mrs Flexor' throughout. Further, the author refers to "the two living founders" of the SEC belonging to different organizations that is Clifford Bias and Robert Chaney. The original third founder of the SEC John Bunker died in 1956. This places the interview in 1957/58 as Dorothy is quoted as speaking as a member of the SEC and the Flexers' church as being a member church of the SEC. Further, Juddah has Mrs Flexor moving the SEC Head Quarters to Florida and Mrs Flexor is named as the 'Presiding Officer' of the Annual Convention. Juddah does add that Mabel Riffle, the Secretary (or was she President?) of Camp Chesterfield forbade the SEC from holding its seminary meetings at the camp, and later forbade SEC mediums from working there. This prohibition would have included Dorothy and Russell and may have some element of truth to it.

In addition, Juddah who clearly had never visited the Sarasota or Tampa churches speaks of the "the resemblance of the architecture to the traditional New England Congregational Church with its tall steeple." Anyone who has been to Browning Street will know that there is no steeple and further that the Tampa Church had the same architecture as Sarasota. The author also added that healing was part of the morning service – at that time it was part of the evening service. The 'interview' appears to have occurred by telephone, or by a meeting away from Florida ,or less likely, by letter. Juddah, having researched his topic then printed the interview, without revision some ten years later.

Not all the errors originated with J Stillson Juddah and the trail is taken up by J. Gordon Melton in 1978 in his study *Encyclopaedia of American Religions*. In the study devoted to Spiritualism the 'Headquarters' of the SEC is stated as being at Camp Chesterfield. "Reverend Dorothy Flexor (sic) moved the Church HQ to Lansing Michigan." The Camp leaders according to Melton then forbade the rump of the SEC to hold teaching seminaries at Chesterfield. Melton cites Clifford Bias, Lillian Dee Johnson and Robert Chaney as "those who sided against Mrs Flexer" – Melton eventually, gets the correct spelling. However, Robert Chaney had left the SEC in 1951, to found the Astara Foundation as a Mystery School in California, and almost certainly wasn't at the 1956 conference and did not become part of the Universal Spiritualist Association.

The internet has continued to reproduce and embellish the above story. One site, *Encyclopedia.com*, adds that the split in 1958 from the SEC was due to accusations of fake mediumship. Such accusation did occur but not until 1960.

The true story is as follows. The Spiritualist Episcopal Church was founded on May 5th 1941, by John Bunker, Clifford Bias and Robert Chaney at Eaton Rapids, Michigan. The 'National Offices' are at Eaton Rapids where the original 'Mother Church' of the movement is. (Please see the Logo from their stationery with details opposite). The SEC was never Headquartered at Camp Chesterfield. The relationship to Camp Chesterfield was as venue to hold a seminary for the training of mediums and clergy. In addition, the SEC issued credentials on behalf of Camp Chesterfield to Spiritualist ministers and healers who were trained and licensed at the Camp. The SEC lost this facility after the 1956 crisis.

The facts of the AGM are somewhat different from the errors that have developed. The 1954, AGM was held at Flint, Michigan in which it is noted that Bias was succeeded by Richard Berry as President of the National Board. John Bunker continued to serve out a five-year term as Presiding Clergyman until his death in early 1956. The SEC Church organized the US into districts. and District 3, the south east, listed Dorothy Flexer as District Clergyman.

The 1955 AGM, held at Congress Hotel, Chicago, on June 5th, lists for the "Board of Clergy" John Bunker, as Presiding Clergyman and Austin Wallace as Appellate Clergyman. Reverend Dorothy is listed as a board member. Dr. Russell is listed as Vice-President of the "National Official Board," thought to be the administrative committee. Clifford Bias had been Appellate Clergyman in 1951 but appears to have had no role on either Board after the 1954 AGM. It is worth noting that in the Psychic Observer account of the AGM for 1954, that John Bunker as Presiding Clergyman opened the 1954, SEC Annual Convention but there is no account given as to who chaired the AGM; except a reference to "Bias Presides". There is then no evidence that Reverend Dorothy chaired the 1956, AGM. The Presiding Clergyman's role in 1954, was to open in prayer and give an address that set the tone of the convention. The task of chairing may well have fallen to the Secretary or President of the National Board.

The *Golden Rays Magazine* of the SEC for 1956, reported that the AGM was held at Lansing, Michigan. The Official Board had Richard Berry elected as President and Reverend Dorothy elected for the standard five-year term as Presiding Clergyman of the National Board of Clergy. Appellate Clergyman was Ruth Walling. We can assume that Dorothy, Ruth Walling and Richard Berry saw eye to eye on the problem of the day. The paper also gives the location for the 1957 Annual Convention as Eaton Rapids.

BOARD OF CLERGY
Rev. John W. Bunker, Presiding Clergyman
Rev. Austin D. Wallace, Appellate Clergyman
Rev. Ella J. Sutton   Rev. Dorothy B. Hiatt
Rev. Irene R. Slocombe   Rev. Lloyd M. Chase
Rev. Dorothy G. Flexer   Rev. Noah M. Rice
Rev. Nellie Curry Hicock   Aletha Hawk
Rev. Ruth L. Walling, Missionary-at-Large
GOLDEN RAYS: Rev. Austin D. Wallace, Editor

OFFICIAL BOARD
Richard N. Berry
Rev. Russell J. Flexer
Cyril C. Sayles
Irene Hathaway
W. Clifford Birchfield
Estyl Fuller
Bernice McGrew

The Spiritualist Episcopal Church   National Offices EATON RAPIDS, MICH.

Mast Head of the SEC stationery 1955.

The events of the AGM may never be fully known and no full report has come to light. However, the following is a summary of what happened. Following the sudden death of Reverend John Bunker in early 1956, Reverend Dorothy succeeded as the acting Presiding Clergyman of the SEC. This role was confirmed by the election at the 1956, AGM at Lansing, Michigan. The Board of Clergy would have had a credentials function in which the eligibility of candidates for Church office was examined. As such it would have been Dorothy's role to chair the 1956, Board of Clergy just prior to the convention that heard the accusations or the 'charge' against the errant clergyman.

The timing is important. The events must have occurred at the Convention as Russell and Dorothy lived 1,500 miles away and would have travelled to attend the AGM. However, under a brief outline of the constitution of the SEC, issued in 1951, the Annual Conference convened the third Friday, Saturday and Sunday in September. "Friday is devoted to the Clergy Conference, during which all matters of Religion are acted upon. Saturday and Sunday are devoted to the General Conference which decides the business affairs of the Church." Therefore, Reverend Dorothy may well have chaired the Clergy Conference in the role of Presiding Clergyman, and then relinquished the chair to another for the General Conference. Committee workers will appreciate that decisions and disputes have a habit of being decided before the start of the meetings. The dispute may then have become public at the Friday Conference and then carried over into the General Conference.

The clergy were accountable to the Board of Clergy for their behavior; "rigidly examined" was the phrase used and it is therefore likely that this Board heard the "morals charge" brought against the candidate. It is not known who the controversial candidate was, nor what the "morals charge" consisted of. The "accused" then sought office at the SEC at the Annual Convention. The charge would have become public and caused the dispute at the AGM of the SEC. Clearly, there was a schism in the SEC and Dorothy is accounted as leading the anti-candidate faction: with Clifford Bias and Lillian Dee Johnson leading the pro-candidate faction. The Church split; with presumably the pro-candidate faction abandoning the convention at Lansing and the remainder continuing the AGM with the election results confirming Dorothy as Presiding Clergyman and others as given in the *Golden Rays Magazine* for 1956.

Reverend Dorothy as Presiding Clergyman, was responsible to the Board for the training of clergy and mediums decided; with the co-operation of the Board of Clergy to move the Seminary of the SEC away from Camp Chesterfield. In addition, Camp Chesterfield gave authority to the new USA to issue credentials on its behalf to Spiritualist ministers and healers who were trained and licensed at the Camp; removing that role from the SEC. It is known that Clifford Bias had or did live at Camp Chesterfield, was born near there and had long had associations with the Camp. The possibility of the rump SEC continuing to use the Camp Chesterfield premise, which was the Center for the new 1956 Universal Spiritualist Association, must have looked unrealistic.

Finally, Dorothy may have suggested to the Convention or Board of clergy that the 1957 Northern seminary be held at Lansing, Michigan, and as we saw in Chapter Two, the Southern seminary be held at St Petersburg Florida.

Bradenton Church SEC,
Rev. Lillian Dee Johnson top row 2nd left.

Appendix Three

Dorothy and Russell Flexer:
An Appreciation by Reverend Tom Newman.

I met Reverend Dorothy Flexer and her husband Dr. Russell Flexer on 27th October 1962 at a Halloween party that the Shrine of the Master Church of Tampa was holding. My mother took us four children with her to the party to see if we liked the Church and the people associated with it. I was ten years of age at the time and tied for oldest with my twin brother. Something inside of me told me we had found our spiritual home. I had an immediate rapport with Reverend Dorothy and Dr. Russell. Little did I realize that these two charismatic people would become like second parents to me and my sister Pat.

Fifty-four years later as I write these words, I can safely say that Reverend Dorothy is the person who has had the greatest influence over my life and that she stands out as one of the most dynamic and interesting people I've ever met. Simply put, her life was dedicated to bringing the truths of life to everyday people. She was a tireless instrument of the Spirit People in carrying out this mission.

Reverend Dorothy was a natural medium and by her mid-thirties had developed the ability of materialization, apports, deep trance, lectures and trumpet (direct voice) work, much to the delight of Church members who were invited to sit in her classes. For many years, she and her team of Spirit Guides gave four classes a week – three of the classes were for Mediumship Development where her primary Spirit Teacher, Dr. Charles Davis, would come through and teach the classes. The fourth class was the Master Class where Master Teachers from all over the Spirit World would come and speak on topics given them by the class members.

The Flexers started two Shrine of the Master Churches – the first in Tampa in 1947 and the second in Sarasota in 1949. As you can imagine Metaphysics and Mediumship were not widely understood at this time. There were some who did not understand these teachings and set out to put roadblocks in the path of these small Churches as they began their efforts to reach out and find progressive thinking people. Dorothy and Russell did not let the efforts of ignorance stop them and the Churches began to grow.

Reverend Dorothy and Dr Russell were the least ego-oriented people I've ever met. They were not self-promoters nor were they interested in the idolization of those who had experienced their fantastic spiritual abilities. They were on a mission to bring spiritual teachings to the public and were following, with humility, the guidance of their Spirit teachers. Dorothy and Russell did so with great understanding and humor. Forgiveness and tolerance of ignorance were strong characteristics of both Flexers. One could safely say they lived the philosophy they taught.

I salute my friend, Gerald O'Hara, for his dedicated efforts to bring to light the life and teachings of Reverend Dorothy Graff Flexer one of the twentieth century's greatest mediums.

I hope you have enjoyed this journey into the lives of the Flexers and many of the thousands whose lives they touched. Truly they were instruments of the Divine Power and will not be forgotten.

Reverend Tom Newman, Senior Minister
Sarasota Shrine of the Master
September 1996 to May 2013

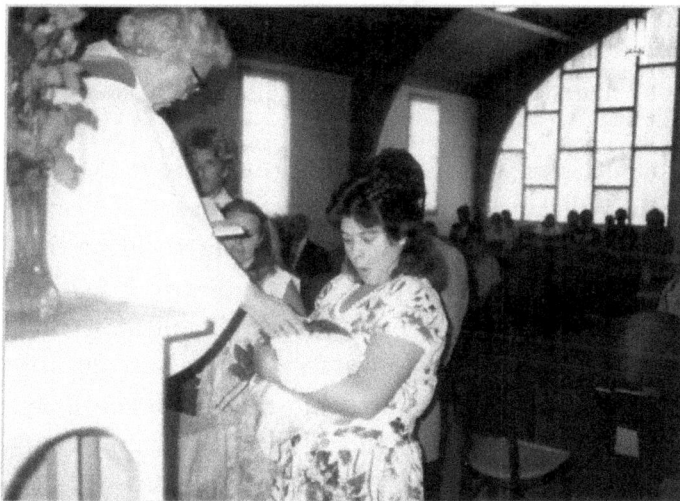

Reverend Dorothy christening Marie Rowe's grandchild

Appendix Four

An Extract from Alda Madison Wade's book *At the Shrine of the Master*, giving an impression of what it was like to attend a Class of Reverend Dorothy at Tampa SOM in 1952.

31
CLASS OF MAY 20, 1952
OUTSTANDING LEADERS -
LUTHER, WESLEY, MYERS

"This is Dr. Davis. Good evening, friends. Before I step aside to admit the speakers of this occasion, it is well that we lay our plans for our remaining class sessions before closing this summer. First of all, I would like to have you decide as a class on the number of meetings we will still have. Perhaps, Alda, we had better ask you to suggest a number if you will."

"To complete our manuscript, I would like to have at least three classes, and four or five would not hurt."

"We will let it stand at that, then – anywhere from three to five more periods. Now that that matter has been settled, have you any suggestions as to subjects for discussion or the nature of the classwork you would like to have considered during these closing sessions?"

"For one thing, I would greatly enjoy a session or two in which our departed loved ones and friends would be given an opportunity to manifest, if that is agreeable to the rest of the class," I suggested. "How do you feel, as a class, regarding this proposal?"

The general response being highly favorable, the doctor continued: "It will all depend on a question of time. Such an evening should serve as a fitting conclusion for the work. However, have you any suggestions regarding the other classes?"

"We have dwelt on the philosophy of mediumship; of spiritualism in general; we have listened to a great inventor; we have heard the stirring words of two former Presidents. How would it be if we were given the opportunity of listening in on certain great religious leaders – Protestant, Catholic and Jewish, or even any other religions whose fundamental tenets are derived from sacred literature not included in the Bible? I have recently listened in on a Jewish radio broadcast which had to do with the life of a rabbi who was respected by people of all denominations and creeds. That great leader was Stephen S. Wise. Would it be possible to bring him in on one occasion?"

"That will be possible only if his commitments will allow. We must not forget that men whose lives on earth were kept busy, as they surrendered their time to the benefit of their fellow men, are just as busy on this side in their continued effort to improve the status of mankind. We cannot demand their presence here when they are otherwise engaged, but we can at least try. If we cannot engage the services of the one you request, we can try to bring in a satisfactory substitute. Now that you have made known your desires, I shall do my best to fulfill them. "I will now stand aside. Russell, will you start a song as a means of increasing the power?"

After we had sung two stanzas of a hymn, Red Wing broke in to say: "Good evening, everybody. I just wanted you to know that I am here. I love you all."

"Good evening, Red Wing. We love you too," we responded to her greeting, always so refreshing and filled with levity. That was the limit of our conversation with Red Wing for the time being. Out of the distant past came another voice which said, "This is Martín Luther."

Our tongues were tied with introduction of a name so prominent in the annals of Christianity. At best, we could but sit and listen, in the hope of absorbing some of his message as this man of pre-eminence entered into his discourse:

> You have asked your teacher to supply you with speakers who had something to do with religious leadership; specifically, persons who were responsible, to a degree at least, for bringing about a change in the religious thinking of the times.
>
> Those of you who are familiar with the history and progress of Christianity will recall that I was born and raised a Roman Catholic.
>
> After having been educated at a Franciscan Seminary, I entered a Monastery of Augustinian Monks and thereafter became a priest. At a subsequent date, I was appointed to a professorship at the University of Wittenburg. While there I taught Dialectics, that branch of logic which teaches the rules and modes of reasoning, or of distinguishing truth from error.
>
> It was during this time that I visited Rome, and became greatly disturbed at what I considered to be evils which were cloaked under a garb of the so-called piety of the Church. Although protesting what I considered to be wrong, I had no thought whatever of quitting the Catholic Church. On the contrary, my desire was that the Church be purged from within.

On my return from Rome, as a result of my teachings, I was appointed superintendent of eleven Franciscan Monasteries. In my lectures, I condemned the sale of pardons and releases from purgatory authorized by the Pope of that day. It is not necessary that I go into all details which followed, other than to say that I was excommunicated from the Catholic Church. This was the beginning of the Protestant Reformation.

The Lutheran Church was the outcome of my effort of that time. Since my passing from the earth plane into the realm of spirit in the year 1546, it has been my great hope and ambition that all churches unite under one head – a universal religion having back of it one great fundamental policy. That policy will not be concerned with creeds or dogmas; but, established on a basis of Love, its controlling Law will be the Golden Rule, as laid down by Jesus of Nazareth and other great religious leaders before and since His time.

The man who will follow me as speaker tonight is a long-time friend – one whose life on the earth plane had its beginning many years following my passing; a man who made history as a great religious leader. I now stand by in order that he may enter,

During the interval taking place between the speakers, it seems desirable that we pause to consult briefly the historical record setting forth the time of Martín Luther. This record shows that he was born in the year 1483; and, agreeable to his statement, his passing occurred in the year 1546.

The next speaker announced himself,

This is John Wesley, referred to historically as the Father of Methodism. It would have been better stated that I was one of the founders of Methodism, for there was my brother Charles, who was just as active in the work. We were staunch members of the Church of England, in which we had been ordained as clergymen, and our thought and ambition in the beginning was not in the least concerned with the formation of a new denomination. Our idea was to introduce into the established Church methods of evangelism which were more aggressive, and having greater spirituality than those which were being practiced at the time.

We conducted our campaigns to bring about these changes both in England and America. While I insisted on staying with the mother church until the last, I was finally forced into a separate church, having been denied communion with the Church of England.

In this manner, Methodism, which came to have various branches, had its beginning. Like the speaker who preceded me, however, I am no longer in accord with the idea of dividing the people into many lines of religious thought. You are all struggling with one thought in mind, and that is not for the betterment of any particular group or church or synagogue or Moslem or whatever it might be, but for the betterment of all mankind.

Know by this that when you have come to your full spiritual heritage, you will not be Roman Catholic nor Episcopal nor Methodist, Presbyterian or Baptist, nor any other denomination or religion into which man of flesh is divided, but you will be taken up into one great universal religion whose foundation is Love and whose law is the Golden Rule. It will not be a religion of Creed which says 'I believe this and I believe that.' On the contrary, it will be a religion based on absolute knowledge. This knowledge will rule out any thought of the Resurrection of the Dead or a Day of Judgment. It will recognize the fact that man, at the instant of his conception, becomes both physical and spiritual. In death, he loses only the physical body, but the spirit lives on throughout eternity.

In this manner, John Wesley spoke eloquently for fully ten minutes. It seems hardly necessary to record everything he said, but, rather, to establish the fact of his presence as a speaker during our class session last night.

History shows that John Wesley was born in 1703 and died in 1791. This span carried him over many of our colonial years, well beyond the Declaration of Independence and the establishment of the Constitution of the United States of America. In fancy, we see him in conversation with many of our early patriots. Not the least of these would be Benjamín Franklin, Thomas Jefferson, Paul Revere, the Adamses and George Washington. It is an experience, not to be regretted, to be able to sit in a class during which these shades of the past express themselves orally and intelligently on many matters relating to the betterment of man.

Before the next speaker introduced himself, there was a song, and then came the voice of Red Wing.

"What do you think of Mr. Wesley?" she asked. It was Dea Pomeroy who voiced the feeling of the class: "I think he is marvelous," she said. "As one who has been a Methodist throughout my life, the name Wesley is very familiar to me. I have always thought of him, not alone as the great organizer and founder of Methodism, but as one of the greatest evangelists of all time. I was deeply impressed with his eloquence tonight. It is obvious that he has undergone a change of mind since entering the spirit world, as the Apostles' Creed is still an important part of the Methodist ritual."

Another song, and another voice. "This is Doctor F.W. H. Myers."

I must confess that while I have attended many séances and conversed with many spirits, some of them historical in their earth lives, the name of Dr. Myers was not among the list; nor have I ever had the good fortune to read any of his books. He was not a stranger to all, however, as the Pittmans, who are students of science, especially as applied to psychology, were highly familiar with him. They knew of his lecture work on subjects falling under the general head of Psychic Science, which were delivered before classes at Oxford University. They spoke of him as the first teacher of eminence to bring the subject of Psychic Philosophy into the curriculum of a great university. His two books, *Human Personality* and *The Survival of Bodily Death*, they tell me are broadly quoted wherever spiritualism has taken root.

I am one who comes to you out of the near past. The years of my life had their beginning in 1843 and their closing in 1901. Why should I say 'the years of my life'? It must be obvious to you that I mean the years of my earthly existence, for, believe me, I am now more alive than ever I was while in my body of flesh.

My adult years were given over largely to the pursuit of science. I was an investigator of many things, and during my later years spent much time in the field of psychic. My first impression was the thought that the very foundation of Christianity lay in the field of spirit communication. It was with this in mind that I set forth to investigate mediumship in its various aspects. It was my desire to prove to my own satisfaction whether or not Jesus actually conversed with his disciples following His death upon the cross.

As a scientist, I was unwilling to accept the words of others who recounted many experiences in séance rooms, during which they talked in direct voice with those who had preceded them into the spirit world. It was obvious that my investigations should at least have their start in a séance room in which the instrument of communication would be a direct-voice medium.

Although it was my desire to be neutral, I must confess that there were doubts in my mind which were not entirely erased at the end of my first sitting. My interest was strengthened, however, to the extent that I was determined to press the investigation to a final conclusion.

While there was a question as to an element of ventriloquism on part of the medium as I approached my first séance, I came in the end to the full realization of the truth of spirit return. I knew positively that I had communicated with the spirits of people I had known in their fleshly existence. These facts I recorded in certain books, which have since become texts in their field. As a teacher, I also transmitted this information to classes in psychology in a well-known university.

I regret that the Christian religion, which would be lost without the foundation it has in spiritual return and communication, does not, as a rule, accept the story of the Upper Room, and put it to a conclusive test in this modern age.If churches could only realize it, the Upper Room, in all reality, was a séance room. It is in a séance room that one learns the true meaning of God; that His laws are nature's laws; and that Communion with the Saints is not a mythological expression, but is actually a statement of fact.

My good people, I must express a deep feeling of satisfaction for the invitation which brings me here tonight. I am glad to report to you that yours is not the only meeting place tonight that concerns itself with the subject in which you are engaged. There are literally thousands of such gatherings everywhere going on all over the universe; not only this night but every night of the week.

Men and women are seeking the truth as they have never sought it before. The fear of war, made most direful with the mastery of atomic destructiveness, is turning their minds as never before to things which have a permanent value; to man's eternal future, where happiness is engendered by service as one reaches out, not to destroy, but to be of benefit to man. I thank you, and goodnight.

"This is Dr. Davis. How have you enjoyed the meeting tonight?"

"Immensely," was the general attitude of the class. "Have you any comments or questions to ask?"

"I was deeply impressed," volunteered one, "with the change of thought that has apparently come to John Wesley since his entrance into the world of spirit. He no longer upholds that statement in the Apostles' Creed which says 'I believe in the Resurrection of the Dead.' During the time that he lived on earth it was the general belief that bodies of flesh would be literally raised from the dead."

"Yes, that is true," answered the doctor. "In those days they would scare people by drawing pictures of men rising out of their graves, as they rushed to the throne where Christ was to judge the 'quick and the dead'. They filled their churches but it was not with the positive thought of the Love of God, but, rather, with a negative thought of the fear of God and His hatred for certain elements of His own creation. ... Are there any further questions?"

"How would you classify fortune-tellers, as distinguished from mediums?" asked Loren Pittman.

"Fortune-tellers deal strictly with material things. Their work has to deal with predictions as regards one's future physical well-being. Sometimes they even go so far as to give negative prognostications, ruinous to constructive thought and doing more damage than good. Fortune-tellers who restrict their predictions to things which are good, are able to set up a positive psychology on part of the seeker. Such forecasts cannot help but have a beneficial result, and are greatly to the fortune-teller's credit.

"While it is true that mediums are sometimes called upon in respect to material things, the real purpose of mediumship is spiritual and is not to be confused with fortune-telling.

"This work could be prolonged far into the night, but I see that it is now time to bring this session to a close, and I must now bid you goodnight."

"Did you suggest a séance, Alda, in which all the loved ones in spirit come in and talk to the different ones in this class?" Red Wing asked. "Do you know that that will require much more time than is allotted to one of these class periods? We must find a night when my Medi is not otherwise engaged."

"That will be O.K.," I answered.

There were two absent from the class – Isla Lippincott and Eva Hewett. This left seven of us to enjoy the work of the evening. When the lights were turned on, it was observed that two names were written on the pad which had been left on the table. One, written in large script, was that of Elmer, brother of Cathryn and Marianna; the other, written in very small script, was Mary, the companion who departed from me and this life, February 1st, 1932.

After the consecration in 1987.
Illustrating an ordination service. (CCC.)

Appendix Five

Four Sermons given by Dorothy and Russell Flexer:
the thoughts that shaped the Shrine of the Master.

All Saints Day

A Trance Sermon by Reverend Dorothy Flexer,
31st October 1971.

Greetings, good friends of Earth! It is always a privilege and a responsibility to bring to your truth that's not only needed by you, which will be helpful to you in the years of your life.

Perhaps you have been reminded in the last few hours of a very special occasion, an occasion which has been neglected by the churches, or by the most of them, and that is the time of honouring saints. Tomorrow, I believe, according to the earthly calendar is that day which is known as All Saints' Day, and tonight, Hallowe'en, is the eve of that hallowed date.

I am certain that most of you in this congregation, if, not all of you, have lost the full significance of this occasion through the years, with the result that Hallowe'en, the eve of All Saints' Day, has become a time of fun and games, of masquerading, of playing tricks on people and having what you call treats. But nevertheless, the religious significance of it is fast fading into the past. I believe that not only should an occasion such as this but many others connected with religion and the guidance of angels have faded and will continue to fade until people like you who have the knowledge and the understanding of the guidance of angels will continue to support them as a very necessary part of your life, knowing that it is a very necessary part of the life of every individual.

Perhaps the reason for this neglect on the part of the churches is due to the fact that few people understand what makes a saint. Few people understand who is a saint, and few people have any knowledge of the communication between the earth world and those so-called saints.

Let us think for a moment about every great project that has been made on this earth in your lifetime. Now that span of time varies, certainly, but the youngest person here has been taught the history of the foundation of this country. Many of the outstanding occasions, if studied properly, will reveal the guidance of angels.

Throughout the past, the angels have played a very important part in the growth and progress of man. It is important to know this because man, of himself, is nothing, but man with the guidance of angels becomes an instrument of the God spirit.

Throughout the short span of your life, whether you are aware of it or not, you have enjoyed the blessings of angel guidance. Angel protection and of the truth brought by angels.

None of what I am telling you is new; it is only new to those who have never heard of it. But since the beginning of time man, who is spirit living in a physical body, has reached out beyond the confines of his physical being and of his mortal knowledge to the invisible power for help.

Now those churches and organisations who do not accept the guidance of the angels as you do will suggest you call upon your god for help. They suggest that God, the Lord, Jesus the Christ, will always be there to answer your prayers, to be a personal saviour to you. Much of whom is no longer acceptable by thinking people.

Surely anything that is good and worthwhile should be recalled, should be remembered and should become a part of your being and your life. I am well aware of the fact that, unless one has knowledge and understanding of the angel world and of the power of spirit, he cannot be expected to believe. He cannot be expected to understand.

Why have churches withheld such truth from the multitudes seeking such help through the churches? My only thought is that many are drawing apart from the real source of help and allowing themselves to be more orthodox, thereby giving the men of the church, or men-of-the-cloth, greater power. All of these things and many more have created a gap between man and his power. And if man does not understand that within his reach are the invisible angels. Ready willing and happy to help. How can he be expected to call upon them, or to open his mind to receive that help? Angel help is not forced upon any Individual. Four of the greatest teachings of the Master Jesus are found in his sermon on the mount, "Ask and ye shall receive, knock and the door will be opened." Nowhere in his teachings will you find any statement that says, "just believe and don't ask. Just take for granted that what is needed will be provided and there is no need for any reciprocal activity on your part, physically or spiritually."

Surely you know that you must take the Bible in its entirety. You can take any statement in the Bible, or any verse or group of verses out of context and you will have a particular meaning which may be helpful. But you cannot say that if any particular group of verses does not explain the guidance of angels that the guidance of angels is all evil or the work of the devil.

Every great soul who has ever made progress, who has ever reached the point of success in his or her life, gives credit to the invisible power and the guidance of angels. Many of these individuals do not understand that power, but they do know they have feelings, they have sensations, they have what is called 'hunches', impressions. They have visions, they have dreams. They have a sense of knowing and not knowing how they know, but they know. And all of these things, my good friends, are contained in the guidance of angels.

A very favourite verse of yours, I trust, and of all the angels, is that one found in the ninety-first psalm which reads, "He shall give his angels charge over thee, to keep thee in all thy ways." Now this means that not only in your moments of strength and of great success the angels are present to help you, but that they are also present in your times of failure and defeat and depression, and in your moments of illness and negation they are there also. The angels do not exercise any right to be highly sensitive, to be hurt or annoyed.

It is quite possible that we from the world of spirit expect a little more of you than you are willing to give or to perform, but this is due to the fact that we know you as a spirit entity in a body, and we know that you have the strength of mind, of character and of spirit to overcome all the conditions of the world. You have the power and the knowledge and, with our assistance, you can overcome any failures. You have the ability to turn everything that is negative into something that is positive, to turn everything that is seemingly bad into something that is good. We know you have the power and the desire to improve your being, to be successful, to be happy, to be congenial, to be all of the things that your heart desires.

We also know that nothing is impossible when one lives in harmony with divine law. And here again we find the need for the guidance of angels, for without that help your sight is limited, your awareness is dulled, and you become so filled with your own personality, with your own ideas, with the knowledge that you have accumulated, that there is little room left for the influx of divine consciousness and the divine power, which to us is divine law. Your lives are enhanced by that divine power, divine love and divine energy. It is the action of the angels with your understanding of it and your ability to activate that power in your life.

Is it any wonder that many people have felt that God is a respecter of persons, that some individuals of earth are sorted out, and some are given more talents than others? That some can expect to receive all kinds of help while others have none? Surely, if you are intelligent, and I know you are, you cannot believe that such things exist in the world of spirit, which is the world of God. All things are equal. Inequality is created by man, or men. And surely you can understand that while you have access to this unlimited power, to this unlimited knowledge, you can have no benefit of it unless you put forth the effort to attain that knowledge, to reach out for it, to ask for it and then, receiving it, to use it wisely.

Some churches in ages past have recognized the manifestation of angels as being miracles, and to many of those angels, or so-called saints, have been accredited the action of divine healing, of divine protection in unusual situations. But can you possibly believe that this power is limited to such a few, or that it is directed only to one certain group of people. Perhaps Catholicism has benefitted materially, financially, and in many other ways by clinging to the worship of these saints. But let me ask you to think clearly and be wise in your understanding, and realize that there are many, many, many angels who have done even greater things than those which have been attributed to the so-called 'saints' associated with Catholicism.

It is true that this power is used by you, and it may well be that many of you within the hearing of my voice are responsible instruments of the spirit, and through your desire to help and to serve mankind, you have made it possible for so-called 'miracles' to be performed. We do not believe in miracles as such. We believe in everything, known or unknown to man, is governed by divine law, by natural law, and therefore is a natural experience. But the unusual experiences in a man's life, the things he cannot explain by man-made laws or by scientific theories, are usually classified as miracles.

Since the beginning of time such things have manifested, and they will continue to manifest so long as man has need of them, and so long as man continues to have faith. Look into the short years of your earth life and try to recall times when you awakened in a dream, a dream that had a message for you, or perhaps a message for you to give to someone else. Think for the very important moments of your life when you were in a state of indecision, not knowing what to do, or which way to turn, when there may have been a dozen ways to go. But out of the great invisible world came the vibrations of an angel who helped you to solve your problems, to direct your thoughts and your footsteps, and to bring about that help that you needed. Think about the many times when riding in some earthly vehicle you suddenly felt a hand reach out to protect you, to stop the car, or to cause it to swerve in time to avoid a serious accident. A miracle? The guidance of angels! Think of these times when you or your friends or relatives were lying on sick beds at death's door when all the knowledge and experience of earthly doctors had been expended, and there was no way to cling to life in that body except by prayer and the power of healing. Yes, a miracle occurred, but all of this was directed to you by way of the angels.

So I would like to place in your minds the thought that are not just a few saints to be remembered, to be honoured, on All Saints Day, but that every entity, known and unknown, who has lived in this earth life, who has made progress, who has learned from experience the great lessons of life and who has come back to give you the love, the joy and the blessing of peace which is yours is a saint. Sainthood does not mean perfection, but it singles out those people who are responsible for the great acts of the God spirit.

And you, my friends, while living in your physical body, should be instrumental, not once, but many times, in hearing the voice of spirit and relaying the message to others. So in my estimation you, too, are on the path with all other saints. You are angels living in physical bodies, disguised in yourselves, sometimes disguised by your ego, by your personality, by your change of dress. But I still speak to you as angels. And the more knowledge you receive, the more enlightened that comes into your life will help you as an enlightened soul to bring peace and understanding to the world.

Let us honour truth. Let us honour all saints, all entities who are saints, for by them, by their service and through their guidance your lives are made more perfect, your lives are enriched and the world becomes a better place because of you and because of your association with the angels.

All Saints' Day should be part of every religious ceremony, and one day out of the year you should give special thought, special prayer, that this power given to man and to all the angels will continue to manifest. For it is the only way that the world can be at peace.

God bless you.

Master of Light – A Christmas Message
through Dorothy Flexer, 13th December 1978.

Greetings friends of Earth, this is the Master of Light. What a beautiful time of year to gather round the centre of light that represents Divine Intelligence, Divine Illumination, Divine Love. I know that as you draw closer to that special day, Christmas Day, you will be faced with a lot of decision-making, vibrations of love, vibrations of giving, vibrations of serving, but do not lose sight of the fact, my children of Earth, that the light which led the wise men is symbolic of the divine light which is ever present to all of you. You just need to look up to see that which is Divine.

Looking downward lets you recognize shadows, the effects of your shortcomings, of your mistakes, of your bad judgement. Looking upward helps you to see the light which is the source of your energy, the source of your power, the source of all things right and good. And as you follow that light as the wise men that followed the star of the east, you will see new doors opening to you that will allow greater blessings to enter your environment, greater thoughts and vibrations to enter your mind, new friends, new conditions. For once you realise where your help and strength lies, then you will surely give praise, show gratitude for that power. The light of love, the joy and the peace of the Christmas season we give to you.

But always with the thought that you're entering a new year shortly thereafter. A year of opportunity, a year of joy and love.

Expand your consciousness dear friends or Earth to accept all of the good things and do not deny yourselves any of the help that is there, invisible though it may be, it is ever powerful and you'll never be without that beam of light that can brighten your heart as well as your pathway.

I know you're aware of the invisible ones, your loved ones, your angel guides. They too will be present with you through all of your joyful experiences during the Christmas holidays. We feast upon your love as you feast upon the food. Just knowing that you think of us and want us to be near is joy and gratitude enough for us and you can be sure dear friends, that we stand watch over your night and day.

We touch with our healing, we bless you with our knowledge and our protection.

So together, you of earth and the invisible ones of the great world of spirit unite prayers and thoughts and forces of energy to make your life more wonderful but especially that you will enjoy your holidays more than ever, that you'll recognise the blessings that are brought to you. (The gift from the spirit is everlasting.)

We expect nothing in return but the recognition that it is there. So wherever you are, whatever you are, whatever you do, know that the angels are present with you giving their love and their blessings.

Peace to all of you. Peace in your heart. Peace in your home. Peace in your church. Peace in your world.

Good Evening

The Magic Of Praise.
A Sermon by Dr. Russell J. Flexer,
Shrine of the Master Church, Sarasota, Fla.
23rd November, 1968.

To praise is to express admiration for, or to glorify. When we praise God we express admiration for all that God means to us. We admire the power which gives us life and which places life into everything about us even in each blade of grass. One seldom gives thanks for anything he does not admire and so we assume that when we pray we also give thanks that those things exist in our realm of being.

What is God?

To us, God is Spirit, love, life and truth. God is omnipresent, omniscient and omnipotent, so to us, God is all. God is that power which heals when the body has been injured or abused. It is that force and energy which attracts things of like nature to each other. It is the power and energy that is directed by man to do good. One of the laws of nature is that everything has a positive and a negative side to it, a male and female aspect. And so that power can be used by man for evil and destructive purposes as well as for good and constructive purposes.

Man learns how to make use of this God Power according to his own personality and character traits. He will build his own success or his own failure. Man learns too that the God Power is no respecter of persons. And so he learns that he must abide by the laws which harmonize with good if he desires to reap the good.

Another thing man learns about the laws of nature is that since they do not conform to man, man must learn to conform to them. And in so doing he is able to create desire and with effort of mind and body, bring those desires into reality. If man needs a reason for praise, here it is. The laws of the universe are dependable laws and man develops an awareness of their power and energy and so he praises and gives thanks for his knowledge and for the opportunity to put his knowledge to work to get the results that he desires.

Praise and thanksgiving are a form of blessing and part of our way of life. If we have an urge to criticize or to use unkind words we are creating chaos within. This being the case we should realize that kindness, love, praise and giving thanks are powerful forces for good. Instead of condemning we should praise. The power of praise never fails. Allowing the Christ within us to recognize the Christ in others will help to overcome and discord that might otherwise exist. It is not easy to judge according to what we see, but it should be our desire to do good and to seek good in all cases. Regardless of our feelings of animosity, when we praise and give thanks, things usually adjust to better states of being. Praising and giving thanks is a powerful harmonizing force to be used daily.

Praise and giving thanks creates great liberating power within us. Before we can enjoy good health continuously we must praise, we must give thanks for that good health. We must learn to praise the God manifesting in all things until we feel every cell and every nerve of our being vibrating with new life. When the body is energized in this manner we are able to raise the consciousness to receive the benefits from Divine law. Our blessings of health, happiness, love and peace continue to grow as we recognize that we are co-creators with the God Spirit and thus are responsible for our use of Divine Power.

As we praise the laws of nature we will enjoy better health of mind as well as health of body. As we praise the need and the use of money we will see our prosperity increase and the better we use our money and the wiser we are in understanding the laws of abundance, the better we are able we are of retaining a state of prosperity. Our power of praise affects people as well as things. Many need to be praised and age eliminates no one. The child wants to be praised for the little deeds he accomplishes and when he is not praised he loses the desire to improve. He needs the praise to stir within him the urge to please others. Adults also need praise because they are children at heart and like to be noticed and want to be needed. Praise makes them feel that [there's] something inside of them [making them] into being better people. Praise of another when all seems dark for him may be the key to his getting ahead or even to his whole future happiness. Can anyone know what moment in any person's life is the very moment he will find himself? We should also learn to praise the smallest bit of good that comes to us and then we shall also recognize that good increasing and developing into radiant living conditions for us. We must not be too concerned with our own feelings so that we are hurt when we seem to be left out or seem not to be praised. We should know that the law takes care of us at all times. We must think in terms of doing the praising and setting into motion a force that has a magical increasing power. When we condemn another or even ourselves we lower our spiritual vision. Let us not take ourselves to task for our mistakes, but rather let us seek to measure ourselves by the standard for the Christ within us. Let us give thanks instead of criticizing and let the perfection develop according to the law. This is the way – walk ye in it. Praise has magic in it.

Through praise we will discover blessings that we never knew existed. There are blessings all around us and they are ours to enjoy. The word of praise when set into operation through our material affairs will bring prosperity. However, we cannot think of poverty when we desire to bring prosperity, for the one counteracts the others. If we keep the consciousness filled with happy and positive thoughts, there will be no room and no times for negative conditions and vibrations. Praise should be used to offset undesirable conditions. Expressing praise can be a good habit and when formed deeply within the mind will act a barrier to failure and as a magnet to all the good things that we desire in life. If we have the wrong attitude toward life we are sure to be awarded some experience that will cause us harm and many times, confusion.

The Christ Consiousness.

A Sermon by Dr Russell Flexer, 1972.

The indwelling Christ is man's inner Christ Consciousness, or his spiritual consciousness. The kind of spirit which manifested Jesus the Christ and which expressed within him so beautifully in love and service. This is the kind of spirit that reflects the Christ Consciousness.

The unfoldment of this Christ Consciousness is the goal of every sincere Metaphysician for it brings to us the opportunity of expressing without conscious effort the inner Divine Power.

When we recognize the origin of our spiritual powers we will seek, think and act in accordance with our highest ideals. The Christ is a part of the infinite in man. It is the idea of a perfect pattern which Jesus speaks to us as the inner voice, or the still small voice. If this inner spirit did not manifest within us we would never seek healing for our sick bodies, or happiness when we are despondent. If for any reason one should stray from this Christ pattern, he will most certainly return to it at some future time. We cannot leave it completely because it is the real true self which is expressed harmoniously with the God Spirit. I am sure that everyone has felt at times a sense of knowing that there is a higher self within that is ever lifting us up and leading us on toward bigger and better things

The Christ is the perfect inner self which is never sick, never defeated, never discouraged; never fearful or never worried. This inner perfect man knows nothing of a negative nature because it is a God Spirit, therefore we must resolve to become one with God through the Christ Consciousness.

Each of us has a Christ idea within as did the Master Jesus, however we must recognize it and then bring it forth into manifestation. We will never find our true self until we learn to draw within ourselves and see there the reflection of our higher ideals and attributes and then bring them into being, in our words our thoughts and in our deeds. The Physical body is merely the temple indwelling Christ and unless we live at the center of this inner spiritual being as did Jesus, we are not fulfilling the law of our being.

As some people might think it is not sacrilegious to compare ourselves to the Christ, for in reality we are speaking of that perfect Christ center which is within the heart of every individual, saint or sinner. The difference between the two extremes is that the saint has recognized his inner Christ Spirit while the sinner has not recognized any part of it. We do not have to search in some far off place for an abiding place of the Indwelling Christ Spirit of Christ Consciousness. We have to look within to find it. Wherever we go we take with us that Christ Spirit. It brings us a feeling of peace and a feeling of security. We must learn to radiate the Christ Love through our body, our mind and all of our affairs. It must also permeate every cell and organ of our body until we become alive with the Christ Spirit and when we have a clear understanding and realization of the presence and the power of that Christ within, we will become a tower of strength and power – power to heal ourselves and to heal others. The Christ is a God Current which illuminates the whole being. The light of the Christ is a healing light. In fact, it is the most powerful light in the universe. It is impossible to visualize a light with such brilliancy and whose healing power is so great that it can heal, cleanse, renew and restore diseased tissue. The Christ

Consciousness acts as a great physician and surgeon which is ever ready to restore us to perfectness. Jesus was so filled with this Divine Power that he had but to speak the word, or lay his hand on the sick and the people were healed and comforted. His body was so aglow with Divine Light that others could recognize the power and feel its penetrating rays. In First John the chapter we read that: "If we walk in the light as He is in the light, we have fellowship one with another and the blood of Jesus his son cleanseth us of all sin." Here we can see that the light of truth which energized the Master and the life force symbolized by the blood can cleanse our bodies from all illness and from all weakness.

To us sin is the transgression of the law and the result of this transgression is manifested in illness and unhappiness. When we walk in the light we can avoid the destructive conditions that so often hinder our progression. Jesus said "I am the light of the world, he that followeth me shall not walk in darkness, but shall have the light of life." The following words are taken from Jesus' Sermon on the Mount: "Let your light so shine bright before men that they may see your good works and glorify your father which is in heaven." Was Jesus not speaking of the inner Christ Consciousness? Did he not tell us that the Kingdom of Heaven is within? The Christ Light is not slow to bring us results if we properly direct that light. We must go within and have faith that it will work successfully for us.

Faith is key to many opportunities and it does unlock the door of the inner Christ-Consciousness, to let in the Divine Light of understanding. Faith helps us to become spiritually strong. We must have a living, growing faith before we can understand the full meaning of the word – "Thy faith hath made thee whole." No matter how low we may sink into materially the indwelling Christ Spirit can lift us, redeem us and restore us. Our faith must be identified with the Christ within so that as we look within we will know that all things good are coming to us.

Paul wrote these words to the Galatians: "Ye are the sons of God through faith in Christ."

When the Christ Consciousness is in control of our being, we recognize only the good such as health, joy, peace, power, abundance and prosperity. When we have the true faith we know that what we desire is already ours. Our faith must be steadfast in that Christ Spirit. And it must never waver.

Then we will cease to live in a world of materiality where we are apt to judge by appearances instead of righteous judgement. Those who live in harmony with the Christ Spirit are free from discord and discontent. We must show our willingness to serve others in selfish devotion to truth as the Master Jesus did when we washed the feet of his disciples. At that moment the Christ was in him, was enacting a Divine service which not only gave others pleasure, but gave pleasure to him as well. We too must learn to enjoy our work however menial it may be. Nothing of a negative or destructive nature can remain in the vibration of the Christ Love. The Christ Love cannot be fully expressed or appreciated in sickness, in anger, in jealously or hatred. The Christ Consciousness being Divine is perfection through the human consciousness. We need to know that it is possible to make ourselves over, to become someone better and stronger and more spiritual. The inner Christ Consciousness leads us into paths of enlightenment, into which we find the right work, the right environment and we make the right decisions.

In the 8th Chapter of John we find these words: "If the Son therefore shall make you free, ye shall be free indeed." In other words, when you are freed from the oppressions of the world by the Christ Spirit you never again allow yourself to live in material or physical bondage. When you are freed by the truth your whole life is changed into something beautiful. You will want to identify yourself with the God Spirit as an expression of your appreciation for your angel guidance, for you too will be able to say, "I and the Father are one." The Christ Consciousness develops to act as a buffer board to protect us from all harm and all evil. It helps us to respond to angel guidance and to the power of the Divine Spirit which sustained us. Jesus said, "My yoke is easy, my burden is light." Meaning this his way of life is easier than any other. The Christ Consciousness within us makes us realize that we are blessed in many ways. It helps us to recognize and to appreciate truth. When the Christ Consciousness is developed as it should be it is easy to form that habit of praising and giving thanks for all experiences, great or small. What we must do then to understand the Christ Consciousness: first we must recognize it and then we must release it, use it and benefit by it. We must strengthen it by our attunement with the God Spirit of the Universe. We must keep ourselves mentally, physically and spiritually aware of the Divine Presence and love, which when activated within us makes it possible for us to be channels, an instrument of that God Spirit. We must make our own choice to walk in the light and to let the darkness be dispelled. Where there is light there can be no darkness. Where the Christ Consciousness manifests there can be no failure, no destruction and no hatred. Let us all become masters of our fate, masters of our whole being, masters fit for the service of the God Spirit. This is done by releasing the Christ within, developing the Christ Consciousness.

Thank You.

Appendix Six

Dorothy's Astrological Birth Chart
by Margaret Hodge.

Date of Birth: November 7th 1913 in Pennsylvania.

The time of Dorothy's birth is unknown, so this analysis is based on planetary aspects and signs alone. Dorothy was born under the sign of Scorpio. Scorpio and its ruling planet are associated with transformation through the 'evolutionary journey of the soul', psychological growth and emotional development, combined in Dorothy's chart, with mysticism, devotion and profoundly deep emotional power. This was the foundation upon which Dorothy entered this earthly life. Dorothy harnessed and developed these inherent qualities with courage and determination to fulfil her destiny, which was connected with the collective and the universal mind – Metaphysics.

Early initiation into life's difficulties came with the death or separation of a parent and the need to support the remaining parent and siblings. Dorothy's powerful intuition and nurturing nature was driven by her need for independence and to change the lives of those around her for the better, often making sacrifices for others. Devotion to her family was unquestionable as it was to her other family, The Shrine of the Master.

A natural leader, she was an instinctive and compassionate provider; Reverend Dorothy drew people to her through her strength of character and her ability to steer them through the rough sea of life – to develop and grow.

Dorothy's pioneering spirit, her tenacity and idealism compelled her to transcend the ordinary. Dorothy was not afraid to fight for her beliefs, even if they were contrary to the prevailing social confines. A powerhouse of emotional and physical energy, determinedly protective of her family and congregation, Dorothy held the reins tightly, if not rigidly. At times, unable to allow people to make their own mistakes and develop in an organic way, Reverend Dorothy expected a great deal from herself and expected the same from others. Dorothy was not averse to letting them know when they fell short of her expectation in an impartial and succinct way.

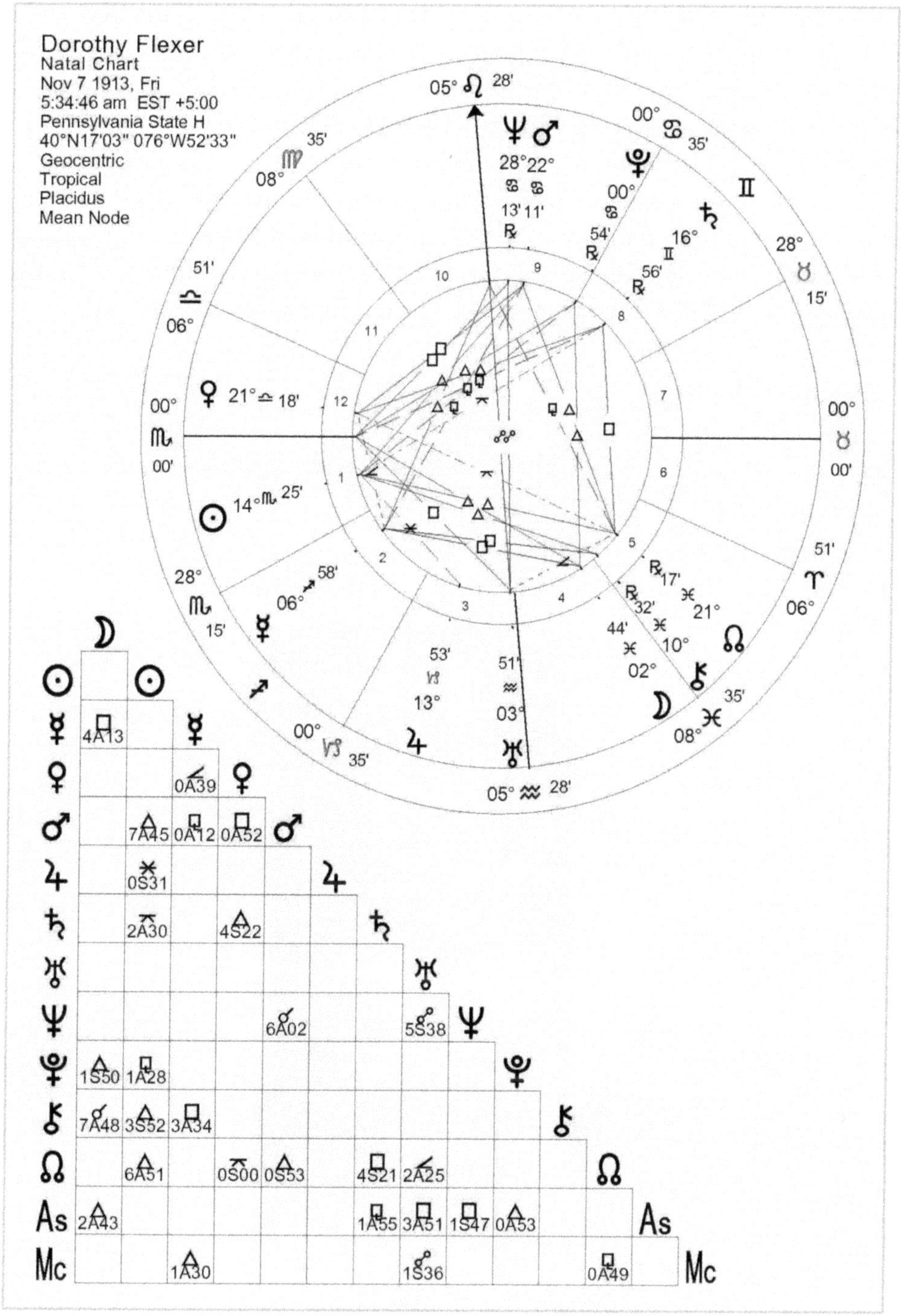

Dorothy Flexer
Natal Chart
Nov 7 1913, Fri
5:34:46 am EST +5:00
Pennsylvania State H
40°N17'03" 076°W52'33"
Geocentric
Tropical
Placidus
Mean Node

Dorothy Graff's Astrological Birth Chart.

Tension through overwork may have been a problem, as her keen intellect and memory would have driven her to achieve her goals and not rely on quick fixes to solve problems. Headaches and digestive problems may have troubled Dorothy.

Dorothy was not afraid to be a figurehead and to shine in her own right. Her creativity and imagination provided her with the impetus to act on her dreams and ideals. She was a visionary with compassion, a charismatic orator and a natural healer; she believed in setting and attaining high standards. Dorothy sought to build a foundation that was unique to her and had its roots in faith, belief, spirituality, discipline and education. Dorothy was charitable, generous and a good friend to all those who sought her counsel.

Margaret Hodge*

Reference: Green, Jeff: *Pluto, The Evolutionary Journey of the Soul, Volume I*

Dorothy Graff Flexer, Tampa 1946

* To contact Margaret, email: margarethodge@talktalk.net .

Appendix Seven

Vibrational Healing Protocol:
given by Dr. Charles Davis – September 1985.

Mentally greet your Healing Guide and ask for her assistance.

Begin by standing behind the Patient

We don't touch the patient; we work with the etheric field

Place hands approximately 1 inch above the shoulders

Move hands to the top of the head

Move hands to the eyes – index fingers touching, just over the bridge of the nose

Move hands to the ears – each palm close to the corresponding ear

Move hands to the throat area

Step to the left side of the patient

Place left hand at the forehead; right hand at the back of the head

Place left hand over the top of the chest; right hand at the top of the back

Step behind the Patient

Place hands at the tops of the arms; finish healing prayer and thank your Healing Guide for her assistance

Place hands at the top of head move hands along the etheric field from the head to the shoulders and the back with each part of the closing prayer.

Mentally say:

"I pray this in the name of the Father (represents God)
Through the Son (represents Mankind)
And by the Holy Spirit (represents Spirit)"

Whisper into the left ear: "God Bless You."

Appendix Eight

A Guide to American Definitions
of Spirit Guides.

Angels – These are spirit guides, entities who are dedicated to helping you achieve peace, happiness and success. They have been trained to assist you in every aspect of your lives. They know us better than we know ourselves. Their personalities are very similar to yours, simply because they are trying to feel what you feel and desire what you desire. They try to understand what is needed to bring about inner peace and success to you.

The angels go by titles that may vary in other areas of the country or the world. The names are determined by the master teachers who take charge of the classes. In Dr. Charles Davis' classes, the names given to the various members of the spirit band are:

Doorkeeper (also known as the Joy Guide or the Gate Keeper) – The Doorkeeper helps you with your everyday concerns. They often manifest as children but yet are mature in terms of wisdom and good judgment. They work closely with the Spirit Doctor to ensure that the many facets of your life are coordinated and harmonious.

The Doorkeeper helps to prepare you for someone who plans to call you so you will be by the phone; or at a place where you can meet someone whose presence will be meaningful to you. The Doorkeeper reminds us of appointments that we have forgotten or will awaken us if we have overslept.

Spirit Doctor (also known as the Doctor of Philosophy) – He assumes overall responsibility for the coordination of your spirit helpers.

The spirit people have access to all knowledge of earth and of spirit. They choose the knowledge they want to gather just like we do on the earth. They educate themselves by learning, searching and through conversation. The angels talk to others, listen to what they have to say and accept their suggestions. They listen to those who have had a chance to learn more than they have. They can be educated as much as they desire. The Spirit

Doctor must have a thorough knowledge of the spiritual laws and the laws of the Universe.

There are schools in the spirit world similar to those on the earth. Studying people constitutes a large part of their education. They observe and analyze our personalities, habits, emotions and responses. There are different levels of education and different degrees of spirituality among the angels.

Master – The spirit master has already passed through the experiences of being a doctor, of working with healers and helping others with conditions similar to ours. Most doctors and masters are men but there are women doctors and masters too. Each one is looked upon according to his or her mentality, wisdom and ability to serve.

The potential for mastership is within everyone; because each is spirit now and always will be. The Master is highly evolved spiritually and vibrationally and is interested in helping us with our spirituality.

There are degrees of Masters just as there are different degrees of progress and learning. Many work toward those ends just as we do for our master's and doctor's degrees on the earth.

Healing Sister (also known as the Healing Nun) – Healing Sisters are entities who enjoy working for the health of individuals of earth. They have the ability to direct the vital life energy which can help heal and cleanse the body. Working closely with the Laws of Nature, healing sisters are great instruments dedicated to helping humanity. Their power of healing is directed through love, the desire to help and the request that you make. Their first obligation is to you and then to all those in your personal world in whom you have some interest.

Chemist – The Chemist in your angel band helps to keep your physical body in balance according to the foods you eat, the exercise you take, the air you breathe – all the things that must be kept in balance to assure good health.

When we don't feel well, the Chemist will impress us about ways to make the necessary corrections through a change in diet or physical habit. The Chemist will help bring everything in your body of balance. The Chemist impresses us to supply the body with the proper foods and vitamins and then works with the Law of Nature to distribute the nutrients so the organs and glands of the body function harmoniously.

Indian Guide – The Indian Guides come mostly to give you physical protection, when you are walking, driving your car or visiting a place where vibrations are not of the highest state. American Indians are highly sensitive to the Law of Nature and are very close to the Great White Spirit. They are intelligent, spiritual, sensitive souls. Your Indian Guide is very important to your well-being and protection.

Secondary Guides – There will be secondary guides who come in and out of our lives to help us with specific tasks or projects. Guides of this nature may have an expertise that you require in your vocation, social or personal life. These guides coordinate their efforts with the Spirit Doctor and inner guides.

Communication with Our Spirit Guides – Communication between us and the angels is built on trust. First you must maintain your faith that the angels are there. They love you and want to work with you. Know that they are there and begin to talk to them.

Inside the Sarasota Center of Light today, note the Sculpture above the platform.

Appendix Nine

How to be A Good Metaphysician.
from a pamphlet published by the
Church of Metaphsyical Christianity, Sarasota.

A good Christian Metaphysician is one who believes in the life, the teachings, and demonstrations of the Master Jesus as part of his religion. A Metaphysician goes beyond the teachings of Orthodox Christian churches not only believing in communication but also developing his own gifts of the Spirit so that communion between the two worlds becomes a very natural part of his life and being.

A good Christian Metaphysician will first of all develop his own spiritual qualities. This includes the development of the mind and the spiritual consciousness.

He understands the value of material things and of his physical nature, but never allows these things to be worshipped or to be uppermost in his mind. He knows that, being a spirit in a body, his life is eternal, therefore, the things of the Spirit are most important. When he understands this, he can guide his everyday life accordingly.

The Christian Metaphysician learns about all the Spiritual Laws, and then he learns to live in harmony with them so that he will be able to build successfully in every way: physically, mentally, and spiritually. He knows that what is his, is his to earn, to share, to give; and he knows, too, that thoughts being things, his success or failure depends upon himself.

The Christian Metaphysician tries to use his mind power for good not for foolish things; not for criticism or judgment, but rather for analyzing, thinking, building, creating and inspiring – all of the things that will make it possible for him to create a good life for himself and for others. He always lives in the future. He remembers the lessons of the past so that he will not make the same mistakes again and again, but he never lives in the past with thoughts of regret, remorse, unhappiness, or depression.

The Christian Metaphysician realizes that as he serves others he is also being served; as he shares with others, he is keeping the Law of Abundance active in his life. This means that he will never want for anything as long as he deals wisely with all that he has of material wealth.

188

Great peace of mind comes to the Christian Metaphysician in knowing that when one door closes another always opens. This is why he can be happy. This is why he can let go of fear thought. This is why it is easy for him to accept some circumstances as they develop, make the best of them, and create something new, something better.

The Christian Metaphysician lives a life of progress, moving forward upward, improving, advancing, sharing, and giving. Every moment is lived with the thought of being an instrument of the God Spirit, of being a channel through which many wonderful things will manifest knowing that every ounce of strength needed will be supplied.

The Christian Metaphysician reminds himself that he does nothing alone; that the inspiration is directed to him from the Divine Source. He knows that there are angels who attract themselves to him as helpers; and therefore, when in doubt, he will make attunement with one of his Spirit and or his angel loved-ones, to make certain that he has not made a mistake, or to be sure that his plans are right, good and of the highest and the best. He knows that his responsibility is to God, to man, to himself, and to his family. His is a life which is lived in service, in harmony, in love, and in sharing.

There is not any other kind of life or religion that can give one as much peace of mind, as much strength and energy, as much progress and prosperity as one can find in Metaphysical Christianity; for a Christian Metaphysician is one who

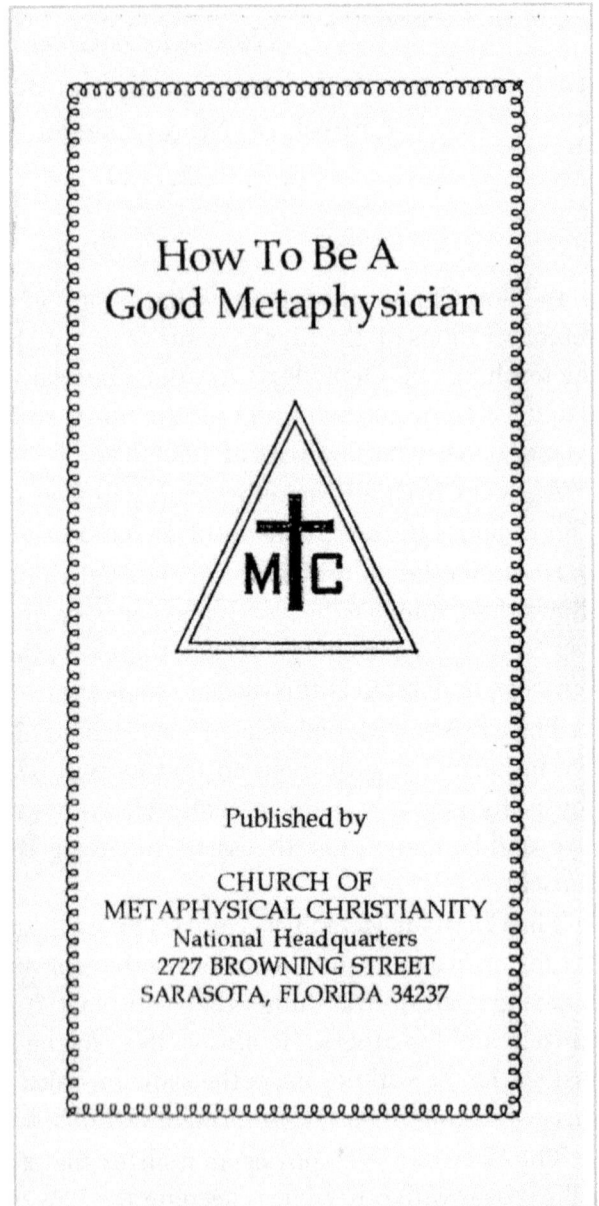

How To Be A
Good Metaphysician

M C

Published by

CHURCH OF
METAPHYSICAL CHRISTIANITY
National Headquarters
2727 BROWNING STREET
SARASOTA, FLORIDA 34237

Front of the trifold pamphlet.

builds his life as closely to that of the Master Jesus and all other Masters down through the ages as is humanly possible.

The Christian Metaphysician knows that every mistake can be overcome by making reparation for it. One is never held in a state of evil. One is never kept from progressing, from working out his problems and conditions. He knows that man must never be led to believe that he is unworthy to receive any kind of help just because he has made a mistake. He lives his life spiritually and materially and under all circumstances is aware that he is a co-creator with the God Spirit.

The good Christian Metaphysician supports his church and its activities. He refrains from doing anything that would bring hurt or shame to his ministers or to his church. Instead of talking about others, he stands up to protect them. He does not criticize, belittle or judge others. He does not think more highly of himself than he ought to think. He has a good sense of values. He is careful in his actions and in his speech to bring honor, praise, and respect to his church family.

*****

Appendix Ten

The Principles of Metaphysical Spirituality at the Sarasota Center of Light.

* We believe in God, the source of all creation.

* We affirm that Metaphysical Spirituality is a way of life based upon the teachings and demonstrations of all Master Teachers.

* We believe that a sincere application of these teachings and living in accordance with Spiritual Law leads to true spirituality.

* We believe in the healing power of God and that all things are possible when done in accordance with Divine Law.

* We believe that the highest morality is contained in the Golden Rule, "Do unto others as you would have them unto you."

* We believe in personal responsibility and that we make our own happiness as we co-create with Divine Law.

* We believe the purpose of human life is to experience and learn from life lessons in order to progress spiritually.

* We believe in the immortality of the soul.

* We believe in communicating with those who have made their transition into the Spirit World.

* We affirm that the doorway to reformation is never closed to anyone here or hereafter.

"These principles of Metaphysical Spirituality represent key focuses of the Center's beliefs and philosophy. Each individual principle is a pathway to a deeper connection, understanding and relationship with God, our own spiritual nature and of life. Together they are guidelines to a clear inner knowing and vibrant expression of true spirituality."

For more information see the website at http://www.sarasotacenteroflight.com

Appendix Eleven

Books and Journals consulted by the Author in his research for this book.

Allen, James: *As a Man Thinketh.* Rise of Douai Publishing, UK (2013).

Awtry, Marilyn: *Light from Beyond the Tomb, Spiritualism Survived.* She-men publishing, Sanford (2010).

Barnes Jefts, Peggy: *Lo, I am With You Always.* NASC Lilydale (various dates).

Britten, Emma Hardinge: *Autobiography.* SNU Publications, Stansted,UK (1996).

Butterworth, Eric: *The Power Within You.* Harper One, New York (1992).

Butterworth, Eric: *The Universe is Calling.* Harper One, New York (1994).

Chaney, Rev. Robert: *Mediums and the Development of Mediumship.* Psychic Books, Eaton Rapids (1946).

de Mello, Anthony: *The Way to Love.* Image, New York (1992).

Elder, Amy A: *Sarasota, Images of America.* Arcadia Publishing, Charleston SC, (2003).

Elliott, Maurice: *Psychic Life of Jesus.* Spiritualist Press, London, (1964).

Ellsberg, Robert: *A Saint's Guide to Happiness.* Darton, Longman and Todd, London, (2003).

Fillmore, Charles & Myrtle: *Metaphysical Bible Dictionary.* Truth Unity Ministries, Kansas City, Missouri (1931).

Fox, Emmet: *The Sermon on the Mount.* Harper One, New York, (1989).

Goldsmith, Joel; *Beyond Words and Thoughts.* Citadel Press, Secaucus, (1968).

Hartman's: *International Directory of Psychic Science and Spiritualism.* Occult Press, Jamaica, New York,(1927 and 1931).

Leonard, Todd Jay: *Talking to the Other Side.* iUniverse, New York, (2005).

Madison Wade, Alda: *At the Shrine of the Master (Glimpse of Immortality).* Kissinger Publishing (repub 2001).

Madison Wade, Alda: *Evidences of Immortality.* William Frederick Press, New York (1943).

O'Hara, Gerald A: *Dead Men's Embers*. Saturday Night Publications, SNPP Books, York (2006)

O'Hara, Gerald A: *Mrs Miller's Gift, the CD*. From the author (2009)

O'Hara, Gerald A. & Harrison A: *Mrs Miller's Gift*. Saturday Night Publications, SNPP Books, York (2007).

Peck, Scott: *The Road Less travelled*. Arrow Books, London (2006).

Stillson Juddah, J: *The History and Philosophy of the Metaphysical Movement in America*. The Westminster Press, Philadelphia (1967).

Tagore, Rabindranath: Saddhana, *The Realisation of Life*. Forgotten Books.org (2008).

SNU Philosophy and Ethics Committee: *The Religion of Spiritualism*. SNU Publications.org (2010).

This is Spiritualism. Federation of Spiritual churches and Associations. Inc, New York (1948).

Trine, Ralph: *In tune with the Infinite.*, G. Bell, London (1942).

Underhill, Evelyn: Practical Mysticism. J. M. Dent, London (1948).

Walsch, Neale Donald: *Conversations with God 1*. Hampton Roads Publishing, Charlottesville VA (1997).

Watson, Lillian Eichler: *Light from Many Lamps*. Simon and Schuster, New York (1951).

Yogananda, Paramhannsa: *Whispers of Eternity*. Crystal Clarity Publisher, Nevada City, (2008).

Journals Consulted

The National Spiritualist: NASC, May/June 2014

The Summit: NASC Dec: 1964

Psychic Observer: Sept 10th 1938, Feb 10th & 25th; May 10th & Nov 10th 1943, Sept?; 1944, Jan?; 1949, Aug 10th; 1954

Chimes Magazine: Dec:1961

The Direct Voice: August 1930

Psychic Observer and Chimes: Nov;1969, June; 1970, Dec; 1972, June;1973, Aug;1973, March;1974, July-Sept; 1974, Jan-March; 1976, April-June; 1976, July-Sept 1978,

Light Magazine: June 1958

Appendix Twelve

Reverend Tom Newman's recommended reading list.

Spiritual Philosophy

The Key to Yourself. Venice Bloodworth (1952)
The Grand Design Volumes 1 & 2. Paddy McMahon (2000)
Meditation. Eknath Easwaran (1978)
The Sermon on the Mount. Emmet Fox
The Unknown Jesus. Robert Siblerud (2003)
The Science of the Soul. Robert Siblerud (2001)
The Keepers of the Secrets. Robert Siblerud (1999)
In the Beginning. Robert Siblerud (1998)
The Way to Love. Anthony de Mello (1991)
From Atoms to Angels. Paul Walsh-Roberts (2000)
Interview with an Angel. Stevan Thayer & Linda Nathanson (1997)
Secrets of Attraction. Sandra Anne Taylor (2001)
Teachings of Silver Birch. A.W. Austen (1938)
The Silver Birch Book of Questions & Answers. Stan A. Ballard (1998)
Bridges. Aart Jurriaanse (1978)
A New Earth. Eckhart Tolle (2005)
Subtle Energy: Awakening to the Unseen Forces in Our Lives. William Collinge
The Religions of Man. Huston Smith (1986)
Power vs. Force. David R. Hawkins (1995)
The Essence of Spiritual Philosophy. Haridas Chaudhuri (1990)
Jesus and the Essenes. Dolores Cannon (1992)
The University of Spiritualism. Harry Boddington (1947)
This is Spiritualism. Maurice Barbanell (1959)
Any Book by Edgar Cayce

Any Book by Arthur Ford
Any Book by Arthur Findlay
Any Book by David R. Hawkins

Healing

You Can Heal Your Life. Louise Hay (1984)
Science of Breath. Yogi Ramacharaka (1904)
Psychic Healing. Yogi Ramacharaka (1905)
The Healing Intelligence. Harry Edwards (1956)
A Guide to Spirit Healing. Harry Edwards 1950)
Spirit Healing. Harry Edwards (1960)
Hands of Light. Barbara Ann Brennan (1987)
Vibrational Medicine. Richard Gerber (1988)

Spirit Communication

Life in the World Unseen. Anthony Borgia (1954)
More About Life in the World Unseen. Anthony Borgia (1956)
Here and Hereafter. Anthony Borgia (1959)
Your Soul's Plan. Robert Schwartz (2007)
Anna, Grandmother of Jesus., Claire Heartsong (2002)
The Afterlife of Billy Fingers. Annie Kagan (2013)
The Blue Island. W. T. Stead (1922)
Talking to Leaders of the Past. Toni Winninger (2008)
Spirit World Wisdom. Toni Winninger (2010)
How I Died and What I Did Next. Toni Winninger (2010)
Life Lessons. Toni Winninger (2012)
Listening to Spirit Wisdom. Toni Winninger (2013)
A Wanderer in the Spirit Lands. Franchezzo (Originally 1896)
I Walked with Spirits. Jeanette Strack-Zanghi (2010)
The Earth Adventure. Ron Scolastico (1988)
Séance 101. Elaine M. Kuzmeskus (2007)
Testimony of Light. Helen Greaves (1969)
Any book by Dolores Cannon
Any of the Silver Birch Books
Any of the White Eagle Books

Mediumship

An Extraordinary Journey. Stewart Alexander (2010)
The Book of Mediums. Allan Kardec (1874)
There are No Goodbyes. Paddy McMahon (2010)
The Silver Cord. Marha Barham & James Green (1986
Bridging Two Worlds. Marti Barham ((1981)
On the Side of Angels. Gordon Higginson (1993)
Mediumship and Its Laws. Hudson Tuttle (1960)

Christian Bible Interpretation

Asimov's Guide to the Old Testament. Issac Asimov (1969)
Asimov's Guide to the New Testament. Issac Asimov (1969)

List Updated April 25, 2016

Gerald o'Hara is researching U.S. mediums and mediumship between 1932/1996 and is interested in any research leads, memoirs, illustrations, accounts of séances and Spiritualist Camp Meetings.

If you can help please contact the author on
historymedium@yahoo.com
and visit the website at
http://www.historymedium.com

Lightning Source UK Ltd.
Milton Keynes UK
UKHW032203061118
331889UK00004B/335/P